Crisis and Restructuring in East Asia

Crisis and Restructuring in East Asia

The Case of the Korean *Chaebol* and the Automotive Industry

Seung-Il Jeong

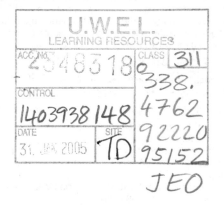

palgrave
macmillan

First published 2004 by
PALGRAVE MACMILLAN
Houndmills, Basingstoke, Hampshire RG21 6XS and
175 Fifth Avenue, New York, N.Y. 10010
Companies and representatives throughout the world

PALGRAVE MACMILLAN is the global academic imprint of the Palgrave Macmillan division of St. Martin's Press, LLC and of Palgrave Macmillan Ltd. Macmillan® is a registered trademark in the United States, United Kingdom and other countries. Palgrave is a registered trademark in the European Union and other countries.

ISBN 1–4039–3814–8

This book is printed on paper suitable for recycling and made from fully managed and sustained forest sources.

A catalogue record for this book is available from the British Library.

Library of Congress Cataloging-in-Publication Data
Jeong, Seung-il.
    Crisis and restructuring in East Asia : the case of the Korean *chaebol* and the automotive industry / Seung-il Jeong.
        p.   cm.
    Includes bibliographical references and index.
    ISBN 1–4039–3814–8 (cloth)
    1. East Asia—Economic policy—Case studies.   2. East Asia—Economic conditions—Case studies.   3. Financial crises—East Asia—Case studies.   I. Title.
    HC460.5.J46 2004
    338.4'7629222'095195—dc22   2004044279

10   9   8   7   6   5   4   3   2   1
13   12   11   10   09   08   07   06   05   04

Printed and bound in Great Britain by
Antony Rowe Ltd, Chippenham and Eastbourne

Contents

List of Figures

List of Tables

Acknowledgements

This book was originally written as a PhD thesis presented to the Free University of Berlin. In writing this book, I have benefited a lot from the kind assistance of many people.

First of all, Ulrich Jürgens, my supervisor, gave much intellectual stimulation and helped me in shaping the book. Wolf-Dieter Narr made helpful comments on the early drafts. I am also thankful to my colleagues and friends in Berlin, Thomas Sablowski, Thomas Kalinowski, Mathias Gleim, Jochen Hille and Sulai Akbary in particular, for their help and useful advice.

The field research for this book was conducted in South Korea between 1999 and 2001. This was a period in which South Korea was going through tumultuous restructuring towards Anglo-American style capitalism. Fieldwork in the automotive industry at the time led me to doubt the liberal views of the crisis and restructuring. In building new viewpoints, I benefited enormously from interactions and dialogues with Hong-Jae Park of the Korea Automotive Research Institute (KARI) and Chan-Keun Lee of Inchon University. They gave me insights and ideas regarding the corporate system and the financial system, which guided me to develop many arguments in this book.

I would like to thank other people in KARI. I owe a special debt of gratitude to Seong-Jae Cho (now at the Korea Labour Institute) who introduced me to his colleagues and other researchers and provided me with helpful information and materials.

I am also grateful to all the people in Hyundai, Daewoo, Kia, Samsung and Ssangyong who spent time with me for interviews. Their willingness and openness to discuss various issues regarding the crisis and restructuring of the carmakers were critical for this book. Dae-Ho Kim of Daewoo deserves particular mention since he introduced me to various individuals in Daewoo who gave interviews for this book.

A special thank you goes to Michael Hobby, who improved my English in the manuscript. Without his help, I could not have written this book. In completing the book, I also owe a debt to Ha-Joon Chang of Cambridge University who was visiting Seoul in 2003.

Finally, I wish to thank my parents for their love and understanding.

SEUNG-IL JEONG

The author and publishers are grateful for the following for permission to reproduce copyright material: The Economist Newspaper Ltd for Table 7.2 from *The Economist*, 27 January 1996; The University of Chicago Press for Table 2.1 and 2.2 from T. Itoh, 'Capital Inflow in Asia', in S. Edwards (ed.) *Capital Flows and the Emerging Economies*, 2000; Oxford University Press for Table 5.3 from H.-J. Chung *et al.*, *Cambridge Journal of Economics* (22, 1998); The Copyright Clearance Center for Table 2.3 from The West Bank, *Global Development* (1999). Every effort has been made to contact all the copyright-holders even, but if any have been inadvertently omitted the publishers will be pleased to make the necessary arrangement at the earliest opportunity.

List of Abbreviations

ASEAN	Association of South-East Asian Nations
BIBF	Bangkok International Bank Facilities
BIS	Bank for International Settlement
CAD	computer-aided design
CAM	computer-aided manufacturing
CEO	Chief Executive Officer
CIS	Commonwealth of Independent States
CKD	completely knocked down
CVs	commercial vehicles
DC	Daewoo Corporation
DMC	Daewoo Motor Company
DMP	Daewoo Motor Polska
D-RAM	dynamic random access memory
DS	developmental state
FDI	foreign direct investment
FSC	Financial Supervisory Commission of Korea
FSL	Fabryka Samochodow Lubline
FSO	Fabryka Samachodow Osowych
FTC	Fair Trade Commission of Korea
GATT	General Agreement on Tariffs and Trade
GDP	gross domestic product
GM	General Motors
GNP	gross national product
HCI	heavy and chemical industrialization
HECC	Hyundai Engineering and Construction Company
HMC	Hyundai Motor Company
HHI	Hyundai Heavy Industry
IDEA	Institute of Development in Automotive Engineering
IDL	Industrial Development Law
IMF	International Monetary Fund
IMVP	International Motor Vehicle Programme
IPO	Initial Public Offering
IT	information technology
KAMA	Korea Automobile Manufacturers Association
KARI	Korea Automotive Research Institute

KD	knocked down
KDI	Korea Development Institute
KERI	Korea Economic Research Institute
LTCM	Long-Term Capital Management
MHI	Mitsubishi Heavy Industries
MITI	Ministry of International Trade and Industry
MMC	Mitsubishi Motor Company
NBFIs	Non-Bank Financial Institutions
NGO	Non-Governmental Organization
NICs	Newly Industrializing Countries
OECD	Organisation for Economic Co-operation and Development
OEM	Original Equipment Manufacturer
R&D	research and development
RAM	random access memory
ROA	return on assets
RVs	recreational vehicles
S&L	savings and loan
SKD	semi-knocked down
SMCs	small and medium-sized companies
TNCs	transnational companies
UD	unrelated diversification
WTO	World Trade Organization

1
Introduction

1.1 East Asia's miracle and crash

East Asian economies once attracted particular attention from the world. They in fact fuelled the greatest expansion of wealth in the history of modern capitalism. The annual gross domestic product (GDP) growth of South Korea (hereafter Korea), Taiwan, Hong Kong and the Association of South-East Asian Nations (ASEAN) five founder members (Singapore, Malaysia, Indonesia, Thailand and the Philippines) maintained the highest level in the world over the three decades until the mid-1990s. In the same period real per capita income increased tenfold in Korea, fivefold in Thailand, and fourfold in Malaysia, while per capita income in Singapore and Hong Kong today exceeds those in some industrial countries.

The period from the mid-1980s to the mid-1990s was truly East Asia's decade. In Western countries the 'East Asian way' and how to learn from it was a popular topic of discussion at that time. Researchers praised Japanese business, as reflected in the classic studies of Toyota (see, for instance, Womack, Jones and Roos 1990; Clark and Fujimoto 1991). Some compared Western and East Asian ways of doing business and identified characteristics of firms and markets in Japan, South Korea, Taiwan and other East Asian countries, relating these to their particular social, political, historical and economic contexts (Whitley 1992; Fallows 1995). There were also those who, confident of the advent of an 'Asian century', warned of the threat from rising East Asia (Rohwer 1995). In its report on the 'East Asian Miracle' (1993), the World Bank also praised these economies for balanced budgets, high savings and investment rates, low inflation and openness to the world market.

However, belief in the invincibility of East Asia was first shaken by Japan's ongoing recession in the 1990s, and then shattered by the crash in East Asia in 1997. A financial market panic struck first in Thailand, before spreading to Malaysia, the Philippines, Indonesia, and eventually South Korea. The 'miracle economies' now went into free fall. Stock markets and currencies plunged and financial institutions and industrial companies defaulted on debts. Banking systems were paralysed and financial markets collapsed. In South Korea and Indonesia, governments changed in the aftermath of the crisis. The miraculous 'Asian Tigers' were abruptly transformed into 'Paper Tigers'.

The East Asian crisis has sparked a large body of literature seeking to explain its causes and development,[1] and this literature can be divided into two broad categories. One argues that the crisis was home-grown, the product of crony Asian capitalism (Krugman 1998a; Corsetti, Pesenti and Roubini 1998b). In this view, the crisis reflected institutional and structural distortions in the region, and mismanaged microeconomic structures, which produced moral hazard problems in financial and corporate governance. The other emphasizes the role of the financial panic arising from the instability of globalized financial markets. Proponents of this latter view argue that, in spite of some macroeconomic weaknesses and governance problems, the extent and depth of the crisis cannot be attributed to such factors but rather to the panicky reaction of global financial investors (Furman and Stiglitz 1998; Radelet and Sachs 1998).

Such divergent interpretations naturally implied fundamentally different policy prescriptions for the crisis. If the crisis was primarily one of panic, then the goal should be to control unstable global financial markets by creating new, reassuring regulatory rules that would limit financial liberalization. But if East Asia's crash was essentially the inevitable result of the specific features of Asian capitalism, then systemic reforms needed to be geared towards dismantling the East Asian type of capitalism.[2] The International Monetary Fund (IMF) adopted this view and urged the crisis countries radically to reform towards an Anglo-American style of capitalism (IMF 1997a, 1998a and c). The transformation of East Asia's corporate system to an Anglo-American one was one of the most important reform policies.

One of the hotly debated issues around the East Asian crash was the role of East Asian corporations in causing the crisis. Until the mid-1990s, East Asian firms were generally viewed as the main vehicle of the Asian Miracle. The Japanese *keiretsu* companies, South Korea's big business groups (the *chaebol*), and the Taiwanese small and medium-sized companies succeeded in catching up their Western counterparts through vigorous investment in technological and managerial learning, but the

1997 crisis raised serious doubts about the efficiency of the East Asian corporate system. The question arose: were the East Asian firms responsible or partly responsible for the financial crisis or were they victims of a financial crisis brought on by other factors (Claessens, Djankov and Xu 2000)?

Literatures emphasizing crony Asian capitalism see East Asian firms as the villain of the crash because, they argue, moral hazard problems arising from East Asia's 'wrong' corporate structure are at the root of the crisis. Therefore, according to this view, institutional reforms aimed at instituting Anglo-American standards are necessary to help East Asia recover from the crisis. This criticism focused on the Korean *chaebol* because Japan and Taiwan were not significantly affected by the 1997 crash, and the other crisis countries had no such large industrial companies.

1.2 Crisis of the *chaebol* and the Korean economy

The *chaebol*, South Korea's large family-controlled conglomerates, have been praised as the engine of Korea's rapid economic growth prior to 1997. Having grown out of small companies in a developing country, *chaebol* firms such as Samsung Electronics and Hyundai Motors have developed to the point where they compete with US, Japanese and European firms in world markets. The rise of the Korean economy was as phenomenal as the *chaebol*'s growth. Korea in 1960 was one of the world's poorest nations, with the majority of its population engaging in agriculture. Over the next 35 years, however, Korea transformed itself into the world's eleventh largest economy with significant heavy and high-technology industrial sectors.

The success of the *chaebol* and the economy was once the subject of extensive studies that praised Korea's idiosyncratic institutions such as state interventionism, bank-based finance and big business groups. 'Korea Inc.' was the term given to this close cooperation between state, banks and business and which was regarded as the hallmark of Korean industrialization.

However, the East Asian crisis in 1997 dramatically changed the research landscape. Neoclassical critics argued that the crisis revealed structural weaknesses in Korea's idiosyncratic economic institutions. The *chaebol* were criticized for features such as moral hazard, low transparency, low accountability, low profitability and high debt. Shareholder value literature emerged and maintained that distortions in corporate governance structure were at the core of moral hazard among the *chaebol*, and that this, in turn, fostered overborrowing, overinvestment and overdiversification. So, according to this view, without radical change in the *chaebol*'s corporate governance, the Korean economy would inevitably plunge into another crisis. Some critics even claimed that the *chaebol* system needed to be dismantled.

As this opinion predominated among international and Korean policy-makers and economists, it was decided that fundamental reforms of the *chaebol* and other institutions would be undertaken. These measures, which were introduced after the onset of the financial crisis, were intended to transform Korea's corporate governance and financial system into new ones resembling Anglo-American models.

Between 1997 and 1999, the *chaebol* system went through a radical change. One-third of the 30 largest *chaebol* groups collapsed and were completely dismantled. Another third lost assets in radical ways. Only the remaining third proved strong enough to recover from the crisis without such asset curtailments, but they also had to significantly reorganize governance, business and financial structure.

This acute discontinuity in theory and practice of the *chaebol* and Korean economy raises many questions. Why had the *chaebol* been successful for such a long period of time and then fallen into such deep trouble so quickly? What happened to them in the period preceding the crisis? If the *chaebol* really invested excessively, from where did the money come? Did Korea's financial system contribute to the financial crisis and, if so, how? And, furthermore, why did all *chaebol* groups not collapse, although they had similar corporate structures? What were the differences between surviving and failed *chaebol*?

This book tries to find out answers to those questions. It aims to understand how the crisis occurred in the context of Korea's financial, industrial and corporate institutions, and how it was influenced by the business dynamics of the *chaebol*.[3] In this regard, the questions running throughout this book are divided into two aspects: first, the possibility of a correlation between Korea's corporate governance, as well as its financial system, and the crisis; second, the analysis of the *chaebol*'s crisis and restructuring with regard to firm-level differences in strategies and capabilities.

These two points assume that the failures which caused the crisis included financial, institutional and business aspects. Since all of these aspects were closely linked, we will emphasize the need to see them in combination in order to fully grasp the crisis, and further-more, the post-crisis restructuring of the *chaebol* and the Korean economy.

We will take Korea's automotive industry as a case study. This industry is selected for the following reasons. First, it is one of the leading sectors in the Korean economy. With suppliers included, the industry is indeed the largest manufacturing sector in Korea, accounting for 10 per cent of industrial production.

Second, all five carmakers belonged to the largest *chaebol* groups: Hyundai (the largest), Samsung (the second-largest), Daewoo (the third-largest), Kia (the sixth largest), and Ssangyong (the seventh largest).[4] Hence, a study of the industry will vividly show the growth and crisis of the *chaebol*.

Third, the successive collapse of the four carmakers significantly affected Korea's financial system. Kia's collapse in mid-1997 played an important role in triggering a panic in financial markets. Furthermore, Daewoo Group's default in 1999, which was largely due to its automotive sector, was one of the world's largest bankruptcies, and alone contributed two-thirds of the total US$100 billion of non-performing loans that jeopardized Korea's financial system. Hence the study of Daewoo can explain a great part of Korea's financial crisis during 1997–9.

From the study of the *chaebol* and the automotive industry, we will argue that, first, liberal reforms in the period of the Kim Young-Sam government (1993–7) concerning deregulation and globalization were substantially related to the crisis. We will show, second, that those *chaebol* firms which, enthusiastically embracing financial and industrial deregulation, expanded businesses into geographically and industrially new areas collapsed eventually, whereas others that instead chose innovative growth, while consolidating technological and organizational capabilities, survived the crisis.

1.3 Controversy over East Asia's industrial growth

Before investigating the 1997 crisis, we need first to look at how pre-crisis literature explained East Asia's past economic growth. This is because explanations of the crisis are a continuation of pre-crisis explanations of East Asia's past growth.

In the discussion about East Asia's industrial growth there have been three main approaches: the neoclassical approach, dependency theory, and the developmental state perspective. We will propose the third as the most suitable for explaining East Asia's past growth because it answers questions that are not answered (or even addressed) by the other two. Despite this, however, it will be helpful to review the main concepts and questions of all three approaches in the light of East Asia's recent crisis. Let us begin with the neoclassical explanation.

Neoclassical interpretation of East Asian newly industrializing countries' economic growth

Neoclassical literature explained the success of East Asia with its trade theory, following the traditional Ricardian ideas of comparative advantages (Krueger 1979, 1980, 1990, 1995; Balassa 1981, 1991). Contrary to other developing countries, which relied on protection and import-substitution, East Asian NICs (newly industrializing countries) – South Korea, Taiwan, Hong Kong and Singapore – pursued a policy of export orientation and openness to the world market. By shifting from protection or import-substitution to an outward-oriented policy, according to this view, positive benefits were gained.

The primary gain was 'getting the prices right': while higher tariffs cause greater distortions and lower growth, reduced trade barriers eliminate distortions, lower the prices of capital goods and materials, and reallocate investments to sectors with comparative advantages. East Asian economies were more successful than others because they gave relatively more scope to the market; so Hughes (1988: p. 38) maintains, 'neoclassical economic principles are alive and well, and working particularly effectively in the East Asian countries. Once public goods are provided for and the most obvious distortions corrected, markets seem to do the job of allocating resources reasonably well, and certainly better than centralized decision-making.'

Government intervention is rejected. A critical issue is the possibility of rent seeking. Neoclassical economics emphasizes that a major source of inefficiency is the collusion between government and business through the provision of rents that advance the interests of politicians, bureaucrats and their private-sector clients at the expense of social welfare. In economies with import substitution, protective tariffs, price controls and other government interventions, heavy losses can occur as individuals allocate resources to seeking out preferential benefits associated with controls. Krueger (1990: p. 4) observed, 'Businessmen devote much of their time to circumnavigating government regulations and controls, rather than to producing goods and services.'

To summarize, neoclassical economists argued that Korea and other East Asian NICs could avoid rent-seeking activities among enterprises by introducing an export promotion policy. This policy would force private firms to be exposed to fierce competition in the world market, which would discipline their misbehaviour. Therefore, according to conventional neoclassical economics, '(product) market pressure' is the ultimate solution for problems of economic governance.

By the 1970s, it had become evident that the East Asian NICs were growing more rapidly than other developing countries that relied on protection and import substitution. In spite of the First and Second Oil Shocks, and following recessions in most Western and developing countries, the East Asian NICs – together with Japan – continued to grow rapidly. This had a profound influence on the theory and practice of political economy of industrialization.

The challenge from dependency theory

In the 1970s, the dependency approach emerged in Latin America and challenged the neoclassical approach. Dependency theorists argued that underdevelopment and stagnating growth in Third World countries resulted not from their lack of certain Western characteristics such as free market principles, but from their structural position in the world capitalist system (Frank 1967; Dos Santos 1970). As in the Marxist concept of a capitalist society, the world system is conceived as a hierarchically structured system of dominance, in which various political, economic and cultural mechanisms exist that reproduce inequality and the gap between rich and poor nations. So, without breaking away from the world trade and finance regime (the General Agreement on Tariffs and Trade, or GATT, IMF and World Bank), developing countries could not catch up with Western economies.

Neoclassical economists criticized dependency theory by citing the East Asian NICs (Krueger 1979; Hughes 1988). In the same world system of trade and finance, the East Asian economies succeeded because they took advantage of the system, instead of rejecting it, and promoted export industries with comparative advantages.

A weakness of the neoclassical interpretation is, however, that it generally ignores the importance of particular political and institutional frameworks which allowed the East Asian NICs to adopt an export-promotion policy (see Haggard 1990). The export promotion policy itself was combined with various government interventions.

For example, the neoclassical interpretation ignores the importance of firms and their nationality. An outstanding feature of the Korean, Taiwanese and Japanese economies was that local companies, under national ownership and control, predominated, rather than transnational companies (TNCs) from Western countries. This is in striking contrast to Latin American NICs where TNCs dominated local industries. The governments of the three Northeast Asian countries provided various financial and fiscal subsidies for local companies to encourage exports, and protected domestic markets from TNCs. The *chaebol* in Korea flourished in this institutional environment.

Dependency literature focused on the hazards of TNCs for developing economies. Evans (1979), for instance, in his efforts to develop the concept of 'dependent development', criticized TNCs for negative influences on economic growth in Latin American countries.[5] He argued that TNCs were the primary partner in a 'triple alliance' of state elites, foreign firms and local firms, and played a crucial role in establishing and deepening an import-substitution regime because the regime defended TNCs' market position within the economy. The TNCs' interest in developing countries is in exploiting the local market rather than the export market. Their power, based on superior technology and market position, constituted a fundamental constraint on national policy. This was shown, for example, in the dependent development of the Latin American automobile industry (Bennett and Sharpe 1985).

There were efforts to extend the dependent development approach to Korea (see Lim 1985; Kim E.-M. 1987).[6] But they did not succeed, as in Korea the state and local firms played more important roles. Lim recognized that the Korean state, by establishing various legal and economic institutions, had constrained the entrance of TNCs to Korea. TNCs' ownership and control of local firms were allowed only in the form of joint ventures with local partners. Even in cases of joint ventures, TNCs were not allowed to acquire majority equity participation that would guarantee full management control. In Latin America, however, the presence and dominance of TNCs and foreign ownership and control of local firms were established facts.

Consequently, Evans (1987) acknowledged that, 'if transnational domination of industrialization is the core of contemporary dependency, then South Korea and Taiwan are not dependent in the same way that Latin American NICs are dependent'.

To summarize, dependency theory's critique of neoclassical economics with reference to the dominance of TNCs in developing countries raised important questions about particular political and institutional frameworks which enabled the East Asian NICs to overcome dependency. Yet, by itself, dependency theory did not succeed in explaining East Asian growth: it was developmental state literature which established a new approach.

The perspective of developmental state capitalism

In the latter half of 1980s, the Korean economy performed remarkably. Associated with the appreciation of the Japanese Yen after the Plaza Agreement in 1985 between Japan and America, exports of Korea's main industrial products, most of which were in direct competition with their Japanese counterparts, grew rapidly. This resulted in noticeable improvements in both the macro and micro economy. Korea reported a trade surplus, the first one since the start of industrialization in 1961 and, consequently, Korea's sovereign foreign debts (the fourth largest in the world after Brazil, Argentina, and Mexico in 1984) were reduced to the smallest, below US$25 billion, by 1990. *Chaebol* firms, the main engines of export growth, doubled turnovers and returns. As a result, some of the largest *chaebol* firms were included in *Fortune* magazine's list of the world's largest 500 non-oil producing firms, and foreign scholars became interested in their success.

One of the best-known foreign studies of the *chaebol* and Korean economy in this period is Alice Amsden's *Asia's Next Giant: South Korea and Late Industrialization* (1989), which illustrated the way that the state in Korea facilitated the growth of *chaebol* firms by effectively intervening in finance, corporate governance, export promotion and technological learning. Together with Chalmers Johnson's monumental 1982 work, *MITI and the Japanese Miracle – The Growth of Industrial Policy, 1925–1975*, and Robert Wade's *Governing the Market: Economic Theory and the Role of Government in East Asian Industrialization* (1990), Amsden's work helped to establish a new perspective on political economy, the 'developmental state' approach.

Advocates of the developmental state (DS) approach, sometimes called 'revisionists', documented cases of state interventions in the three Northeast Asian countries during the fast growth periods, from the 1950s to the mid-1970s in Japan, from the mid-1960s to the late 1980s in Korea, and from the 1950s to the 1980s in Taiwan.[7]

Taken together, all these interventionist policies were called 'industrial policy'. An important contribution of the DS approach is that it elucidated industrial policy and made it a legitimate concern of economics (Johnson 1982, 1995; Amsden 1985, 1989; White and Wade 1985; Wade 1990).

By contrast, neoclassical economics does not acknowledge the 'contributions' of industrial policy, and instead insists that the East Asian success occurred in spite of (rather than because of) industrial policy.[8] Korea's Big Push for heavy and chemical industrialization in the 1970s in particular, together with the Japanese Ministry of International Trade and Industry (MITI) failure in its computer chip push in the 1980s, were evaluated as typical failures of industrial policy (World Bank 1993: p. 86).

Indeed, neoclassical policy-makers in the World Bank opposed Korea's promotion of capital and technology-intensive industries. They instead proposed that Korea concentrate on existing labour-intensive industries such as clothing and textile production because they had more comparative advantages (see, for instance, Balassa 1981).

Nonetheless, in view of the triumph of Japanese industries and the decline of their American counterparts in the 1980s, DS literature acquired broad support even in the USA, the stronghold of liberalist public policy (see Johnson 1984; Nester 1998).

A critical issue regarding industrial policy, as with other state interventions, is the hazard of rent-seeking behaviour, recently called 'moral hazard'. We have already seen that neoclassical literature emphasized the export orientation of Korea and other East Asian NICs, which exposed private firms to 'product market pressure' in the world market. What, then, is the hazard of an industry policy that supports export orientation?

The question of moral hazard with regard to industrial policy is at the core of opposing interpretations of the East Asian miracle as well as its crisis. This question in turn can be referred to the governance system: that is, to the various political, economic and legal institutions that constituted the industrial policy.[9]

The DS approach argues that the governance system of the three Northeast Asian countries was efficient in preventing rent-seeking activities. Amsden (1989) explains as follows:

> In late-industrializing countries, the state intervenes with subsidies deliberately to distort relative prices in order to stimulate economic activity. This has been as true in Korea, Japan, and Taiwan as it has been in Brazil, India, and Turkey. In Korea, Japan, and Taiwan, however, the state has exercised discipline over subsidy recipients. In exchange for subsidies, the state has imposed performance standards on private firms. Subsidies have not been giveaways, but instead have been dispensed on the principle of reciprocity. With more disciplined firms, subsidies and protection have been lower and more effective than otherwise. (p. 8)

It is noteworthy that Amsden observes that the discipline exerted by the state and the rise of big business groups in Korea were interactive, as big business consolidated its power in response to the government's performance-based incentives.[10]

Chang (1993, 1994) and Haggard and Lee (1995) also emphasize the state's role as a corporate discipliner, both relying on Williamson's transaction cost and hierarchy-market theory (1975, 1985).

In the 1980s and 1990s, international debates on corporate governance emerged among industrialized countries. It was argued that in the USA 'the market for corporate control' via mergers and acquisitions, based on the highest priority of shareholder value, works as an effective corporate governance mechanism (Jensen and Ruback 1983; Jensen 1988). In Japan, which does not have a well-functioning capital market, the main bank system associated with *keiretsu* is seen as playing an important role in corporate governance (Aoki and Patrick 1994). In continental Europe, the primary roles of the German *Hausbank* in corporate governance, and also the German two-tier board system in which diverse stakeholders participate, attracted attention (Schmidt and Drukarczyk 1997).

The existing literature on corporate governance and financial systems usually refers to only two archetypes: a capital market-based model (the Anglo-American model) and a bank-based model (the German-Japanese model). In view of the crucial role of the state in corporate governance and finance in state-led capitalism, however, another archetype can be suggested: a state-based model (see Woo 1991; Chang 1993, 1994, 1999).

This model existed not only in Japan, Korea and Taiwan in their high growth periods, but can also be found elsewhere as late-industrializing developmental states emerged, for instance, in post-war France until the mid-1980s (Lorianux 1999; Walter 2000) and in Finland and Austria from the 1950s to the 1970s (Vartiainen 1999). This is not surprising because, according to DS literature, the developmental state was not invented by Northeast Asia in the twentieth century, but dates back to medieval Venice, whose absolutist state effectively supported the rise of modern capitalism by fostering nationalistic and mercantilist goals. The mercantilist states in Europe in the seventeenth and eighteenth century also had features of the developmental state. The most eminent case of a developmental state in the last century has been the Bismarck–Meiji model of German and Japanese late industrialization. This model significantly – and directly – influenced Korea's military and economic leaders in choosing the path of industrialization (Amsden 1989; Woo 1991; Kohli 1999).[11]

In the early 1990s, the DS perspective became one of the dominant interpretations of Korea's industrial success. At the same time, however, Korea's liberalist policy-makers and scholars, including neoclassical economists who strongly criticized the developmental state, gained increasing influence and undertook liberal reforms, particularly in the period 1993–7. The IMF, World Bank, World Trade Organization (WTO) and Organisation for Economic Cooperation and Development (OECD) acclaimed and supported the reforms. By the time that the crisis in

Korea occurred, in late 1997, the developmental system had been largely dismantled. The crisis therefore renewed the debate about the developmental state and liberal reforms.

1.4   Controversy over the 1997 crisis in East Asia

Two main interpretations of the crisis

There is a wide range of explanations of the East Asian crisis, from a bank-run model to a socio-cultural interpretation which attributed the crisis to a failed 'neo-Confucianism'.[12] However, insofar as economic institutions are associated with the crisis, there are two different lines of argument: one is from neoclassical economics and the other from the developmental state perspective. We will here only briefly sketch these two main types of interpretations of the 1997 crisis because they will be analysed in detail in the following chapters.

In line with its critical attitude towards industrial policy, neoclassical economics interprets the 1997 crisis as a case of 'government failure', a result of the East Asian developmental state. This argument attributes the crisis to supposedly specifically East Asian factors such as industry policy, close state–business links, bank-based finance and large business groups, all of which produced moral hazard, cronyism and corruption (Greenspan 1998; IMF 1998c; Krugman 1998a). As these institutions are rooted so deeply in East Asian capitalism, the problem is seen as essentially a structural one. In particular, East Asian enterprises were the 'villains' of the piece because their unsustainably high debt ratios, low profitability and excessive diversification caused the financial crisis (Claessens, Djankov and Lang 2000). The rapid growth of East Asia was not sustainable and it finally collapsed in late 1997. From now on, we will call this interpretation the 'finally collapsed' argument.

In contrast with the neoclassical critique of East Asia's institutions, DS literature argues that the East Asian financial crisis was a result of the decline of the developmental state in the region in the 1990s (Chang 1998, 2000; Wade and Veneroso 1998; Woo-Cumings 1999; Amsden 2001). They point out that in Korea, a unique case among the three Northeast Asian countries affected by the crisis, the interventionist state retreated in the 1990s. Indeed, the Kim Young-Sam government in 1993–7 abolished industrial policy and other interventionist institutions. Thus, according to the DS literature, liberalization was responsible for the crisis.

Discussion in Korea about the 1997 crisis

Discussions within Korea about the 1997 crisis closely follow these same two lines of argument. The unprecedented and destructive character of the financial crisis not only surprised the Korean people; they also felt shamed by the IMF bailout programme because it imposed various limitations on Korea's sovereignty in economic policy.

Despite this, the majority of Korean scholars and policy-makers followed the neoclassical interpretation of the crisis, and welcomed the Kim Dae-Jung government's free market reform initiatives. What is more, in some circles, the crisis was welcomed since it gave Korea the opportunity – with the help of the IMF – radically to change economic institutions and thereby guarantee Korea's quantum leap to advanced economy status.[13] Publications from the KDI (Korea Development Institute), a leading public economic research institute that represents dominant opinions among policy-makers and scholars, clearly show this optimistic trend (see, for example, Nam *et al.* 1999).

There were and are, of course, critics of the reform policies, but in most cases they sought even more radical free market reforms (see, for instance, Kim K.-W. 1999; Choe J.-P. 1999). The majority of Korean scholars and policy-makers, many of whom were trained in America in the 1980s and 1990s, have a strong tendency to believe that institutions deviating from Anglo-American standards are 'abnormal' and 'distorted'. Korea's conglomerates, together with bank-based finance and industrial policy, are now criticized in this way. For example, Kang C.-K. (1995) and Choe J.-P. (1999) maintain that the *chaebol* is a distortion of market economy, a rent-seeking business organization. According to them, these deviations were responsible for the 1997 crisis.

Following the same line of argument, a serious attack on the *chaebol* came from advocates of shareholder value in Korea. Associated with some non-governmental organizations (NGOs) that support liberal public policies, they concentrate on the *chaebol*'s ownership and control structure. They regard the concentrated ownership and control of the *chaebol* as not merely a distortion of small shareholders' rights, but also as pre-modern and abnormal because it deviates from Berle and Means' (1932) model of a modern corporation with dispersed ownership and control. Because this distortion and abnormality in the *chaebol*'s corporate governance is a real weakness of the Korean economy, strengthening shareholder value will substantially improve productivity (Kim K.-W. 1999; Jang 2001). Consequently, the majority of the Korean literature holds that a fundamental reorganization of Korea's governance and financial system along capital market lines will bring the nation up to date.

There are some critics of the neoclassical interpretation of the crisis and the subsequent capital market-oriented reform policy; but their respective lines of argument are ambiguous, and often mixed with the neoclassical one. Hence they failed to provide a clear-cut alternative approach to important issues such as reform of the *chaebol* (see, for example, Kim and Kim 1999; Yoo 1998, 2000).

The most critical attitude towards the majority view can be found in Cho Y.-C. (1999, 2001) and Chang and Park (2000). Following the DS interpretation of Korea's growth and recent crisis, Chang and Park criticize the moves towards a capital market-based model. They argue that this ignores the importance of path dependency in national institutions. So, instead of the pro-Anglo-American reforms, Chang and Park suggest reinforcing interventionism, including a partial revival of a developmental state (a democratic one this time) because, they believe, the 1997 crisis was a result of liberalization. In contrast, Cho prefers a bank-based model as the future of Korea's governance and financial system because the banking system, he argues, is expected to remain the primary channel of finance for Korea's corporations rather than the capital market.

Economic institutions and business dynamics

When we began this study, our primary concern was the business aspect of the 1997 crisis. It was assumed that *chaebol* firms' risky investments – particularly their excessive diversifications and capacity expansions – had been the primary cause of the crisis. Furthermore, we supposed that a study of the *chaebol*'s business dynamics would suffice to explain the crisis, and therefore that institutions of corporate governance and finance need not concern us. As a matter of fact, we shared the 'finally collapsed' argument of the crisis, assuming that the neoclassical interpretation of Korea's 'distorted' corporate governance and financial system had turned out to be true.

However, our research into Korea's automotive industry led to the realization of the importance of industrial policy in limiting the *chaebol*'s diversifications and expansion of capacity. Then, a series of questions arose: what precise form did industrial policy take? What role did it play? Why did it disappear? Our research showed that the abolition of industrial policy occurred as a part of liberalization in the 1990s.

Rethinking previous assumptions, and re-examining the literature on corporate governance and financial institutions, led to the conclusion that the neoclassical interpretation of the East Asian crisis is significantly at odds with the historical facts of Korea's past growth, as well as the liberalization in the 1990s. Another approach, found in DS literature, seemed to provide a more comprehensive perspective. Consequently, our interpretation of the 1997 crisis follows the DS approach, insofar as Korea's economic institutions are concerned.

Nonetheless, the existing DS literature could not satisfactorily explain another important aspect of the crisis: the crisis arising from the *chaebol*'s business dynamics. The successive collapses of *chaebol* groups that had diversified into major industries in the 1990s, for example, needed another explanation. A fundamental question was why had they excessively invested in capacity expansion and diversification, instead of research and development (R&D) and other technology-based assets. Failures in firms' strategies and organizational capabilities seemed as important as institutional failures for explaining the collapses. Therefore we needed an approach that emphasized firms' strategies and organizational capabilities.

1.5   Business dynamics and theory of the firm

A weakness of pre-crisis literatures on Korea's success, not only in neoclassical but also in DS literature, is that they tended to concentrate on successful companies in major industries, such as Hyundai Motors, Samsung Electronics, Posco Steel and so on, while neglecting the failures. Failed Korean firms such as Daewoo Motors and Hyundai Electronics, did not attract attention, and therefore the large-scale collapses of many *chaebol* groups in 1997–9 came as a shock.

Now, paradoxically, after the crisis, existing literatures have a strong tendency to exaggerate the structural weaknesses of the *chaebol* system and forget successful aspects. For these 'crisis literatures', the rapid recovery of the Korean economy, led by exports from the big *chaebol* groups, and the record-breaking performances of some *chaebol* companies since 1999 (again, Hyundai Motors, Samsung Electronics, Posco Steel, etc.), must be a surprise.

We need to correct this tendency to be overselective which is found in the existing literatures. In this book, we will investigate both successful and failed *chaebol* firms and their differences in order to gain a more comprehensive perspective. In the following, we will discuss neoclassical and neo-Institutionalist theories of the firm and then introduce the 'dynamic capabilities approach' to see what a firm is and what makes it succeed.

Limitations of the neoclassical and neo-Institutionalist theories of the firm

The fundamental question for a firm is how it achieves and sustains competitive advantage in dynamic market competition. However, traditional neoclassical economic theory is not interested in differences between firms.[14] A firm is regarded as a legal entity, in which a production team (management), acting rationally with full information, chooses a production set (a set of feasible production functions) that is most likely to minimize production costs so as to maximize profits or present share value of the firm (Alchian and Demsetz 1972; Hart 1989), but the production set itself is regarded as a 'black box' (Nelson 1972).

Furthermore, the theory completely represses the uncertainty and contingency that often characterizes strategic behaviours of firms, and it also ignores the differences in vision, opinions, bets and efforts among firms (Nelson 1994). Accepting the proposition that relevant information is fully accessible for every firm and its management is fully rational, it is assumed that all firms are operating in the same economic context and hence that they have the same strategies to do the same thing. The question of a firm's competitive advantage, which is the central concern of business management literature, is regarded as too trivial to answer. As Nelson (1991) points out, 'the theoretical preconceptions shared by most economists lead them to ignore firms' differences'. Hence, the theory offers no real basis for understanding why at certain times some firms are successful in product market competition but others are not.

The principal-agent theory of the firm accepts the neoclassical firm as proposition but adds to it the notion of a control hierarchy. This theory concentrates on the ways in which the owners can discipline the managers with whom they have contracted. Its main concern is the owner's (shareholder or creditor or something else) problems of coping with asymmetric information, measurement of performance and incentives of the management, all of which are reduced to the problem of agency cost.

Like agency theory, transaction cost theory as proposed by Coase (1937) and Williamson (1975, 1985) also focuses on informational asymmetry and the resulting information costs. The difference is only that, while the former is concerned with the asymmetric information involved in designing contractual relations between principals and agents, the latter focuses on the information costs (transaction costs) involved in transaction.

Transaction cost theory has more relevance to explanations of the meaning of differences among firms because it tries to understand the asset-specificity that incorporates firms' investment in facilities and skills (Williamson 1985). However, the theory's concern is transactions involving existing assets, rather than the creation of such assets. At issue is the firm's decision on whether to buy or produce (i.e., whether the costs of transaction carried out by the firm are lower by relying on the market or by internalizing them within the firm). Transactions are the unit of analysis, while everything else, including asset-specificity, remains constant and static. The creation of new firm-specific assets, particularly in production and R&D, is not of interest.

Therefore, in analysing transactions and legal contracts, the 'bounded rationality' (Simon 1957) and 'opportunism' (Williamson 1985) of all concerned parties are more important concepts than asset-specificity. The theory is not at all concerned with the competitive advantage and disadvantage of firms.

As Amsden (1997a) argues, transaction cost theory cannot help us understand the behaviour of firms in late industrializing countries because they have not yet acquired firm-specific assets, and hence have to concentrate resources on creating new assets in production and R&D, rather than on transactions of existing assets.[15]

All three theories regard the firm as a legal entity in which the owner contracts with insiders (managers and workers) and outsiders (suppliers, dealers, financial institutions and so on). None of these endeavours to look into the 'black box of production' and the management's concerns with creating and dealing with the firm's competitive advantages (specific assets) that produce the current return and ensure the sustainable growth of the firm.

Dynamic capabilities approach to the firm

In contrast, the dynamic capabilities approach provides a more coherent framework for understanding features in developing firm-specific capabilities and the manner in which corporate competencies are built and renewed (Teece and Pisano 1998).[16] This approach concentrates on two aspects: first, the shifting character of the environment, and second, the key role of strategic management in properly adapting, integrating and re-configuring internal and external organizational skills, resources and functional competencies in the rapidly changing environment. In the dynamic capabilities approach, also called the 'competence-based theory of the firm', the firm's assets such as facilities, skills and other capabilities are important, rather than the transaction or agency relationship (Chandler 1992a).

In the theory of dynamic capabilities, the focus is on the 'three different if strongly related features of a firm that must be recognized if one is to describe it adequately: its strategy, its structure, and its core capabilities' (Nelson 1991). Let us look at these concepts.

Knowledge and capability

As seen above, both the principal-agent and the transaction cost theory are concerned with information problems. These theories conceptualize the firm as a system of processing information-related problems (Simon 1957).[17]

Information is, however, a closed set of data. In contrast, the capabilities approach developed by Penrose (1959), Nelson and Winter (1982), Chandler (1990, 1992a, 1992b), Teece (1993) and Teece, Rumelt, Dosi and Winter (1994) focuses on the specific knowledge created by the firm and transferred among firms, seeing the firm as a repository of knowledge. Firm-specific knowledge is the core of the firm's specific assets. Knowledge is essentially an open set of data, so that the process of knowledge creation and transfer – a central problem for all firms – includes interpretative ambiguity and uncertainty, and subjective and intersubjective data and relationships (Fransman 1998). Firm-specific knowledge is the core of the firm's capability.[18]

Firms in late industrializing countries have to build knowledge-based competence through technology transfer from advanced countries. But this is a complex process because it includes 'uncertain', 'subjective' and 'tacit' factors. Some *chaebol* firms have successfully acquired relevant capabilities in spite of these difficulties, but others have failed.

Strategy and vision

For the firm as a knowledge organization, a significant problem is to present a strategy and vision that embodies insight into the future. The firm's strategic planners are 'image creators' and the images emerge from the experience and knowledge that is generated within the firm. The firm's strategic vision is not merely the solution of a profit maximization problem as many neoclassical economists assume; the strategic commitments are as much a matter of faith in top management as well as tradition, as they are of cost-benefit calculation (Nelson 1994).

In contrast with game theorists, who analyse the nature of competitive interaction between rival firms to reveal how a firm can influence the behaviour and actions of rival firms and thus the market environment, Teece, Pisano and Shuen (1997) point out that firms which have a distinctive competitive advantage over their rivals ought not be transfixed by the latter's moves and countermoves. Only where competing firms do not have deep-seated competitive advantages and core capabilities can the manipulation of the market environment by the strategic moves and countermoves among rival firms be usefully formulated in game-theoretic frameworks.

In this regard, the role of entrepreneurs – in its Schumpeterian meaning – is crucial in firms in late industrializing countries. Some *chaebol* entrepreneurs, closely cooperating with the developmental state, created the vision and strategy that led their firms to successfully build distinctive capabilities.[19]

Structure, organizational routine and path dependency

The structure of a firm relates to how a firm is organized and governed, and how decisions are made and carried out. As organizational capabilities – such as managerial and technological capabilities – are the result of sequential successful solutions to problems, there is a tendency for firms to establish fixed routines to solve problems.

According to Chandler (1962) a firm's strategy determines its structure, but this means only that changes in strategy come chronologically before those of structure. Structure has as much impact on strategy as strategy has on structure. This is evident from the fact that structure is difficult to change, often far more so than strategy. To significantly change the way a firm is organized and decisions are made and carried out is time-consuming and costly (Nelson 1994).

Thus organizational structure is resistant to change because it embodies the core capabilities of the organization. What an organization, a firm, can do well has something of a life of its own. 'The essence of competencies and capabilities is embedded in organizational processes of one kind or another' (Teece 1997). To explain the sticky nature of organizational structure, Nelson and Winter (1982) propose the 'hierarchy of practised organizational routines' as a key building block in the notion of organizational capabilities. Because of this 'stickiness', the developing path of a firm's strategy and capability follows an evolutionary line: path dependency.

A company's core competences become core rigidities when it continues to rely on established routines to solve problems, even where the environment has changed fundamentally. Leonard-Barton (1992, 1995) develops the idea of core organizational rigidities. The conditions at the time of the company's founding and flourishing create an internal consensus about the ways things should be done to succeed. Successful routines and capabilities are established. However, they solidify to internal inertia over years, and the firm loses the ability to learn and create new routines to solve radically new problems.

In Chapters 6–9, we will use these concepts of the dynamic capabilities approach to compare successful and failed *chaebol* firms and analyse their differences. Korea's carmakers will be researched as a case study.

1.6   Existing studies of Korean carmakers and the industry

Academic research into the Korean automobile industry began in the mid-1980s as the 'dependent development' approach of Latin America was introduced. In the beginning, its critical view of the capitalist world regime was widely accepted in Korea. Soon, however, the approach's assumption of the primary role of TNCs in economies was found to be incorrect with regard to Korea. It was recognized that, without the government's industrial policy and the existence of strong local companies, the rapid growth of the Korean automobile industry from the mid-1980s, which was led by car exports, would not have been possible.

Despite this, some argued that the Korean automobile industry also followed the pattern of dependent development because Korean carmakers, in spite of national ownership and control, also were dependent on TNCs in technology (see, for example, Shin S.-S. 1988). Thus, the debate focused on dependency in technology.

Ryu J.-H. (1989) was the first to study firm-level differences. He surveyed the three main Korean carmakers, Hyundai, Kia and Daewoo, and compared corporate structure and strategy. It was shown that Hyundai Motors, supported by government policies, grew quickly because it developed and launched its own cars without relying on TNCs' technology. In contrast, Daewoo Motors (under GM – General Motors – control) and Kia Motors (assembler of knocked down kits for various TNCs and then an original equipment manufacturer (OEM) supplier for Ford) did not perform well because their ability to expand exports and build technological know-how was constrained by agreements with TNCs. Daewoo's failure in the 1970s and 1980s showed that national ownership and control of firms was a necessary condition for export orientation and catching up successfully in technology. The failure of Kia, however, which was owned and controlled by local capital but which chose to rely on TNCs in exports marketing and technology, showed that the strategic determination of *chaebol* entrepreneurs was also important.

In the late 1980s, it became more obvious that Hyundai would grow faster in the future than Kia and Daewoo. Daewoo in particular faced chronic crises. The focus of studies among Korean scholars shifted to technological learning. There remained the question of how Korean firms overcame the knowledge-barrier formed by the technological monopoly of TNCs. The surveys of Lee J.-J. and Hyun Y.-S. (1985) and Hyun Y.-S. (1988) showed that Hyundai had achieved remarkable progress in acquiring new product development technology, as well as in developing manufacturing engineering. In the 1990s, when all Korean carmakers attempted to develop in-house designed cars, Hyun surveyed new car development at Hyundai, Daewoo and Kia (see, for example, Hyun 1997, 1999). The surveys were conducted for the IMVP (International Motor Vehicle Programme) organized by the Massachusetts Institute of Technology.

The mechanisms of technological learning and technology transfer had not yet been studied in detail, however. The dissertation of Kim G. (1994) was the most successful in this respect. Relying on the neo-Schumpeterian theory of learning and innovation, he surveyed engine development projects by Hyundai, and showed a variety of paths of learning and transfer of knowledge. Also, innovation studies of Korea's electronics, D-RAM, and other main industries showed that successful Korean firms overcame the problem of technological dependency through vigorous strategic efforts to seek out multiple ways of learning and knowledge transfer (see, for example, Choi 1996; Lee K. 1997; Kim L.-S. 1997, 1999; Kim S.-R. 1997).

In the mid-1990s, as Korea was becoming a member of the OECD, the *Zeitgeist* of liberalization and globalization, accompanying a certain triumphant and optimistic trend among Korean economic leaders, overwhelmed critical study. Diversification and capacity expansion by *chaebol* firms were positively evaluated, without careful research. Scholarly articles dealing with Daewoo's overseas automotive ventures in the 1990s, for example, consistently reflected optimism among Daewoo managers as well as Korean business administration scholars (see Seo, Kwack and Song 1998).

Another example was Samsung's entry into the car industry in 1994. Coming at the time of the abolition of industrial policy, which had previously limited new entry into major industries, it caused a controversy between liberals and state interventionists (see Hu S.-S. 1994). In spite of its intensity, however, the controversy did not lead to meaningful studies on critical issues such as diversification by *chaebol* groups.

This optimistic trend was completely reversed by the 1997 crisis. Yun J.-H. *et al.*, for example, wrote in 1998 that the Korean automobile industry was suffering from all the problems of the Korean economy that caused the crisis. In reality, the crisis hit the automobile industry in an extreme way: only Hyundai survived and all the other manufacturers – Kia, Daewoo, Samsung and Ssangyong – collapsed.

Nonetheless, strangely, there was no meaningful study on the failed carmakers. The only exception is Cho S.-J.'s dissertation on Kia's growth and collapse (2000); but he regards the collusive relationship between management and trade unions that allegedly distorted the corporate governance of the company as the cause of the corporate collapse, rather than strategy, capabilities and organizational routines.

In spite of these defects and weaknesses, we will use the existing studies extensively in Chapters 5–9. However, we will add new findings and interpret from new viewpoints.

1.7 Structure of the book

In analysing crisis and restructuring, which had, on one hand, an institutional dimension and, on the other hand, a dimension relating to firms' business dynamics, we start with a discussion of the former. This is because firms' business cannot be thoroughly understood without reference to the broader context of the overall economy.

Chapters 2–4 will investigate the growth and crisis of East Asia with particular reference to the governance and financial system. Chapter 2 will provide an overview of the controversy surrounding the East Asian crisis. The neoclassical critique of crony Asian capitalism will be evaluated in a critical light. This chapter will instead take up the argument that emphasizes financial panic as an essential element of the East Asian crisis: large-scale foreign capital inflow into the region preceding the crisis created a boom and its panic reverse caused the crisis. Therefore, this chapter will discuss the liberalization in East Asia in the 1990s because, in our view, it was this which not only made the inflow and outflow of foreign money possible, but also eroded East Asia's governance system.

Chapter 3 will continue the examination of the East Asian crisis, but focusing on the Korean economy. We will first examine some of Korea's idiosyncratic institutions which existed until the late 1980s, and see how the corporate governance and financial mechanisms worked in the context of developmental state capitalism. Then we will look at the effects of financial liberalization and industrial deregulation in the 1990s in relation to the 1997 crisis. Two aspects will be examined: first, the role of financial liberalization in allowing the large-scale inflow of international money into Korea, fostering overlending by banks and over-investment by *chaebol* groups, and making the economy vulnerable to panic; and second, the role of liberalization in creating *laissez-faire* in the governance, which encouraged moral hazard among *chaebol* enterprises.

Chapter 4 focuses on the corporate governance structure of the *chaebol*. The question is whether the concentrated ownership and control structure of the *chaebol*, being regarded as 'abnormal' and 'distorted' by liberalist critics, was responsible for the crisis. The chapter will emphasize that corporate governance may not be reduced to a microeconomic structure of firm-level ownership and control; it is the national institutions of governance and financial system which determine the nature of corporate governance mechanisms.

Chapter 5 will provide a historical overview of the Korean automobile industry and carmakers, in relation to the various interpretations of Korea's growth and crisis. The various roles of industrial policy in promoting the industry will be examined. This chapter will, however, emphasize that not all carmakers followed the industrial policy. Responses to the policy and to the strategies of TNCs were, in fact, varied. In relation to institutional changes in the 1990s, the chapter will briefly show the market dynamism in the industry caused by the entry of Samsung and Ssangyong, and capacity expansion by the three existing carmakers, Hyundai, Kia and Daewoo.

Chapters 6 and 7 will look at the strategies of Hyundai Motors and Daewoo Motors before and during the crisis. Following the dynamic capabilities approach, the focus is on differences between the companies in the same institutional environments. The importance of vision and strategy, created by *chaebol* entrepreneurs, will be examined, especially in relation to three areas: relationship with TNCs, the drive to export, and technological learning. These chapters also examine the differences in strategic responses of the two companies to institutional changes in the 1990s. These differences are certainly indicators of path dependencies. Consequently, these chapters will argue that Hyundai Motors, closely cooperating with the developmental state, followed the path of successful big business as described by Alfred Chandler for the industrialized countries, whereas Daewoo Group and Daewoo Motors in the 1990s, which were deeply integrated into deregulated global markets, followed the spirit of globalism and liberalism that dominated the 1990s.

Chapter 8 continues the discussion on the respective strategies and capabilities of Daewoo and Hyundai, but this time with the focus on the development of product technology. The different approaches taken by Daewoo and Hyundai to new car development, new engine development and organizational processes in R&D will be analysed. In particular, the advantages and disadvantages of Hyundai's national approach and Daewoo's global approach to R&D will be compared.

In Chapter 9, we will discuss the problem of diversification by the *chaebol*. This chapter will apply the dynamic capability approach to interpreting the shifting nature of diversification, and argue that, whereas once 'legal barriers' imposed by the government were important in limiting diversification, after liberalization the 'knowledge barrier' and other firm-specific assets established by first mover companies were to become crucial.

In summary, this book will argue that the 1997 crisis in East Asia, particularly in Korea, had various aspects. It was one of the financial boom-and-bust syndromes that appeared in the global economy in the 1990s, and caused financial crises not only in East Asia. It was also an institutional crisis, a crisis resulting from liberalization and globalization. At the same time, we will argue that the crisis revealed the evolving nature of Korea's business dynamics, in which innovative *chaebol* firms with technologically-based capabilities increasingly predominated, while *chaebol* firms which expanded whilst relying on existing capabilities did not survive. It is true that the first two aspects were the primary causes of the crisis and the last was secondary. Nonetheless, all three aspects should be taken into consideration if we want to fully explain the crisis and, at the same time, to assess post-crisis restructuring policy properly.

2
The Asian Crisis in 1997 and its Causes

East Asian economies, with their unprecedented growth in investment and national income, were once considered to be models for other developing countries. The World Bank's *East Asian Miracle* (1993), for example, lauded positive features and policies of the East Asian model. Optimism spread and East Asia attracted almost half of the total capital inflows to developing countries (nearly US$100 billion in 1996). It was hardly ever considered that East Asia might become embroiled in one of the worst financial crises in the post-war period.

The Asian crisis occurred suddenly after several years of the so-called Asian miracle. The foreign exchange crisis that began in Thailand in July 1997 quickly spread to other countries in Asia and eventually to South Korea. Between June and the end of the year, the currencies of five East Asian crisis countries – South Korea, Malaysia, Indonesia, Thailand and the Philippines – had depreciated by 80 per cent and their stock market prices had fallen by 50–70 per cent. This accompanied the worst ever decline in GDP in these countries, which was estimated at minus 7.7 per cent in 1998, with the fall in Indonesia a spectacular minus 17.7 per cent. Large numbers of financial and industrial firms defaulted on debts, banking systems were paralysed, and financial markets collapsed.

What went wrong? What caused the East Asian crash? In this chapter, we will examine two fundamentally different interpretations of the Asian financial crisis. In section 2.1, we will examine the critique of special features of East Asian capitalism: cronyism, industrial policy, and other government interventions. By contrast, section 2.2 will examine the role of the financial market panic and, more broadly, the financial liberalization which preceded the crisis.

2.1   Structural inefficiency of East Asian capitalism

As Sachs and Woo (2000b) stress, the most troublesome question about the East Asian crisis is whether there was a common element in the development strategies of the five crisis-affected countries that rendered them vulnerable to a sudden fall. The critics of East Asian capitalism found common structural problems. In their view, state intervention was a primary cause of the sudden collapse, and the crisis was an 'inevitable disaster that finally happened' (Krugman 1998a).

The role of structural inefficiencies inherent in Asian capitalism at the onset of the Asian crisis has been discussed by a number of authors (see, e.g., Dornbusch 1997; Fischer 1998; Greenspan 1998; Krugman 1998a, 1998b). This argument attributes the economic crisis to domestic causes such as moral hazard, crony capitalism, industrial policy, and ultimately government failure. The crisis resulted from deep-rooted weaknesses in the national institutions of the Asian countries that created moral hazard among their financial and industrial enterprises, leading to reckless risk-taking, inefficient investment, large external deficits, and property and stock market bubbles (see also IMF 1997b, 1998c; Corsetti, Pesenti and Roubini 1998a, 1998b).

According this view, the countries became victims of their own successes as Asia's growth strategy inevitably led to the financial crash. Developmental state interventionism, close state–business links in fostering heavy industry and large state subsidies to help exporters gain market share, which were said to have achieved the Asian miracle, are identified as the common deficiencies that created moral hazard and crony capitalism. Krugman (1998b) explains: 'The crisis, in short, was a punishment for Asian sins, even if the punishment was disproportionate to the crime.'

Therefore, associated with ongoing economic troubles in Japan, which was the case par excellence of Asian-style capitalism, it is asserted that 'the age of the developmental state is now gone and East Asian capitalism can neither be engineered nor saved ... Convergence toward Anglo-American capitalism is likely to be accelerated in the name of globalization and global standard' (Moon and Rhyu 2000).

These arguments have profoundly influenced the prescription for policy change and institutional reforms of the crisis countries. The International Monetary Fund released bailout money for the countries only on condition that they accepted programmes of radical liberalization, deregulation and privatization (IMF 1997a, 1998a, 1998b). It was a new version of 'Shock Therapy' for East Asia.[1] The Fund openly intended to dissolve what have been regarded as the main ingredients of the so-called East Asian economic model. But these 'finally collapsed' arguments have significant weaknesses, as we will see in the following discussion.

Cronyism

The most popular variety of the Asian inefficiency argument is that of 'crony capitalism': it is the political connection of individuals, firms and institutions, rather than entrepreneurial abilities, that determines who gets access to public credit and other public resources. This includes implicit and explicit government guarantees for domestic bank loans as in the cases of the Thai finance companies, members of the Suharto family in Indonesia, and *chaebol*-controlled merchant banks in Korea (*The Economist*, 8 April 1998; Krugman 1998a, 1998b; Corsetti, Pesenti and Roubini 1998b). Pomerleano (1998) also points out that cronyism is at the core of the crisis because the corrupt bank–business relationship encouraged excessive investment.

However, this argument has a significant weakness: it cannot explain why cronyism did not cause similar crises during the previous period. In fact, the 'corruption perception index' compiled by Transparency International shows that corruption was diminishing in all the crisis-affected countries on the eve of the crisis (Chang 2000). In an international comparative index of corruption, Radelet and Sachs (1998) also come to the conclusion that, in spite of extensive corruption and cronyism in East Asia, its level was not significantly associated with the financial crisis as there was little difference in the level of perceived corruption between the crisis economies and other emerging market economies.

Industrial policy and moral hazard

Another argument relates Asian inefficiency to the moral hazard associated with industrial policy: Asian governments, in their attempts to promote targeted industries, explicitly or implicitly guaranteed private investments against risks, which naturally encouraged the tendency of Asian firms towards over-optimistic investment and excessive risk-taking (Corsetti, Pesenti and Roubini 1998a, 1998b; Krugman 1998a). This was especially true for Korea, where 'the government has treated the banks as tools of state industrial policy, ordering them to make loans to uncreditworthy companies and industries' (*The Economist*, 15 November 1997).

However, the extent of industrial policy in Southeast Asian countries had been rather limited. The World Bank itself pointed out in its report, *The East Asian Miracle* (1993: p. 86), that from 1965 to 1990 Thailand, Indonesia and Malaysia – like Singapore and Hong Kong – had grown fast without the so-called East Asian type of industrial policy, which had been found primarily in the three Northeast Asian economies of Korea, Taiwan and Japan. Johnson (1998) and Chang (1998, 2000) also emphasized the difference between Korea, where industrial policy had been extensive, and the other crisis economies, where a strong developmental state had never existed (Thailand, Indonesia and the Philippines), or had been relatively weak (Malaysia).[2]

Even in Korea, industrial policy disappeared slowly from the late 1980s, and very rapidly from 1993. President Kim Young-Sam's administration, during its term in office from 1993 to 1997, abolished industrial policy so that Korea could join the WTO and OECD. If industrial policy was absent in Korea and the other crisis countries before the crisis, it is difficult to blame the Asian crisis on it (Johnson 1998; Radelet and Sachs 1998; Chang 2000).

On the other hand, it has been argued that the economies in East Asia had their own mechanisms for preventing moral hazard problems and that, from the late 1980s to the mid-1990s, however, these mechanisms disappeared because of financial and industrial deregulation, making the moral hazard problem serious for the first time (Chang 2000). If so, the efforts towards open and free market economies throughout East Asia may have been responsible for the appearance of the moral hazard problem in East Asian capitalism.

Government guarantee and moral hazard

Krugman (1998a, 1998b) and McKinnon and Pill (1998) regard deposit insurance and other public guarantees for banks and industrial corporations by governments as the major source of moral hazard in East Asia, causing overborrowing and overinvestment.[3]

Following this line of argument, the IMF demanded that crisis countries, in the midst of the financial panic in late 1997, let insolvent banks close immediately and introduce limited deposit insurance. In the case of Korea, the IMF required that nine out of 30 merchant banks suspend operations immediately in December 1997. However, the measure intensified the panic so much that all Korean banks were driven to the verge of outright default. Instead of restoring market confidence the measures intensified the panic among depositors, bank managers and international lenders, among others, and increased the turbulence in the Asian and international financial markets.[4]

Consequently, the Fund was forced to change its strategy. The new principles, introduced in early 1998, included government guarantees of all bank liabilities (in contrast to the IMF policy in November for

Indonesia, in which only small depositors in the closed banks were protected), reduced focus on bank closure in the short term, and placed greater emphasis on longer-run restructuring and bank recapitalization by injecting public funds and temporary nationalization (Radelet and Sachs 1998).

The US government itself, which together with the IMF had severely criticized the moral hazard of the bailout guarantee for banks by the East Asian governments, has shown a readiness to intervene in its own home-grown financial troubles. For example, the US Treasury intervened to help the Federal Deposit Insurance Corporation remain solvent by providing US$30 billion of credit as the fund went to the edge of insolvency because of bank failures in America between 1986 and 1990.

The problems in savings and loan (S&L) banking in the late 1980s were even greater: US government intervention bankrupted the Federal Savings and Loans Insurance and cost the American taxpayer over US$100 billion.[5] Recently, in September 1998, the US Federal Reserve organized a rescue of Long-Term Capital Management (LTCM), a very large and prominent hedge fund which was on the brink of failure.[6] The Federal Reserve intervened because it was concerned about the possible devastating consequences of failure for national and world financial markets.

Besides this US practice of public guarantees, the IMF bailout programme itself can be identified as a public guarantee, and hence as a source of moral hazard. International assistance to countries experiencing financial crisis can only encourage more reckless risk-taking not only on the part of Asian borrowers but also on the part of international lenders and investors, which increases the risk of moral hazard due to the implicit guarantee.

The Fund (1998c) has responded to the criticism with the argument that 'the IMF's lending role stems from the public policy objective of limiting the economic and social costs of crises'. Frankel (1998) also argues that, without the bailout, the crisis could have spread further, and not always to countries that deserved it; the weak Japanese financial system was one possible channel of transmission to America and Europe. This provides a strong justification for a public policy role of the Fund in avoiding unnecessarily deep and damaging crises such as the Great Depression.

However, the Fund's acknowledgement of its public role in limiting the economic and social costs of crises contradicts its own criticism of the implicit guarantee for banks by governments of the crisis countries. If, on general principles, the IMF can, in spite of the danger of moral hazard, give bailout loans to international lenders and borrowers in order to limit the economic and social costs for the international community, why may not national funds (i.e., national governments), as the lenders of last resort, play the same role for domestic lenders and borrowers for the national public's sake?[7]

Consequently, if a public guarantee for financial institutions is not unique to East Asian economies but a usual practice of advanced economies, it cannot be regarded as a cause of the Asian financial crisis.

2.2   Role of panic and financial liberalization

The other explanation for the Asian financial crisis singles out financial panic as the essential element of the crisis. According to this view, large-scale foreign capital inflow into East Asia's financial systems made its economies vulnerable to panic.

There undoubtedly existed significant problems and weak fundamentals in the Asian economies before the crisis. Export growth was falling and current account deficits rising by 1995 and 1996. There were also poor banking supervision, poor corporate governance, excessive lending and reckless investment, to name but a few. However, these factors were not severe enough to warrant a financial crisis of the magnitude of the one that took place in late 1997 (Radelet and Sachs 1998). It could only have been financial panic among international banks and investors that brought East Asia to its knees.

The globalized financial market has a tendency to overreact to both positive and negative news. Just as global investors and lenders had been excessively optimistic about economic prospects earlier in 1994–6, they became overly pessimistic at the end of 1997 (Sachs and Woo 2000b).

Like the financial crises of Mexico and Argentina in 1994–5, the Asian crisis in 1997 may be interpreted as essentially a case of 'self-fulfilling crisis' resulting from 'herd behaviour' in international financial markets. While the individual banker or money manager may act rationally, market outcomes produce irrationally sharp, costly and unnecessary panic reversals in capital flows (Radelet and Sachs 1998).[8] That is to say, each individual may respond more to the actions of others, due to the asymmetric distribution of information among them, than to their own private information (Stiglitz and Weiss 1981). Contrary to Milton Friedman and other monetarists' belief in the rational market, the market occasionally becomes irrational. As Kindleberger (1989) and Minsky (1982) stress, the rational behaviour of individuals may turn irrational and thus drive the financial market to unsustainable heights and subsequently therefore to greater depths than would be rationally necessary.

The East Asian boom and crisis in the 1990s was another example of 'manias, panics, and crashes' (Kindleberger's expression) in an under-regulated financial market, involving international lenders and investors (Palma 1998; Sachs and Woo 2000b). The East Asian financial crisis may therefore be characterized as a 'financial bubble' phenomenon (Hanna 2000).

Financial liberalization and border-crossing capital movement

Most commentators, including those who criticize East Asian capitalism, agree that the massive outflow of capital after June 1997, reversing an equally massive capital inflow in the preceding three years, triggered the financial crisis (see, e.g., World Bank 1998). Therefore, understanding these capital inflows and outflows is crucial if we are to understand the vulnerability of East Asia's institutional system.

The obvious question which arises is: what made the border-crossing capital movement possible? It was the financial liberalization and deregulation throughout the region. East Asian governments, encouraged by the IMF and the World Bank as well as by national business elites, liberalized their financial systems throughout the 1990s. The most important change was the opening of the capital account. This permitted domestic financial and industrial firms to raise finance on foreign credit and capital markets and gave foreign financial institutions access to the domestic financial market. Domestic banks, non-bank financial institutions and private corporations could borrow abroad; foreign portfolio investors could own shares of local corporations on domestic stock markets; foreign banks could enter the domestic banking sector; and offshore branches of domestic banks could borrow abroad and lend domestically (Wade 2000).

The liberalization of capital movement removed the regulatory authority of governments. Those who demanded and welcomed financial deregulation partly acknowledged the need for the strengthening of bank regulation and supervision, but did not want to constrain the push for liberalization (Wade 2000). Furthermore, enthusiasm for the East Asian boom overwhelmed any reservations. Both international lenders and domestic borrowers were excessively optimistic about the future of the liberalized East Asian economies.

In Thailand, radical financial liberalization began in 1988 with the country's first full civilian government, and was accelerated under the second civilian government from 1992. A large number of new financial companies were created and foreign borrowing was allowed. Most importantantly, the Bangkok International Bank Facilities (BIBF), effectively an offshore banking system, was created in the early 1990s (Delhaise 1998: pp. 83–4). This greatly increased Thai companies' access to foreign currency lending (Ito 2000). The increase in BIBF lending accounted for two-thirds of the increase in total foreign currency debt between 1991 and 1997. In this period, the total foreign debt increased by US$61 billion, a jump from US$36 to 97 billion. Almost all of the increases occurred in short-term debt (Hanna 2000).[9]

In Indonesia, where the banking sector had been dominated by a string of state-owned banks, a substantial banking reform was introduced in 1988. Entry and service provision in the financial sector were deregulated. This resulted in a mushrooming of new banks and non-bank financial companies. But there was hardly a regulatory institution that prudently supervised the large number of financial companies (McLeod 1998; Delhaise 1998). The banking sector grew much faster than the rest of the economy, and there was a dramatic decline of state banks as their private sector competitors expanded rapidly. As international banks rushed to lend money to the private banks, Indonesia's foreign currency borrowings rapidly increased by US$50 billion, from US$80 to US$130 billion, between 1991 to 1997. Here also, short-term borrowings accounted for most of the increase.

In Korea, the Kim Young-Sam government accelerated financial deregulation during 1993–7 as part of its efforts to join the OECD in 1996. For the first time, the capital account was opened to foreigners. Merchant banks, other non-bank financial companies, offshore branches of commercial banks and *chaebol* groups all rushed to borrow abroad in order to take advantage of the lower interest rates in the international financial markets; but there were hardly any regulations introduced to supervise their activities. This resulted in an enormous surge in Korea's foreign currency borrowings: a US$97 billion increase for three years between 1993 and 1996, from US$67 to US$164 billion. Most of the foreign borrowings were private and 57–66 per cent were short term (see also Chapter 3).

Lending boom to East Asia

Japanese banks were a main provider of foreign credits to the East Asian economies. After the Plaza Agreement in 1985 between the Japanese and US governments, the Japanese yen appreciated dramatically against the US dollar, from about 238:1 to 80:1 in the period 1985 to 1990. This produced a bubble in the Japanese property, stock and credit market in the late 1980s.[10] After the bubble burst, the Japanese banking system fell into a chronic crisis in the 1990s. On the one hand, because of the collapse of the bubble economy, Japanese banks found themselves with many bad loans. On the other hand, however, they collected more and more domestic savings, because Japanese households wanted to avoid the uncertainty of the financial market. But it became difficult for the banks to find credit-worthy company clients, even though real interest rates for lending were lowered to nearly zero.

Hence, the Japanese banks aggressively sought high returns from foreign lending, much of it in risky loans to the deregulated East Asian economies (Wade 2000). They could lend to East Asian banks and firms at higher rates than to Japanese clients, confident that East Asian currencies would remain stably pegged to the US dollar. They thereby earned an interest gain as well as a currency gain (as the yen depreciated against the US dollar from 1995).

European banks followed Japanese banks, especially after they had fled from Mexico and Argentina in the wake of the 'Tequila crisis' of 1994–5. By mid-1997, European banks accounted for the largest share in East Asia's foreign borrowings, with 40 per cent.[11] Next came Japanese banks, with 32 per cent (see Table 2.1). US banks accounted for only 8 per cent primarily because the soaring prices in the US stock market throughout the 1990s attracted them more than the East Asian boom.[12] On the demand side, banks and firms in Korea and Southeast Asia rushed to borrow abroad because it cost roughly half as much as borrowing domestically. There was an assumption, of course, that their currencies would remain fixed to the US dollar.

From 1990 to 1997, the volume of private capital flow to developing countries rose more than sixfold, from US$42 billion in 1990 to US$256 billion in 1997 (World Bank 1998: p. 5). While world trade grew by about 5 per cent annually, private capital flow grew by nearly 30 per cent annually. Commercial bank loans and portfolio investments – the most mobile forms of capital movement – set the pace. 'Emerging markets' were booming, and offered greater profitability than investment in developed countries, despite their higher risk.

East Asia, including China, attracted almost half of the total capital inflows (bank loans, portfolio investment, foreign direct investment, or FDI, etc.) to developing countries, and 60 per cent of all short-term capital flows to developing countries. As for commercial bank loans, the Bank for International Settlement (BIS) reported by June 1997 that international banks' outstanding loans to East Asia amounted to over US$389 billion and that 62 per cent of this was short term (see Table 2.1).

Table 2.1 International bank lending to Asia, June 1997 (US$ million)

	Total lending (A)	Short-term lending (B)	B/A (%)	A/GDP (%)	B/foreign reserve (%)	Nationality of lending banks		
						Japan (%)	Europe (%)	USA (%)
Korea	103,432	70,182	68	21.3	211	23	35	10
Thailand	69,382	45,567	66	38.1	141	54	28	10
Indonesia	58,726	34,661	59	26.5	163	39	38	9
Malaysia	28,820	16,268	56	29.3	61	36	44	8
Philippines	14,115	8,293	59	16.2	73	15	48	20
China	57,922	30,137	52	7.1	23	32	48	5
Taiwan	25,163	21,966	87	9.2	24	12	57	10
Asia total	389,441	242,273	62			32	40	8

Note: Europe includes Austria, Belgium, France, Germany, Italy, Luxembourg, Netherlands, Spain and the UK.
Source: Ito (2000).

These massive capital inflows fuelled the domestic credit boom throughout the five deregulated countries. During 1993–7, the five crisis economies had experienced rapid increases in domestic bank lending to the private sector in amounts exceeding by 50 per cent or more the level observed in 1992. In contrast, the rise of credit in China and Taiwan, where the financial system was still not deregulated, was clearly more moderate than in the crisis-hit Asian countries (Perry and Lederman 1998: p. 11).

As a result of the increasing domestic credit, broad money (M2) expanded at a near 20 per cent annual rate in 1996 and 1997 in the five countries. This was nearly twice the rate of Taiwan, Hong Kong and Singapore, countries that would later fare better in the storm of the 1997 financial crisis (World Bank 1998: p. 7). The domestic credit boom, in turn, led to an excessive increase in asset prices and industrial investments, creating bubbles in the economies.

The enthusiasm for booming East Asia created two fundamental weaknesses in the region. Table 2.1 shows the two differences between the five crisis countries on the one hand and China and Taiwan on the other. First, the ratio of foreign currency borrowings to GDP in 1997 was substantially higher in the five crisis countries than in China and Taiwan, where it remained below 10 per cent. This reflects the fact that between 1994 and 1997 private capital inflow rapidly increased throughout the five countries. In Korea, the ratio jumped from 11.9 per cent in 1993 to 21.3 per cent in 1997; in Thailand from 20.7 per cent to 38.1 per cent; in Indonesia from 19.2 per cent to 26.5 per cent; in Malaysia from 16.6 per cent to 29.3 per cent; and in the Philippines from 10.8 per cent to 16.2 per cent.

Second, and more significantly, Table 2.1 shows a striking difference between the five crisis countries and China and Taiwan in the ratios of short-term foreign borrowings to foreign exchange reserves. In June 1997, on the eve of the financial crisis, Korea's short-term foreign borrowings amounted to 211 per cent of its foreign exchange reserves.[13] Those of Thailand and Indonesia were also over 140 per cent. This means that these countries did not have enough foreign currency to repay foreign short-term debts if international lenders rejected rolling over existing short-term loans, as actually occurred in late 1997. In contrast, China and Taiwan had enough foreign reserves to repay short-term foreign debts.

Panic, capital flight, and crash

The real economy of the five countries deteriorated from 1995. In particular the current account deficits for 1996 increased in Indonesia, Thailand

and Korea. The worst case was Korea, whose current account deficit in 1996 was US$20 billion, the second largest after the USA. Falling export growth was the main cause of the rising deficits. This, in turn, reflected the falling competitiveness of domestic industry. Appreciation of the domestic currencies due to the massive foreign capital inflow contributed to deteriorating industrial competitiveness, as did rising costs due to the asset-price bubbles throughout the region.

Thailand, Malaysia and Indonesia all experienced a speculative mania in property markets. Furthermore, the lending boom for industrial investments produced an overcapacity problem in manufacturing sectors.

Nevertheless, the worsening current account deficits, deteriorating competitiveness, property market bubbles, excessive investments and so on could not have caused a financial catastrophe of the magnitude that we observed in late 1997 (Radelet and Sachs 1998). Before the crisis, it was only a growth recession. Thailand's GDP growth rate was down from 8.8 to 5.5 per cent in 1995–96, Malaysia's from 9.5 to 8.6 per cent, and Korea's from 8.9 to 7.1 per cent. The capital flow to East Asia was slowing down due to the recession, but continued to be strong. International bankers and money managers still believed in the East Asian miracle. In fact, there was no significant change in FDI and capital flows until the devaluation of East Asian currencies began in July 1997 (Ito 2000).

The crisis began as a domestic liquidity crisis in Thailand. First, the Thai property and stock market bubbles burst in 1995 and 1996 respectively, leaving the banking system in a sort of impending insolvency. This, in turn, led to strong concern among international bankers and money managers in the first half of 1997, when they saw the danger that a possible devaluation of the Thai baht would render domestic borrowers less able to meet the now more expensive repayments on their short-term loans (Wade 2000). With a baht devaluation in sight (that is, a breaking of the peg to US dollar), foreign investors suddenly realized that Thailand's foreign reserves were not enough to cover their short-term lending. So they began to race for the exits.

It was a panic in the globalized financial markets that drove East Asia towards an unprecedented disaster. Kindleberger (1989: p. 38) describes a panic as an irrational sum of rational behaviours by individuals:

> Yet euphoric speculation...may also lead to manias and panics when the behaviors of every participant seems rational itself. This is the fallacy of composition, in which the whole differs from the sum of its parts. The action of each individual is rational – or would be,

were it not for the fact that others are behaving in the same way. If a man is quick enough to get in and out ahead of the others, he may do well...even though the totality does badly...'Devil take the hindmost', *sauve qui peut, die Letzen beissen die Hunde* (dogs bite the laggards), and the like are recipes for a panic. The analogy of fire in a theater comes to mind.

With the Thai central bank's foreign reserve running out, the baht was floated in early July 1997. The IMF entered Thailand in August 1997 with a bailout package, but imposed a freeze on many financial companies as a condition. The IMF blamed the 'crony capitalism' in Thailand's banking sector for the mess. This, however, intensified panic because it sent uninsured Thai depositors into a panic run on banks. Jeffrey Sachs (1998) described the IMF's behaviour as being akin to 'screaming fire in the theatre'.[14] Nonetheless, the IMF later imposed the same condition on Indonesia and Korea with the same result (Wade 2000).

The panic spread to other Asian countries because foreign bankers suddenly began to be concerned about the fact that Korea, Indonesia and Malaysia did not have sufficient foreign reserves to cover the huge amount of short-term foreign debts. As all holders of the countries' currencies tried to sell, the value of the currencies dropped rapidly. Currency speculators also attacked the Hong Kong dollar and the Taiwanese dollar.[15] The crisis grew from a 'Southeast Asian' crisis to an 'East Asian crisis' as the 'contagion effect' acquired momentum.

Between July and December of 1997, European, Japanese and US bankers demanded full repayment of short-term loans from their Asian clients as the loans became due (although they had been lent on the implicit understanding that they would roll over indefinitely). The panicked bankers had no interest in an irrational result of their (individually rational) market behaviours; they only wanted to escape from the economies as soon as possible. Consequently, without enough foreign reserves, the governments of Thailand, Indonesia and Korea had no option but to turn to the IMF. The Asian financial crisis broke out.

Table 2.2 shows that the picture of capital flow changed sharply in 1997 as private capital fled from the five crisis countries. The net private capital inflow (bank lending, portfolio investment, FDI, etc.) to Asia fell from US$110 billion in 1996 to just under US$14 billion in 1997. Bank lending and portfolio investment to Asia became negative in 1997 for the first time since 1990. In the five crisis-hit countries, the net private capital inflow fell to minus US$11 billion in 1997. The sharp reversal of

Table 2.2   Net private capital flows to emerging markets, 1990–7 (US$ billion)

	1990	1991	1992	1993	1994	1995	1996	1997
Emerging markets, total[a]	31.0	126.9	120.9	164.7	160.5	192.0	240.8	173.7
FDI	17.6	31.3	37.2	60.6	84.3	96.0	114.9	138.2
Portfolio	17.1	37.3	59.9	103.5	87.8	23.5	49.7	42.9
Others[b]	−3.7	58.4	23.8	0.7	−11.7	72.5	76.2	−7.3
Asia, total	19.1	35.8	21.7	57.6	66.2	95.8	110.4	13.9
FDI	8.9	14.5	16.5	35.9	46.8	49.5	57.0	57.8
Portfolio	−1.4	1.8	9.3	21.6	9.5	10.5	13.4	−8.6
Others[b]	11.6	19.5	−4.1	0.1	9.9	35.8	39.9	−35.4
Five crisis countries, total	24.9	29.0	30.3	32.6	35.1	62.9	72.9	−11.0
FDI	6.2	7.2	8.6	8.6	7.4	9.5	12.0	9.6
Portfolio	1.3	3.3	6.3	17.9	10.6	14.4	20.3	11.8
Others[b]	17.4	18.5	15.4	6.1	17.1	39.0	40.6	−32.3

[a]Emerging markets include developing economies and transitional economies.
[b]'Others' include short-term and long-term credits, loans (not including use of IMF credit), currency and deposits, and other accounts receivable and payable.
Source: Ito (2000).

Table 2.3   Capital inflows to and outflows from the five East Asian crisis countries, 1996–8 (US$ billion)

	1996	1997	1998
Total capital inflows (A)	83.3	48.9	32.8
Long-term inflows	67.3	52.1	38.9
Short-term inflows	16.0	−3.2	−6.1
Net external finance (B)	−40.8	16.2	19.9
Current account surplus	−55.8	−19.7	66.1
Change in reserves	15.0	35.9	−46.2
Capital outflows (A + B) [a]	42.5	65.1	52.7

[a]Errors and omissions are included.
Source: World Bank (1999: p. 26).

bank lending and credits was the major contributor to this capital flight (see 'Others' in Table 2.2 and also Ito (2000)).

Table 2.3 shows the capital outflow from the five crisis countries more clearly. While the capital outflow of US$42.5 billion in 1996 resulted primarily from the currency account deficit of US$55.8 billion, the capital outflows in 1997 and 1998 were caused primarily by the non-renewal of short-term financial flows. The data for 1998 show this the most clearly: even though the five crisis countries achieved a positive current account surplus of US$66.1 billion, they experienced net capital outflows. This was because short-term capital continued to flow out and, at the same time, long-term capital inflow fell significantly. As a result, the countries had negative foreign reserves of US$46.2 billion. Consequently, around US$120 billion of foreign capital fled out of the five crisis countries during 1997–98. This was equivalent to 10 per cent of these countries' yearly GDP (World Bank 1999: p. 25). The degree of panic is reflected by the fact that most of the capital flight occurred between July 1997 and March 1998.

To summarize, a combination of panic behaviour on the part of the international bankers and investors, poorly designed bailout programmes by the IMF which intensified the panic, and policy mistakes by the Asian governments in fixing their currencies to the US dollar prior to the crisis, turned the withdrawal of foreign capital into a fully-fledged financial panic and deepened the crisis more than was either rational or inevitable (Sachs 1998). Thus, it was a 'self-reinforcing' crisis (panic causing more panic) caused by the panic outflow of international capital (Radelet and Sachs 1998; Krugman 1999). The panic was not simply the 'trigger' or messenger of the Asian crisis; it was the primary cause (Wade 2000).

Asian capitalism and global capitalism

A common weakness of the various criticisms of 'crony Asian capitalism' is that none of them is able to explain why the Asian crisis occurred in the latter half of the 1990s, of all periods. Why had not the East Asian economies faced such a large-scale financial disaster before, since industrial policy, state intervention in the banking system and large corporate groupings, all of which allegedly caused the moral hazard problem, had existed for decades? My own view is that *there were functioning institutions in East Asian capitalism, and that they changed in the 1990s, and that this change led to the crisis* (see also Stiglitz 2001). What, then, was the most remarkable institutional change in the East Asian economies during the period preceding the crisis?

Everybody would agree that nothing was more striking than the financial liberalization (see, e.g., Ito and Krueger 1996). Without the opening of the capital account, there would not have occurred that massive foreign capital inflow into the region which enabled miraculous Asian growth and, at the same time, created the economic bubble that burst in 1997. Without abolition of capital controls, there would not have occurred a panic outflow of foreign capital. Therefore, in discussing the most salient issue of how the Asian 'miracle' unravelled, Furman and Stiglitz (1998: p. 4) argue, 'An important change was the pursuit of rapid financial liberalization and capital account opening without the development of sound supervision and regulation.'

The World Bank (1998: p. 4) itself acknowledges that three forces interacted to leave the five Asian economies vulnerable to external shock or panic: first, the rapid increase in inflows of international private capital, especially short-term capital; second, newly liberalized, but insufficiently regulated, financial companies that were growing rapidly; and third, government policies that permitted capital inflow to fuel booms in credit, investment and the property market. These three forces are all essentially related to financial liberalization and globalization.

The IMF, however, hardly acknowledges the premature nature of the financial market opening in East Asia (see IMF 1997b). Corsetti, Pesenti and Roubini (1998b), for example, consider the financial deregulation to have been unavoidable although they acknowledge that 'the adverse consequences of these distortions [inherent in Asian capitalism] were crucially magnified by the rapid process of capital account liberalization and financial market deregulation in the region during the 1990s, which increased the supply-elasticity of funds from abroad'. Claessens and Jansen (2000: p. 3), representing the World Bank's official position, argue that even though financial globalization raised a number of dangers such as the undermining of prudential controls of financial institutions, the loss of monetary autonomy and the increased volatility of capital flow, many of these concerns are not related to financial liberalization itself.

However, McKinnon (1991) and McKinnon and Pill (1996) had already given warnings about the danger of the deregulated international capital movement, and stressed the need to restrain short-term capital flows. Even Jeffrey Sachs, who had once advised Russian and East European governments to institute radical reform measures towards a free market economy, criticized the financial liberalization in Asia, saying that:

at least in part, the Asian financial crisis has its roots in attempts at financial reforms in East Asia in the early 1990s that were aimed at upgrading financial institutions, but in fact the economies were exposed to the instabilities of the international financial markets... These reforms led to a dramatic increase in the number of banks and their linkage to the international economy, which, in turn, increased the exposure of these economies to international shocks, mainly through the remarkable buildup of short-term debts.

(Radelet and Sachs 1998)

Good evidence of the argument that deregulation was the basic cause of the Asian crisis is provided by China, Vietnam and India. These countries undertook no significant financial sector reforms in the 1990s, and were shielded from the crisis despite the known cronyism in their economies. Furthermore, China's banking system was known to be in worse shape than Thailand's or Korea's both before and after the crisis (Sachs and Woo 2000b).

Therefore the East Asian crisis of 1997 was not an inevitable failure of 'Asian capitalism', but rather a failure of deregulated global financial markets. Financial liberalization exposed the Asian economies more directly to the instability of global financial markets. Rather than an Asian crisis, it was more a type of global crisis that reflects the arrival of global capitalism.[16] In this light, Sachs and Woo (2000b) write:

In general terms, we can say there were few specifically 'Asian' features of the Asian financial crisis. Official Washington, led by the IMF, proclaimed the crisis to be one of Asian capitalism, but the more generic character of the crisis became all too clear during 1998, as the crisis spread to Russia, South Africa and Latin America.

2.3   Conclusion

What liberal critics of 'crony Asian capitalism' call 'Asian' features are not in fact Asian but mainly Korean. Among the five crisis countries Korea was a unique case, possessing strong state interventionism, highly bank-based finance and large industrial conglomerates. In the other four cases, such institutions had never existed or had been relatively weak. Korea had more in common with Japan and Taiwan. However, neither Taiwan nor Japan was significantly affected by the Asian crisis. Therefore, an essential question is whether the five crisis economies had a common element in their structures that rendered them vulnerable to the sudden collapse in 1997.

In this chapter, we have agreed with the view that panic massive outflow of international capital was the common aspect and, at the same time, the primary cause of the financial crisis. Moreover, financial deregulation and globalization in the 1990s in the five countries had been the common institutional background. The opening of the capital account was particularly important because it allowed free cross-border capital movement. Enormous amounts of global capital subsequently flowed into the five countries, particularly between 1993 and 1996, creating investment booms and property market bubbles. Deregulated domestic financial sectors also played a part.

The lending boom to East Asia made the five liberalized economies vulnerable to external shock. First, the ratio of total foreign borrowings to GDP increased rapidly. Second, short-term foreign borrowings grew more rapidly than total foreign borrowings while the countries' foreign reserves – as a buffer for foreign exchange fluctuation – did not increase in proper proportion to it.

The bubble burst in late 1997, however, when global capital started to run out of Asia. International banks were largely responsible for the crisis. In mid-1997, when East Asian currencies began to devalue, international bankers panicked and collected their short-term loans on Asian banks. Some US$120 billion of international capital haemorrhaged from the five countries, and most of the capital flight occurred between July 1997 and March 1998. This amounted to 10 per cent of the GDP of these economies. It was this sudden and large-scale capital flight that was primarily responsible for the unexpected collapse of their financial and corporate systems. The IMF policies that imposed immediate structural reforms intensified the panic.

In summary, East Asia's boom and crisis in the 1990s were essentially associated with financial liberalization. Without it, the enthusiastic inflow and subsequent panic outflow of foreign capital would not have been allowed. Imprudent financial liberalization and globalization created the institutional failures that caused the crisis. In the next chapter, we will look at how liberalization and globalization operated in the case of Korea.

3
Korea's Economic Institutions and the Crisis

Korea has long been praised as an excellent example of successful capitalist economic development. Despite poor natural resources and the legacies of the colonization by Japan and the Korean War, it emerged as an industrial power in a relatively short time, showing a remarkable pathway from the periphery. Entry into the OECD in December 1996 was publicized by the Kim Young-Sam government as the symbol of Korea's economic 'arrival'.

Only one year later, in November 1997, this same Korean government had no choice but to sign up to an IMF emergency bailout programme in order to overcome mounting foreign exchange problems and rapid deterioration of the nation's credit standing. Major industrial and financial companies collapsed one after another and almost all banks were faced with soaring levels of bad debt. The financial market melted down and foreign currency reserves were depleted. The whole country was on the brink of bankruptcy.

In Korea, the reliance on IMF assistance was widely regarded as a national shame, and this effectively ended the Kim Young-Sam government, the first regime change since the start of industrialization in 1961. The new Korean government's first challenge was negotiation with international lenders and the IMF about the US$57 billion bailout loan package programme, the largest ever, of which the IMF contributed US$21 billion directly.

In spite of this aid, the economic crisis worsened in 1998. Just as 'miracle East Asia' suddenly became 'crony East Asia', so too did the crisis dramatically change the landscape of Korean research.[1] Once seen as a highly effective model of industrial catch-up, Korea's idiosyncratic system now came to be regarded as the primary structure that caused the crisis. State interventionism, industrial policy, bank-based finance and big business groups, previously praised as hallmarks of the country's successful industrialization, were now seen as the structures that created cronyism, moral hazard and the too-big-to-fail mentality which, in turn, resulted in reckless risk-taking and excessive investment.

However, this 'finally collapsed' view lacks historical perspective. If we follow this view, Korea's success prior to the crisis appears to have been merely a mirage. Furthermore, this view is not able to answer the question of why Korea had not experienced such a disaster earlier.

In this chapter, we will argue that financial liberalization and industrial deregulation during the 1990s created institutional failures that caused the crisis. Section 3.1 will examine the developmental state system with particular reference to the question of moral hazard. The focus will be on the government's industrial policy and its institutions of corporate governance. In section 3.2, we will examine the institutional changes from the late 1980s, which saw the beginnings of democratization and liberalization, and in section 3.3, we will show how liberalization changed the ways that the *chaebol* were governed and financed themselves. Finally, section 3.4 will first examine the movement of global capital into and out of Korea, and then the 1997 crisis.

3.1   Developmental state, banks and the *chaebol*

Establishment of the state-led economy

The developmental state of Korea was established after Park Chung-Hee, a Korean army general trained in the Japanese military academy during the colonial period, came to power in 1961.[2] Following the Japanese model of the Meiji Restoration, his government mobilized national resources for rapid industrialization in authoritarian ways. It drove industrialists towards the goal, and used carrot and stick methods to govern them. It needed to take control, and power over finance became a major policy instrument (Woo 1991; Cho and Kim 1997). By nationalizing commercial banks, establishing various specialized public banks, and subordinating the central bank to itself, the government was able fully to control the creation and supply of credit to industrial firms.

The government's control over commercial banks was an essential element in government-led economic growth, and much of the investment financing of the *chaebol* was subject to government approval. As long as access to bank credit was the key to the *chaebol's* business success, they were also willing to follow government directives. In this way, the government allocated so-called 'policy loans' to selected *chaebol* firms in targeted industries including automotive, shipbuilding, electronics, and iron and steel. Foreign commercial and public credits to the *chaebol* firms were also mediated and strictly controlled by the government as it guaranteed repayment (Cho and Kim 1997).

Various implicit and explicit government guarantees were important ways of providing public support for industrial firms. They enabled *chaebol* firms to sustain investment by easing the adverse effects of economic downturns. This is one reason why Korean firms were able to keep investing in heavy industries during the 1970s, notwithstanding the First and Second Oil Shocks. In addition, public guarantees were particularly beneficial for borrowing foreign capital, which was essential under the conditions of overall capital shortage during the early periods of industrialization. The government's guarantee on credit repayment could reduce the risks and uncertainties faced by foreign creditors (Woo 1991). The banking sector was repressed since credit policies were seen as the most important tool of government control of the economy; the competitiveness and profitability of commercial banks were not a primary concern. The banks were incapable of screening credit supply and monitoring business firms as they simply served as agents of the government.

Government regulation of the economy during the 1960s and 1970s was expressed also in industry policy. The heavy and chemical industrialization drive (HCI drive) in the 1970s in particular created many interventionist industry policies: government licence of industrial entry and exit, price controls for targeted industries, and government control over ownership and management of selected firms, for example. As the government wanted to maintain the firms' profitability, it protected their market position by introducing entry licence, price control and import restraints. The entry barrier created an oligopolistic position for the existing *chaebol* firms. In return for protection in the domestic market, the government drove them towards an export-oriented strategy. The success of all economic policies depended on this strategy, as it was the primary means of earning the foreign currency which was indispensable for repaying foreign credits.

Credit policies, fiscal policies, industrial policies, export and import policies, and macroeconomic policies were all integrated in the Five-Year Plans for economic development which the Korean government initiated in 1962 and continued up to 1991 (Cho and Kim 1997).

The idiosyncrasies of the *chaebol*, such as numerous and extremely diversified subsidiaries under family control, highly-leveraged corporate finance, and intersubsidiary shareholding were established during the period of government-led growth, especially during the HCI drive in the 1970s.

State control of the *chaebol* and moral hazard

As we have seen, many critics hold that government intervention and the resulting lack of market discipline produced moral hazard among banks and the *chaebol*, and that this resulted in overborrowing and overinvestment and caused the 1997 crisis (IMF 1997b; Krugman 1998a). For this reason, the IMF pressed Korea radically to reform its financial system and corporate governance along free market lines (IMF 1997a).

However, in this regard, two points need to be raised: first, the developmental system had been largely dismantled well before 1997; second, the system itself had incorporated effective mechanisms to solve the moral hazard problem.

In neoclassical economics, moral hazard appears as a problem of economic incentive in situations in which there is incomplete, or asymmetrical, information among the parties concerned (Vickrey 1994). The typical case is adverse selection by an insurant, who may either want an outright loss to occur or may have a tendency to be less than careful with property in order to receive the insurance. However, the underwriter, the insurance company, can detect moral hazard in various ways; by checking the insurant's credit situations, by revealing records of criminal or bankruptcy history, and so on. Similarly, in the case of public guarantee and other supports for banks or big conglomerates, the government can detect moral hazard by introducing various checking and disciplinary mechanisms.

This kind of moral hazard problem can be interpreted as a corporate governance problem; in situations of asymmetric information between agents (managers or insider equity holders) and principals (outsider equity or debt holders), agents can seek private advantage through opportunistic behaviour, damaging principals' interests. In the principal-agent theorem, this problem is supposed to be solved by building an effective monitoring and reward system that optimally reduces agency costs (Jensen and Meckling 1976). In the developmental system of Korea, the moral hazard problem was solved by the same principle: the government created various monitoring and reward systems to detect rent-seeking activities (Amsden 1989: p. 8; World Bank 1993: p. 94).

In the risk-partnership between the government and *chaebol*, labelled 'Korea, Inc.', the former took over the role of principal or senior partner, and the latter became its agent or junior partner (Jones and SaKong 1980). Risk socialization, by definition, means spreading the costs of private sector failure across society as a whole, and therefore there is undoubtedly a potential hazard of rent seeking by the private sector at society's expense. In this context intervention by the government, as a key stakeholder representing society, can be a legitimate method of corporate governance (Park 1999).

Thus the Korean government closely checked the performance of the business firms receiving its support in various forms, and even the largest conglomerates were not free from such disciplinary processes (Chang 1993, 1994). Subsidies were not giveaways, but instead were distributed on the principle of reciprocity. With more disciplined firms, subsidies and protection were lower and more effective than otherwise (Amsden 1989).

In exchange for subsidies and protection, the government imposed performance standards on private firms. When a *chaebol* failed to accomplish export or technology targets set by the government, financial and fiscal supports could be reduced or withdrawn as punishment. The government urged improperly run *chaebol* to merge with efficient ones and sometimes the government insisted on this: it was a kind of hostile takeover (Park 1999).

The government's industrial support and control measures were institutionalized in various industrial promotion laws, enacted in the late 1960s and early 1970s (Chang 1994). A feature of these laws was the tight performance monitoring system. All firms in targeted industries were required to report not only on their export performance but also on their performance in other areas, such as improvement of technological capability.

Violators of such restrictions could be punished with revocation of licences, imposition of fines and, in some serious cases, prison sentences. Therefore, Chang (2000) argues, 'there was actually little room for moral hazard for the government-supported firms in the traditional [*sic*] Korean system, as continued government supports were contingent on their performance and were not guaranteed by just being in the 'right' industries'.

State control of the financial system and the high debt model

According to the 'finally collapsed' argument, the unsustainably high level of corporate debt was a primary cause of Korea's 1997 financial crisis, and Korean firms' moral hazard following the logic of 'too-big-to-fail', based on the long-established practice of public guarantee, was the underlying cause of such high debt build-up. Hahm (1998) and Krugman (1998a) argue that public guarantees created incentives for Korean firms to choose abnormal overborrowing regardless of high risk. Kim and Ryu (1998)

also insist that the developmental state capitalism of Korea, by introducing interest rate control and preferential policy loans for targeted
industries, induced *chaebol* firms to borrow excessively, because 'in such
an environment, the so-called "too-big-to-fail" mentality has been
deeply rooted: the more *chaebol* borrow, the safer *chaebol* are' (p. 10).

According to this argument, the high degree of risk inherent in the
liability structure of Korean firms is evident from the fact that the
corporate debt/equity ratio[3] in Korea had been the highest compared
with other similar countries; for instance, it was about four times higher
than that of Taiwan in the 1990s (see Figure 3.1). In particular, the average ratio for the 30 largest *chaebol* in Korea reached 519 per cent by the
end of 1997. In this regard, it is argued that Korea's financial crisis was
caused by an excessive debt problem in the corporate sector, especially
among *chaebol* firms (see also Claessens, Djankov and Lang 2000).

Given this diagnosis, the IMF and the Kim Dae-Jung government
forced the *chaebol* radically to reduce their reliance on debt financing,
and to bring down their debt/equity ratio to 200 per cent by the end of
1999 by encouraging asset sales to foreigners, new share issues, and the
elimination of intersubsidiary loan guarantees.

Was the level of debt in Korea really abnormal? Chang and Park
(2000), basing their views on a World Bank study (Demigruc-Kunt and

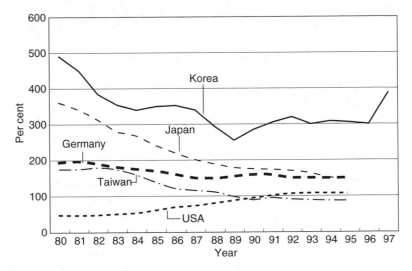

Figure 3.1 International comparison of corporate debt/equity ratios, 1980–97
Note: Data refers to the manufacturing sector for Korea, Japan and Taiwan.
Source: Kim and Ryu (1998: p. 6).

Table 3.1 Capital structure of firms in selected countries, 1980–91

Countries	Debt/equity ratio	Countries	Debt/equity ratio	Countries	Debt/equity ratio
Australia	1.248	Italy	3.068	Singapore	1.232
Austria	2.696	Japan	3.688	South Africa	1.115
Belgium	2.023	Jordan	1.181	Spain	2.746
Brazil	0.56	Korea	3.662	Sweden	5.552
Canada	1.6	Malaysia	0.935	Switzerland	1.75
Finland	4.92	Mexico	0.817	Thailand	2.215
France	3.613	Netherlands	2.156	Turkey	1.996
Germany	2.732	N. Zealand	1.527	UK	1.48
Hong Kong	1.322	Norway	5.375	USA	1.791
India	2.7	Pakistan	2.953	Zimbabwe	0.801

Source: Chang and Park (2000).

Maksimovic 1996), indicate that the debt/equity ratio of Korean corporations, at an average of 366 per cent from 1980 to 1991, was not exceptionally high by international standards (see Table 3.1). During the same period, it was similar to that of Japan (369 per cent), France (361 per cent) and Italy (307 per cent). Moreover, it was much lower than that of Scandinavian countries such as Norway (538 per cent), Sweden (555 per cent) and Finland (492 per cent).

Besides, high debt structure itself does not necessarily cause a financial crisis. For example, Japan did not experience any serious financial crisis in the high-growth period between the 1950s and 1970s even when the debt/equity ratio of its private sector was higher than 500 per cent (Park 1999). On the contrary, Japan suffered a serious financial crisis during the 1990s although the ratio decreased to around 200 per cent. Similarly, Korea did not suffer from any devastating financial crash during its high-growth period between the 1960s and 1980s, in spite of high indebtedness.

The argument that high debt structure was caused by Korean firms' and banks' moral hazard, based on 'too-big-to-fail' mentality, is also questionable. First, as mentioned above, the Korean government (up to the late 1980s) played an active role in governing banks and firms in order to prevent their moral hazard. It succeeded in its efforts as a whole, so that there was no serious financial crisis. The government persuaded commercial banks and big business firms to conform to national industrial strategies by threatening to withhold support. Restrictions on borrowing

Table 3.2   Growth, investment, and savings in Korea, 1962–91 (%)

	1962–66	1967–71	1972–76	1977–81	1982–84	1985–91	1962–91
GNP growth rate	7.9	9.7	10.2	5.7	7.3	10.0	8.6
Investment (% of GNP)	16.3	25.4	29.0	31.0	28.2	32.7	27.4
Domestic saving (% of GNP)	8.0	15.1	20.4	25.5	24.8	34.8	22.1
Foreign saving (% of GNP)	8.6	10.0	6.7	5.6	3.2	2.1	6.0
Foreign saving/ investment	52.8	39.4	23.1	18.1	11.3	6.4	21.9

Source: Cho and Kim (1997: p. 58).

abroad, and coordination of foreign borrowing by the government, were vital parts of this system.

Second, the highly leveraged corporate financing was not the product of a 'too-big-to-fail' mentality on the part of the banks and *chaebol* firms, but resulted from circumstances particular to Korea: that is, as the World Bank (1993) and Wade and Veneroso (1998) indicate, savings had been much higher in Korea and other East Asian countries than in Europe, America or Latin America. The gross domestic savings to gross national product (GNP) ratio in Korea reached about 35 per cent in the latter half of the 1980s, compared to 15–20 per cent in Western systems (see Table 3.2). Households made the most savings, which were held mostly in bank deposits because bank deposits were much less risky than investing in the stock market. Under the circumstances, banks had to lend mostly to industrial firms, as neither households nor the government were significant net borrowers. This resulted in a highly leveraged financial structure for Korean firms. The fact that small and medium-sized companies (SMCs) in Korea have also had similarly high debt/equity ratios shows the invalidity of the 'too-big-to-fail' explanation of the *chaebol*'s high level of liabilities.

A historical perspective on the high debt model

A significant weakness of the 'finally collapsed' argument is the lack of a historical perspective with regard to different timing, paths, and conditions of industrialization (but the ahistoric character of neoclassical economics, which proposes the 'finally collapsed' argument, is well known).

According to Gerschenkron (1962), late-industrializing countries have to overcome the problem of capital shortage. Germany solved the problem with the bank-based system, and Russia and post-war Japan and France with direct state finance and a state-led banking system. The later a country industrializes, the more difficult is the capital shortage and, hence, the greater is the economic intervention of its government. Gerschenkron explains that capital shortage becomes increasingly difficult because production methods become more capital-intensive. Larger quantities of absolute capital are necessary to cover the costs of bigger equipment for historically increasing minimum scale economies. This brings forth new institutional arrangements that entail a larger role for the bank and the state in mobilizing capital for firms (see also Amsden 2001: ch. 10). Especially in the state-based financial systems observed in 'developmental state' capitalism, the state creates various public banks and, at the same time, holds commercial banks under its control. As a result firms become highly dependent on external credits from banks and the state. Korea and Japan provide good examples (Park 1999).

Both Japanese and Korean firms continued to be heavily dependent on external credits up to the 1980s. As seen in Table 3.1, the average debt/equity ratios of their corporate sectors remained at well over 300 per cent in the 1980s. By contrast, Taiwanese firms did not depend on external credit from the early 1970s. According to Ito (1998, cited in Park 1999: p. 40), the debt/equity ratio of large firms in Taiwan in 1972–84 averaged 166.1 per cent, and this ratio improved considerably with the late 1980s' stock market boom, even diminishing to 82 per cent during 1991–96 (see also Figure 3.1).

The reason for the similarly high dependence of Japanese and Korean firms on bank loans cannot be explained solely by the similarly vast amount of domestic savings absorbed by banks as Wade and Veneroso (1998) propose. This takes into account only the supply side of credit. The demand side is more important in determining corporate financial structure. In other words, high savings per se do not necessarily lead to the high indebtedness of private firms. As we have seen, the debt/equity ratio of Taiwanese firms has been much lower than those of Korean and Japanese firms in spite of a similarly high savings rate in Taiwan. In contrast, the modes of corporate financing of Korean and Japanese firms (up to the 1980s) were similar. This can be explained by the fact that Japan and Korea developed similar industries which demanded large amounts of external credits. Following the Japanese model of developing heavy industries, the Korean government promoted the build-up of heavy and chemical industries including the automotive, steel, shipbuilding, electronics and electrical, petrochemicals and petroleum refining, machine and military industries. Japan and Korea's big business firms in the targeted industries aimed to catch up with their Western counterparts as quickly as possible. They therefore had to get their hands on very large amounts of resources, which they could do only by borrowing. As Wade and Veneroso (1998) indicate, 'neither equity markets nor corporate retained earnings are feasible alternatives for mobilizing resources on the scale required to compete in these export markets and continually upgrade'. As a result, highly indebted big business conglomerates – the pre-war *zaibatsu* and the post-war *keiretsu* in Japan, and the *chaebol* in Korea – have dominated in both economies. By contrast, small and medium-sized companies have characterized Taiwan's export industries.[4]

Nonetheless, Japanese firms reduced debt dependency steadily in the late 1980s, thanks to high profits and retained earnings and new equity emission on the booming stock market at that time. Their debt/equity ratio dropped to 203 per cent in 1991, and stayed under 240 per cent up to 1996.

In contrast, Korean firms' debt/equity ratio increased again in the 1990s. The reason for the increase is significantly related to the financial liberalization and industrial deregulation in that period.

3.2   Democratization, liberalization and globalization

Democratization and changes in economic policies

In her book, *Asia's Next Giant*, Amsden raises the question of whether the strong economic measures taken by the Korean state could have been taken under political democracy (1989: p. 18). Moreover, she points out that the relationship between developmentalism and democracy is complicated, 'because reciprocity in the allocation of subsidies requires a strong state vis-à-vis business, not necessarily labor' (p. 148). But she suggests that, in view of the case of post-war Japan and some statist European countries, developmentalism and political democracy can be compatible in principle.

Nonetheless, Korea's Big Push for heavy and chemical industries in the 1970s accompanied a totalitarian political regime. In 1972, President Park Chung-Hee declared martial law and legalized the 'Yushin Constitution'.[5]

The constitution completely banned anti-government political activism, including all criticism of the constitution itself. Presidential decrees replaced laws. The powers of the legislature and judiciary were significantly restricted. Furthermore, the constitution secured the re-election of the president, who wanted to keep the position of commander of industrial promotion.

The Yushin regime collapsed abruptly with the assassination of President Park in October 1979,[6] but the totalitarian regime itself survived because the Korean military re-established military rule in May 1980 after a short period of civilian government. Martial law was declared on 17 May, and all kinds of political activities, assemblies and rallies were banned. After the bloody suppression of a large-scale civilian protest in Kwangju, General Chun Doo-Hwan, head of the Army Intelligence Agency, came to power. In August, he became president of the country.

From this bloody outset, the following seven years saw more and more confrontations between the regime and the protest movement. In June 1987, students as well as opposition politicians, dissidents and religious groups joined forces in strong nation-wide campaigns for democratic reforms. This resulted in the fall of the totalitarian regime, marking a turning point in modern Korean political history. Democratization of the country started, at last, and continued under the government of Roh Tae-Woo (1988–92) and Kim Young-Sam (1993–7), even if it followed a zigzag course.

Democratization brought about some changes in the economy, especially in the area of wealth redistribution. First, increasing union activities by workers led to a rise in wages, which resulted in expanding consumer demand in domestic markets. Second, because industrial policy favouring big business groups had negative consequences, such as concentrating economic power in the hands of the *chaebol*, which in turn drew criticism from the democratic opposition, a reorientation of industrial policy emerged as a new democratic mandate (Moon 1998). For example, in 1987, a basket control credit system (credit ceilings) was introduced to limit the share of commercial bank loans to the 30 largest *chaebol* groups.

Third, at the same time, commercial bank loans, which had previously concentrated on big *chaebol* companies in targeted industries, were now more focused on SMCs and farmers. SMCs benefited from the anti-*chaebol* policies (Cho and Kim 1997; Kim and Mo 1998). Consequently, a growing share of commercial bank loans was allocated to SMCs (50 per cent in 1989 and 59 per cent in 1996), while the share of loans to the 30 largest

Table 3.3   Required minimum lending ratios for banks to SMCs, 1965–92 (%)

	1965	1976	1980	1985	1986	1992
Commercial banks	30	30	35	35	35	45
Local banks	30	40	55	55	80	80
Foreign bank branches				25	25	25

Source: Kim and Mo (1998).

Table 3.4   Share of commercial bank loans to SMCs and the *chaebol*, 1983–93 (%)

	1983	1985	1988	1989	1990	1991	1992	1993
SMCs	33.1	31.5	48.1	50.1	55.5	56.8	n.a.	59.3
30 largest *chaebol*	n.a.	n.a.	23.7	20.7	19.8	20.4	n.a.	n.a.

n.a. = not available
Source: Kim and Mo (1998).

chaebol decreased significantly from some 50 per cent in the early 1980s to 36 per cent in 1985. It fell to 20 per cent in 1990, and 14 per cent in 1995–99 (see Tables 3.3 and 3.4).

Democratization versus liberalization

Besides democratization, the developmental state in Korea faced another challenge in the 1980s: the advent of the neoliberal critique of the strong state. This neoliberalism has manifested itself in policies of liberalization, deregulation and globalization.

Democratic ideas are traditionally associated with economic justice, social welfare and wealth redistribution, bringing certain forms of state intervention into the market economy. By contrast, liberalist ideas are associated with strengthening private sector autonomy, smaller government and a more flexible labour market instead of social welfare and redistribution. History provides innumerable cases in which the two ideas are in contradiction. Only liberal democracy will assert that both ideas can be reconciled.

The governments of Roh Tae-Woo and Kim Young-Sam also failed to balance the two conflicting ideological and political goals. For example, the government policy of providing loan assistance to the agricultural sector, which was threatened by the WTO agreement on trade liberalization, was supported by Korean farmers, many of whom belonged to the poorest social classes in Korea. But the WTO and the IMF strongly criticized the policy. Consequently, the Kim Young-Sam government executed the policy halfheartedly.

To give another example, the basket control credit system to limit the share of commercial bank loans to the 30 largest *chaebol* groups may be regarded as a part of a process of democratization. But at the same time, as we shall soon see, the government allowed non-commercial bank financial institutions (NBFIs), many of which were under the *chaebol*'s control, to extend their business in underregulated financial areas: an example of liberalization. Hence, the policies of presidents Roh and Kim towards the *chaebol* were a mixture of contradictory ideas. Such mixing-and-matching of liberalist and democratic goals was also seen in other areas. The result was inconsistent economic policies (Moon 1998).

The history of Korea shows clearly that liberalization is not related to democratization. The neoliberal orientation in Korea dates back to the early 1980s and the military rule of Chun Doo-Hwan. According to Mo and Moon (1998), the hegemonic spread of Reaganomics and Thatcherism worldwide legitimized the adoption and implementation of the new thinking. Moreover, the USA, the IMF and the World Bank were pushing for the neoliberal reforms. Third, a new breed of neoliberal reformers such as Kim Jai-Ik and Kang Kyung-Sik took important positions in the government bureaucracy.[7] They won extensive support from American-trained economists, who then began to constitute the majority of the academic community in Korea in the 1980s (Mo and Moon 1998).

Nonetheless, the influence of liberal ideas on economic policy in the 1980s was limited, and institutional changes did not alter the framework of developmental state capitalism. It was from the late 1980s that liberalization and globalization started to set Korea's economic policy agenda. Let us now look at how this change affected the *chaebol*.

3.3 Liberalization and *laissez-faire*

The *chaebol*'s autonomy in corporate governance

As mentioned above, the relationship between the government and the *chaebol* in the developmental system was analogous to that of principal and agent. As an insurer and financier providing policy loans, the government monitored and controlled the *chaebol*'s activities.

For this purpose, various industrial promotion laws were enacted in the late 1960s and early 1970s. They enabled the state not only to monitor performance of firms in targeted industries but also to restrict the entry of new firms and the capacity expansion of existing firms.

This kind of policy was criticized as promoting an oligopolistic economy and disturbing free market competition. However, these measures were particularly important as a way to prevent overborrowing and over-investment by the *chaebol*.

There was a moderate change of the industry policy in the 1980s, with the enactment of the Industrial Development Law (IDL) in 1986, which abolished the various industry-specific promotion laws and integrated them into one law. Although the IDL kept major characteristics of the old industry policies, important changes were also introduced (see Chang 1994).

First, the law shifted industry policy away from intensive interven-tion in specific industries and towards function-oriented industrial support, such as support for R&D in all industries. With the law limit-ing the scope of support for *chaebol* firms, the tight performance monitoring by the government, which had disciplined them, gradually weakened. At the individual firm level, direct government intervention in corporate decisions was gradually replaced by indirect or contingent intervention.

Second, the IDL emphasized rationalization programmes with limited lifetimes, usually 2–3 years. The rationalization programmes were intended to provide temporary boosts to industries that needed entry restriction, control of capacity expansion, specialization of production areas, an upgrade of technological capability, and product price control. Between 1986 and 1989, the automotive, heavy construction machinery, heavy electrical equipment, naval diesel engines, ferro-alloys, fertilizers, coal min-ing, textile and dyeing industries underwent rationalization programmes.

Nonetheless, all of these interventionist programmes were only temporary, and industries that finished the programmes began to experi-ence competition from new entries and capacity expansions from the late 1980s.

The government's two pillars for controlling the financial and corporate sectors, industry policies and financial control, disappeared slowly from the late 1980s, and very rapidly during President Kim Young-Sam's administration. Abolition of industry policy and financial control was not only the basic demand made by the IMF and the World Bank, but also the precondition for entry into the OECD. The Kim Young-Sam government demonstrated its willingness to conform when it released its 'New Economic Policies' in 1993, adopting globalization as the government's leading policy motto. The Economic Planning Board, the powerful organ of industrial policy which had a similar role to MITI in Japan, was abolished in December 1994.

The abolition of industrial policy made it possible for the *chaebol* to begin ambitiously investing in new business lines and capacity expansion, without fear of monitoring or punishment by the government. The automotive industry, for instance, was earmarked in 1986 by the Ministry of Commerce and Industry for a rationalization programme. Entry and capacity expansion in it were restricted until 1989, and only Hyundai, Kia and Daewoo were allowed to produce cars. However, from 1990 on no legal restriction existed. Consequently, between 1990 and 1996, the Korean car industry saw two new entrants as well as vigorous capacity expansion by the existing carmakers.

Similarly, diversification and capacity expansion occurred in all major industries from the late 1980s. The number of companies in the petrochemical industry went from four to six as Hyundai and Samsung entered in 1988. Hyundai sought to enter electronics, which had been dominated by Samsung and LG, and succeeded in 1987. Many new companies, mostly *chaebol* firms, entered the construction industry as it seemed to be booming in the early 1990s. In the financial sector, too, the number of companies and amount of investment increased rapidly, as government controls were either abolished or relaxed, and a vast amount of foreign credit and capital began to flow into the Korean financial market. The number of life insurance companies increased from ten to twenty or more, and that of merchant banks from six licensees to 30 between 1994 and 1996.

As most *chaebol* groups wanted to expand and diversify their business lines in seemingly promising sectors, they tended to aim for a similar business portfolio. The result was a huge rise in competition throughout the Korean economy during 1993–7.

The *chaebol* did not merely invest in domestic expansion. Welcoming the declaration of the globalization era by the Kim Young-Sam administration, and basing themselves on vast amounts of credit and capital provided by a globalized financial market, major *chaebol* sought to build and expand overseas empires, also. A representative case is the 'global management' of Daewoo, which we will examine in Chapter 7. Later, when the countries were hit by the Asian and Russian financial crises of 1997–8, it was Daewoo that suffered most severely.

The *chaebol*'s autonomy in corporate financing

The liberalization and globalization of the Korean economy freed the *chaebol* not only from corporate control by the government, but also from financial control. Commercial banks, which had been nationalized in the early 1960s, remained under government control throughout the

1980s, despite their partial privatization in the early 1980s. Even during the 1990s, the government continued to control commercial banks' credit distribution. Only the policy goal changed: from the support of *chaebol* business to social and public purposes. As mentioned above, democratization since 1987 had increased the demand for social equity and income redistribution. Many policy loans were made available to previously disadvantaged sectors, such as SMCs, agriculture and housing, and at the same time, credit control over large business groups was intensified. Consequently, commercial bank loans to SMCs increased, while those to the *chaebol* decreased.

The decreasing role of government-controlled commercial banks in the financing of the *chaebol* meant, however, that the government was losing an important means of keeping the *chaebol* under its control. Furthermore, even though the *chaebol* reduced its dependence on commercial bank loans, it substantially increased external fund raising through so-called NBFIs.

NBFIs include short-term investment companies, mutual savings and credit unions, insurance companies, security broker companies and investment trust companies, and merchant banks. Since the 1970s, the government had encouraged the development of NBFIs in an effort to bring curb funds to the formal financial sector. The government permitted these institutions to offer higher interest rates and to operate with greater freedom than commercial banks. They were not required to make policy loans. Associated with the start of partial financial deregulation in the early 1980s, the NBFI sector grew rapidly in the 1980s, and its share in total saving and credit became larger than that of the commercial banks from 1987 (see Table 3.5). In the 1980s, the government relaxed NBFI entry barriers and permitted them to expand into merchant banking.

An important reason why NBFIs increased their participation in the *chaebol*'s fund raising is that a large number of them were owned and controlled by the *chaebol*. While under the laws regarding commercial

Table 3.5   Share of banks and NBFIs in savings and credits, 1980–94 (%)

		1980	1985	1987	1990	1991	1992	1993	1994
Savings	Banks	69.1	52.7	46.2	40.5	39.3	34.2	32.6	29.2
	NBFIs	30.9	47.3	53.8	59.5	60.7	65.8	67.4	70.8
Credits	Banks	63.8	58.2	53.5	49.7	48.3	45.2	45.2	38.5
	NBFIs	36.2	41.8	46.5	50.3	51.7	54.8	54.8	61.5

Source: Bank of Korea, *Currency Finance*, 1995, cited in Kwack E.-J. (1999: p. 53).

Table 3.6 Domestic lending to the 30 largest *chaebol*, 1993–7 (%)

	1993	1994	1995	1996	1997
Commercial banks' share	53.9	51.2	43.0	32.9	32.4
NBFIs' share	46.1	48.8	57.0	67.1	67.6
Merchant banks	30.4	31.5	38.6	48.0	48.2
Insurance companies	11.0	9.8	7.8	7.4	8.6
Lease companies	4.7	7.5	10.6	11.4	10.6
Rest				0.3	0.2
Total (billion won)	30,158	63,122	78,326	100,200	110,459

Note: as of December each year, except for 1997 where figures given are for June.
Source: Ministry of Finance and Economy, *Report to Parliamentary Investigation*, 1997, cited in Kwack E.-J. (1999: p. 71).

banks only the government could be a controlling shareholder, NBFIs could be owned by the *chaebol* from the outset. The number of NBFI companies belonging to the top 10 largest *chaebol* groups was six in 1972; this increased to 25 in 1987 and 39 in 1995. In 1995, the 30 largest *chaebol* owned 43 non-bank financial subsidiaries, including 13 security broker companies, nine insurance companies, 19 short-term investment companies, and two credit card companies. By means of these financial subsidiaries, the *chaebol* were able to become autonomous in fund raising.

Financial deregulation in the 1990s further contributed to the growth of NBFIs at the expense of commercial banks. In domestic lending to the 30 largest *chaebol* groups, the NBFIs took a larger share than commercial banks from 1995. As seen in Table 3.6, the main financers of the *chaebol*'s investment projects in the 1990s were not commercial banks, which were still under government control, but the merchant banks and insurance companies, which belonged largely to the *chaebol* themselves. In particular, the importance of merchant banks increased rapidly and, from 1996, they alone surpassed commercial banks in domestic lending.

Deregulation, *laissez-faire* and moral hazard

With the partial liberalization in the Korean economy during the period of the Chun Doo-Hwan government (1980–7), the relationship between the state and the *chaebol* moved from one of clear dominance by the state, between 1961 and 1979, to a more symbiotic one (Kim E.-M. 1987). A shift in industrial policy, a gradual reduction of policy loans, and the increasing role of NBFIs made the position of the *chaebol* stronger and stronger. Nonetheless, there still existed public regulation and supervision over financial institutions and *chaebol* companies until the late 1980s, so that there appear to have been no serious cases of moral hazard problems in the Korean economy at this time, but full-scale liberalization and deregulation in the 1990s created one.

As mentioned above, the moral hazard problem can be avoided if the principal or insurer is able to effectively check the agent's or insurant's behaviour and performance. But with the government's industrial policy and financial control abolished, the *chaebol*'s financial and industrial companies were freed from the state's disciplining power.

Furthermore, the liberalized and globalized financial market provided the *chaebol* with the funds necessary for investment. Previously, the *chaebol* could approach the international financial market only via the government or government-controlled banks. Now, however, the *chaebol* gained direct access to foreign capital through deregulated financial institutions such as NBFIs or offshore branches of commercial and merchant banks. In addition, the *chaebols'* offshore subsidiaries were allowed directly to obtain foreign credit from foreign financial institutions.

This created a kind of *laissez-faire* situation: nobody wanted to play the role of a principal to check the agent's business. International fund managers and lending bankers did not take roles in corporate governance because Korea's commercial laws still excluded them. At the same time, they were rarely concerned about this. Korea's commercial banks had never been competent in corporate disciplining and had no reason to change. Moreover, NBFIs, which now became the most important financial intermediaries for the *chaebol*, were under the *chaebol*'s influence.

With full autonomy in corporate governance and corporate financing, the *chaebol* turned out to be a monster let loose. The period of 1993–7 may be characterized as a time when functioning corporate governance institutions did not exist. The too-big-to-fail mentality, a kind of moral hazard problem, arose as a result of these circumstances. As failures of ill-advised investment projects led to recession and deteriorating profitability from late 1996, the *chaebol* borrowed more and more. The average debt/equity ratio (non-financial sector) of the 30 largest *chaebol* soared from 347.5 per cent in 1995 to 519 per cent in 1997 (Koo 1998). But given the predominance of *chaebol* firms' market share and their vertically integrated industrial structure, the economic and social costs of their bankruptcy would have been enormous. In such an environment, the too-big-to-fail mentality appeared. Troubled *chaebol* were able to get rescue loans from banks even though the balance sheets of the banks deteriorated rapidly.

Without industry policy and financial control, the government did not have the tools to discipline failed *chaebol*. Nevertheless, the government continued implicitly to guarantee rescue loans in the last instance. Hence the moral hazard problem arising from the public guarantee of the *chaebol* and banks became serious for the first time.

Moreover, liberalization and deregulation made cronyism into a real economic problem, as Chang (2000) points out. As developmental state intervention with official regulations was dismantled, political corruption, based on unofficial connections between the state and business, spilled over from traditionally corrupt areas such as urban planning and defence contracts into the principal manufacturing and financial industries. Kim Young-Sam's term in office was notorious for its corruption scandals.[8] Premature deregulation and lax financial market opening, strongly urged by the IMF and World Bank, created a widespread moral hazard problem in Korea's financial and corporate system, leading to overinvestment and to the crisis.

3.4 International capital movement and the financial crisis in Korea

Inflow of foreign capital into Korea

In the 1990s, NBFIs became more important to the *chaebol* because they acquired access to the globalizing financial markets. It was the NBFIs that benefited the most from Korea's opening of the capital account.

A significant step in Korea's liberalization was taken in 1992, when foreigners were allowed to purchase Korean stocks for the first time. The Kim Young-Sam administration eased restrictions on foreigners' equity investment step by step.[9] As a result, the cumulative net inflow of portfolio investment in the Korean stock market during 1993–96 amounted to US$ 18.1 billion (Shin and Wang 1999). As the Korean stock market was dominated by NBFIs at this time, much of this foreign funding flowed into *chaebol* companies.

Even more significantly, the liberalist government allowed commercial banks and NBFIs to borrow foreign currency via their offshore branches. One direct result of this deregulation was a rapid and enormous increase in foreign credits, which was equivalent to a sharp rise in the country's external debts (see Table 3.7). Gross external liabilities jumped from US$62.9 billion to 158 billion between 1992 and 1997. Between 1994 and 1996, a period of comprehensive capital account liberalization, they grew at annual rates exceeding 32 per cent. These rates are not comparable

Table 3.7   Korea's external liabilities, 1992–98 (US$100 million)

	1992	1993	1994	1995	1996	1997	1998
Gross external liability (A)[a]	629.0	670.0	887.0	1,197.0	1,643.4	1,580.6	1,493.5
Financial sector[b]	436.0	475.0	651.0	905.0	1,165.3	896.0	719.0
Corporate sector	137.0	156.0	200.0	261.0	417.5	462.0	410.0
Short-term ext. liability (B)	370.0	403.0	584.0	787.0	929.8	632.2	308.3
Long-term ext. liability	259.0	265.0	303.0	410.0	713.9	948.4	1,185.2
B/A rate (%)	58.82	60.15	65.84	65.75	56.58	40.00	20.64
A/GDP rate (%)	19.99	19.38	22.04	24.46	31.60	33.16	46.48

[a] Year-end values. External liabilities include external debts as defined by the World Bank, offshore borrowings of Korean banks, and overseas borrowings of Korean banks' offshore branches.
[b] Including foreign bank branches operating in Korea.
Source: Hahm and Mishkin (2000).

with those of the previous period when it was 8 per cent at most during 1980–92 except for one year, 1984. In a mere three years between 1994 and 1996, gross external liabilities increased by an amazing US$97.3 billion, and their ratio to GDP soared from under 20 per cent to over 30 per cent. In 1996 alone, foreign borrowings increased by US$44.6 billion.

A primary reason for the huge inflow of international credit into Korea was the gap in interest rates during 1990–8: 11–18 per cent in the Korean financial market, compared with 2–7 per cent in the international credit markets. Japanese banks, which suffered from nearly zero interest in their home financial market during the 1990s, were particularly enthusiastic lenders to Korean banks (see also Chapter 2).

Short-term foreign borrowings contributed more to the increase of gross external liabilities than long-term foreign borrowings. The increase in short-term external borrowings amounted to US$52.7 billion during 1994–6, while long-term external borrowings increased by US$44.6 billion. The share of short-term foreign debts in total foreign debts stayed under 30 per cent in the 1980s but jumped to over 60 per cent during 1993–5, as seen in Table 3.7 (see also Table 2.1). Banks, especially offshore branches of commercial banks and merchant banks, were responsible for the increase in short-term foreign borrowings.

Nonetheless, Korea's foreign debt was not at an obviously unsustainable level (Chang, Park and Yoo 1998). The World Bank considers countries with debt/GNP ratios under 48 per cent as low-risk cases, but Korea's debt/GNP ratio was only 22 per cent in 1996, and was still around 25 per cent on the eve of the crisis.[10]

However, Korea's foreign debt had a critical problem with its maturity structure because of the rapidly increasing short-term debt. Merchant banks in particular were exposed to the dangers of short-term foreign debt (Chang, Park and Yoo 1998). These had been recently licensed by the Kim Young-Sam government during the financial deregulation – nine in 1994 and 15 in 1996 in addition to the six that existed before 1993 – and hence were inexperienced. They operated primarily by borrowing abroad and lending domestically. Total foreign borrowings of the merchant banks rose by around 60 per cent annually during 1994–96, from US$7.3 billion to 18.6 billion. Moreover, supervision of the merchant banks, unlike that of deposit banks (commercial banks and local banks), was virtually non-existent, to the extent that the Kim government, on the eve of the crisis, was apparently unaware of the huge mismatch in the maturity structures between their foreign borrowings (64 per cent were short term) and domestic lending (85 per cent were long term).

Capital flows into Korea's corporate sector

Let us look more closely at the net increase in total foreign borrowings of US$97.3 billion between 1993 and 1996 (see Table 3.7). According to a government report (Board of Public Inspection 1999), 39 per cent of the increase (US$37.9 billion) was used to compensate the current account deficit during the period, but 54.6 per cent (US$53.1 billion) flowed into Korea's corporate sector. Consequently, together with the foreign equity capital inflow of US$18.1 billion during 1993–6 mentioned above, a total of around US$71 billion flowed into Korea's corporate sector in the period. The *chaebol* benefited most from the capital inflow.

However, given that commercial bank lending to the *chaebol* continued to be under strict regulation even during 1993–6, the question arises: how had the huge foreign credits flowed into the *chaebol* sector? Financial deregulation had made it possible for the *chaebol* to bypass commercial bank regulation.

Table 3.6 shows that the lending of NBFIs to *chaebol* firms jumped from 13.9 trillion (46.1 per cent of total domestic lending) to 67.2 trillion won (67.1 per cent of total domestic lending) during 1994–6.[11] In particular, merchant banks' lending to the *chaebol* rose by 39 trillion won, from 9.2 trillion to 48.1 trillion. But in the same period, commercial banks' lending to the 30 largest *chaebol* increased only by 17 trillion won, from 16 trillion won to 33 trillion. Nonetheless, Table 3.8 shows that

Table 3.8   Korean banks' foreign currency borrowings, 1992–97 (US$100 million)

	1992	1993	1994	1995	1996	1997
Commercial banks	56,674	63,669	82,104	105,397	127,923	111,614
Special banks	19,365	22,614	28,093	35,429	43,207	48,628
Merchant banks	4,534	5,526	7,265	11,659	18,623	19,113

Source: Board of Public Inspection (1999).

commercial banks received the largest part of foreign borrowings in the same period. The difference between the large amount of foreign borrowings and the small amount of domestic lending to the *chaebol* suggests that commercial banks had various ways of bypassing government control and supplying foreign currency credits to the *chaebol*.

First, commercial banks lent the borrowed foreign currency to merchant banks and other NBFIs, which then lent it to *chaebol* firms. Differences in interest rates between commercial banks and NBFIs made the transaction possible.

Second, the numbers in Table 3.6 do not reflect the offshore transactions between offshore branches of commercial banks and offshore subsidiaries of Korean firms, while the numbers in Tables 3.7 and 3.8 do include those offshore transactions. This means that, although domestic branches of commercial banks did not greatly increase loans to the *chaebol*'s domestic subsidiaries (because of various regulations), their offshore branches drastically increased foreign currency loans to the *chaebol*'s offshore subsidiaries. Such offshore financial transactions between Korean financial institutions and Korean firms fell outside the regulations due to the opening of the capital account.

To summarize, NBFIs and offshore branches of commercial banks, both outside prudent supervision, were the main channels of capital supply to the *chaebol*.[12] Through them a total of US$53.1 billion foreign currency borrowings were supplied to Korea's corporate sector.

Furthermore, there was a third deregulated way for the *chaebol* to obtain foreign credit: in 1993 the Kim Young-Sam government allowed offshore subsidiaries of Korean firms to borrow directly from international banks without any mediation by offshore branches of Korean banks. These transactions, not being regarded as those of domestic residents in a legal sense, did not need to be reported. Consequently, the numbers in Tables 3.7 and 3.8, based on Korean banks' obligatory reports to the Bank of Korea and to the Ministry of Finance and Economy, do not include all the offshore credits obtained by Korean firms from international banks.

All the relevant parties kept the credit relationships as business secrets. Even after the outbreak of the financial crisis, it was either difficult or impossible for Korea's regulators to gain access to these business secrets. As a result, rumours about allegedly gigantic amounts of *chaebol* firms' offshore liabilities spread in the Korean and international financial markets, so that the panic intensified.

The Ministry of Finance and Economy then forced the *chaebol* to report on such offshore borrowings from international banks. Subsequently, the Ministry announced officially that they amounted to US$53.2 billion in mid-1998, including US$37.2 billion borrowed by the five largest *chaebol*s (Board of Public Inspection 1999). The *chaebol* group with the largest of this kind of overseas debt was Daewoo, which financed its global investment projects, worth US$20 billion, mostly with direct offshore credits.[13]

If we add together the foreign equity capital inflow of US$18.1 billion, the foreign currency lending provided by Korean financial institutions of US$53.1 billion, and the *chaebol*'s direct offshore credit of US$53.2 billion, a total of more than US$120 billion of foreign capital was supplied to Korea's corporate sector during the four years 1993–96.

The *chaebol*'s overinvestment based on overflowing funds

The enormous inflow of foreign capital and credit made it possible for Korean firms to invest excessively. After relatively slow growth during 1990–2, the Korean economy entered an expanding phase in late 1993 with a notable expansion in investment (Kim J.-I. 1994, 1995). Large-scale investment was made in major export industries. Figure 3.2 shows that the increase in domestic facility investments by Korean non-financial firms between 1993 and 1996 was remarkable. The rate of annual increase in facility investment averaged 44.7 per cent during the Big Push period of 1973–9, but dropped to 20.5 per cent in the 1980s, and again to 12.3 per cent during 1990–3, following which it suddenly rose to over 37 per cent during 1994–5. Led by the strong increase in facility investment, the Korean economy had been booming since 1994. Gross domestic production grew at a rate of 8.3 per cent in 1994 and 8.5 per cent in 1995, up from 5.3 per cent in 1992 and 5.4 per cent in 1993.

The surge in equipment investment accompanied strong capacity expansion in major industries. However, this expansion turned out to be excessive. As the excessive capacity investment was widely regarded as one of the key factors in bringing about the financial crisis of 1997, the Korean government came up with the so-called 'Big Deal' policy in 1998, in which the five largest *chaebol* were asked to swap their businesses in

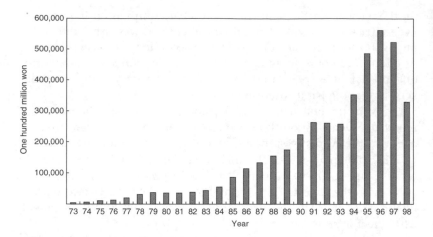

Figure 3.2   Domestic facility investments by non-financial firms, 1973–98[a]
[a] Planned values.
Source: The Korea Development Bank, *Surveys of Facility Investment Plan*, various years. In the bank's website at http://www.kdb.co.kr on 15 August 2001.

eight troubled industries among themselves to alleviate excess capacity. The eight major industries targeted by the policy were cars, semiconductors, electronics, petrochemicals and oil refining, aerospace, railways, and power equipment and ship engines.

On the basis of a statistical analysis of 26 *chaebol* firms' financial statements during 1988–98, Lee I.-K. (2000: p. 33ff) concluded that excessive capacity in the eight industries had been chronic (see Table 3.9). He observed that overly optimistic demand forecasting during the bubble period of 1993–6 led to the excessive facility investments. Money and optimism overflowed in the period.

The Korean economy went into recession from the second half of 1996, when the growth of exports stagnated. The prices of major export goods such as semiconductor chips, steel and chemical products fell significantly during 1996–97, and the terms of trade deteriorated by approximately 20 per cent in the same period. While the annual increase in exports was 16.3 per cent (1994) and 30.8 per cent (1995), up from 6.6 per cent (1992) and 7.3 per cent (1993), it fell to 3.7 per cent in 1996. The current account deficit in 1996 hit a record US$23 billion, the second largest in the world after the USA.

In particular, the export performance of the semiconductor, electrics and electronics, and steel industries, accounting respectively for 14 per cent, 28 per cent and 8 per cent of the total exports of US$125 billion in

Table 3.9 Capacity utilization of the 26 companies of the top five *chaebol* groups in troubled industries, 1988–98[a] (%)

	1988	1989	1990	1991	1992	1993	1994	1995	1996	1997	1998
Cars	64.49	65.26	64.94	62.79	62.01	80.00	88.00	81.87	89.83	76.12	56.56
Semiconductors	90.59	87.64	77.69	88.00	96.49	94.00	102.40	98.33	96.78	91.75	89.55
Electronics	75.90	70.95	78.74	77.01	83.97	76.17	85.96	82.24	83.39	86.12	85.67
Petrochemicals	82.00	86.33	92.98	104.03	93.04	98.66	106.21	96.67	94.50	89.84	88.81
Oil refining	91.52	91.35	91.93	96.30	82.98	89.48	92.52	97.73	98.03	96.29	85.38
Aerospace	58.98	65.52	78.12	77.86	54.19	67.24	140.46	54.65	45.29	68.52	87.07
Rail systems	74.96	72.56	77.26	67.26	66.26	55.91	74.33	71.59	65.83	65.45	84.22
Power equipment and ship engines	86.35	56.43	73.73	70.23	66.96	79.09	82.33	81.62	83.56	85.00	91.50

[a] Top five *chaebol* are Hyundai, Samsung, Daewoo, LG and SK. Capacity utilization rates refer to those announced by the companies, and are not based on uniform production hours.
Source: Lee I.-K. (2000).

1995, deteriorated unexpectedly, and fell by 14.1 per cent, 2.8 per cent and 13.9 per cent in 1996. As a result, the annual rate of growth in net sales in the manufacturing sector fell to 10.3 per cent in 1996, down from 18.2 per cent (1994) and 20.4 per cent (1995).

The trade shock in 1996 put unduly heavy pressure on already thin profit margins in Korea's corporate sector. The annual growth rate of operating income of Korean non-financial listed companies declined by 14.4 per cent in 1996. Their return on assets (ROA) significantly reduced in 1996, and then dropped below zero in 1997 (see Table 3.10).

The profitability of the largest *chaebol*, even if higher during 1994–95, deteriorated faster than that of average listed firms. Table 3.11 shows that the ROA of the 30 largest *chaebol*, particularly that of the sixth to tenth largest, declined rapidly after 1996. In fact, a 'polarization' occurred: the sixth to thirtieth largest *chaebol* were especially exposed to a chronic weakness of extremely low or minus ROA during the boom between 1993 and 1996. This was because many of these small and middle-sized *chaebol* groups, aiming to catch up with the five largest *chaebol* groups, vigorously invested in unrelated diversification and capacity expansion.

The recession's second stage began as major corporate bankruptcies started in early 1997. Some of the sixth to fiftieth largest *chaebol*

Table 3.10 Indicators of corporate sector profitability, 1991–97[a] (%)

	1991	1992	1993	1994	1995	1996	1997
Return on assets	1.8	1.5	1.1	2	2.5	0.8	−0.7
Return on equity	6	5.1	4	6.9	8.7	2.7	−2.9
Annual growth rate of income	29.1	11.9	16.7	21.1	26	−14.4	−22.9

[a] For non-financial corporations listed in the Korean stock market.
Source: Shin (2000: p. 84).

Table 3.11 Return on assets of the 30 largest *chaebol*, 1993–97[a] (%)

Ranking	1993	1994	1995	1996	1997
1–5th *chaebol*	1.86	3.54	4.86	1.41	0.43
6–10th *chaebol*	0.87	1.17	1.10	−0.49	−2.25
11–30th *chaebol*	−0.40	−0.06	−0.08	0.08	−3.00
All 30 *chaebol*	1.11	2.19	3.15	0.23	−2.13

[a] Simple average of each *chaebol*'s return on asset figures reported in Joh (1999).
Source: Shin (2000: p. 84).

Table 3.12 Defaults among the 30 largest *chaebol* in 1997

Chaebol	Default month	Size[a]	Core business	Bankrupt business
Hanbo	January	14	Steel	Steel
Sammi	March	25	Steel	Steel
Jinro	April	19	Alcoholic drinks	Construction
Kia	July	7	Automobile	Steel
Haitai	November	24	Food	Electronics
New-Core	November	28	Retail	Retail

[a] Size is according to the asset value.

collapsed one after another. Woosung, a small *chaebol* with core business in construction, collapsed in late 1996. In January 1997, Hanbo, the fourteenth largest *chaebol*, went bankrupt. This was just the beginning. The year 1997 witnessed defaults by eight of the fifth to thirtieth largest *chaebol* and several more among the lower-ranked in the top fifty.

As large *chaebol* went bankrupt, the recession began having a serious impact on the financial system. The vulnerability of banks, and in particular merchant banks, increased because the *chaebol* bankruptcies burdened them with real and potential non-performing loans of total 28 trillion won (US$33 billion). The most spectacular was the default of Kia, Korea's seventh largest *chaebol* group with core business in the automobile sector (see Table 3.12), which had non-performing loans of 12 trillion won (US$13 billion).

As a result of the greater uncertainty created by these bankruptcies and the deteriorating performances of both financial and non-financial firms, the stock market in Korea fell sharply. From a peak value of 980.9 at the end of April 1996, the market index fell to 677.3 by the end of March 1997, and dropped further to 470.8 at the end of October before the outbreak of the currency crisis.

Panic outflow of foreign capital causing the financial crisis

However, the collapse of several of the *chaebol* and the resultant weakening of domestic financial institutions alone were not enough to trigger a financial crisis. It was the panic outflow of international capital from Korea that magnified the economic downturn into a catastrophic crisis.

The Thai baht and other East Asian currencies were already under speculative attack in mid-1997, and a financial contagion spread over Korea. Given the weakening of Korea's financial and corporate sector and the increased exposure of the economy to foreign exchange rates due to the large amount of external borrowing, Korea was also ripe for a speculative attack on its currency. With the collapse of Asian stock markets and the downgrading of Korea's sovereign credit rating to junk level at the end of October 1997, the danger of attack become even more serious.

However, direct speculative attack on the Korean currency was limited due to the still existing tight regulation on currency account transactions and the absence of a currency futures market inside Korea. Rather, the rapid depreciation of the Korean won was driven by international creditors' panic run on Korean banks to collect their loans, particularly short-term loans (Hahm and Mishkin 2000: p. 97).

Most merchant banks defaulted as soon as foreign lenders refused to roll over short-term credits. This was because of the mismatch problem in the maturity structure, as mentioned above. The default of merchant banks, in turn, jeopardized Korea's entire banking system because, as we have seen, commercial banks were largely involved in financial transactions with the merchant banks. So, the panicked foreign bankers ran on commercial banks, too. A large-scale bank run started in Korea. But this time, it was not depositors, as expected in the traditional model of bank runs, but global bankers who ran on Korean banks.

Korea's short-term overseas borrowings, amounting to US$93 billion and 57 per cent of total foreign currency borrowings at the end of 1996, turned out to be extremely vulnerable in the latter half of 1997. Table 3.7 shows that for two years between the end of 1996 and the end of 1998, a total of US$62 billion of foreign short-term capital (loans and credits) ran out of Korea (see the short-term external liabilities in the table). Even worse, most of the capital flight occurred in the midst of the East Asian currency crisis between November 1997 and March 1998. As a result of the massive outflow of foreign capital, the spot price of the Korean won depreciated by 88 per cent between October 1997 and January 1998.

The speed and size of the panic capital flight were extreme enough to cause a financial crisis. The Bank of Korea, as the lender of last resort, supported troubled Korean banks by providing them with foreign currency. However, this bailout programme rapidly exhausted its available foreign reserves. With no foreign exchange reserves, Korea decided to ask for IMF assistance towards the end of November. This was granted on 4 December. The amount of assistance was unusually large. The IMF would provide US$21 billion, supplemented by US$10 billion from the World Bank and US$4 billion from the Asian Development Bank (ADB).

The USA, Japan and other countries would provide an additional US$36 billion, bringing the grand total to US$57 billion.

The most critical factor, however, was the extent to which foreign banks would roll over their lending to Korean banks. The IMF rescue plan failed to stop the panic run by international banks because the Fund's demands for radical structural reform of the Korean economy intensified their panic further. Sachs (1998) and Krugman (1999) criticized the IMF for 'screaming fire in the theatre' (see also Chapter 2).

The panic run continued into the first quarter of 1998, while the Korean government, representing Korea's 33 borrower banks, negotiated with representatives of more than 100 international creditor banks, including big Japanese, European and US banks. Both sides agreed on a plan to roll over US$25 billion of foreign short-term debts, due at the end of March 1998, and to convert them into debts with longer maturity dates.

Despite the rescheduling of short-term obligations, however, the financial turbulence intensified. With the sharp depreciation of the Korean won, the market interest rate now soared to over 20 per cent, and peaked at 28 per cent in December 1997 (see Figure 3.3). This was because the IMF officially called for high interest rates in an effort to discourage speculation and to induce international bankers to return to the Korean market. However, the IMF policy failed to calm the market; the panicked international bankers did not return. Rather, high interest rates had

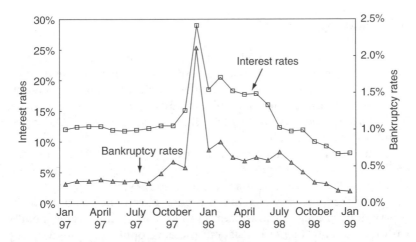

Figure 3.3 Interest rates and bankruptcy rates during the crisis
Note: Interest rates denote yields on the benchmark three-year corporate bonds; bankruptcy rates denote the dishonoured bill ratio.
Source: Bank of Korea, *Online Services of Statistics*, at the home page, http://www.bok.or.kr/.

serious negative consequences for the economy (see, for example, Hahm and Mishkin 2000: p. 101).[14] As borrowing costs blew out and cash flow worsened, the bankruptcy rate skyrocketed, especially among smaller *chaebol* and small and medium-sized companies.

Figure 3.3 clearly shows that interest rates and bankruptcy rates rose rapidly together. And now, a vicious cycle – a 'credit crunch' – began to work: as the corporate sector increasingly failed to meet repayments, they were able to obtain less and less credit, which, in turn, worsened the cash flow of the corporate sector. This downward spiral came to a halt only after the IMF acknowledged its failure and allowed Korea gradually to lower interest rates from February 1998. As seen in Figure 3.3, interest rates fell back to less than 13 per cent in the latter half of 1998 and bankruptcy rates slowly decreased at the same time.

Faced with an unprecedented financial and corporate crisis, the new government – led by Kim Dae-Jung – was forced to intervene strongly in financial and corporate restructuring, in spite of its undertaking to the IMF to introduce a free market economy into Korea. In order to correct the worst results of 'market failures', the IMF itself was forced to allow the Korean government to nationalize troubled commercial banks, inject huge public funding into financial institutions, and give them explicit government guarantees. Of course, it was thought that such state interventions were only temporary, and that the government would, for instance, privatize the banks in line with its market-oriented reforms.

3.5   Conclusion

In this chapter, we deepened our analysis of the East Asian crisis by investigating the case of Korea. Liberalist critics of 'inefficient Asian (Korean) capitalism' criticize 'government failures' such as cronyism/corruption, industrial policy and public financial guarantees for producing moral hazard problems, while attributing the crisis to them. Our investigation showed this to be wrong.

The developmental state in Korea between around 1960 and the end of the 1980s had institutions that effectively prevented moral hazard problems. The government's industrial policy and credit control functioned as mechanisms of corporate governance and financial supervision. Throughout this period the Korean economy grew rapidly without a serious financial crisis. But the developmental system, (i.e., a state-based model of corporate governance and finance) was dismantled in the 1990s. The Kim Young-Sam government was particularly eager to liberalize and globalize. The liberalist reform of institutions, however, created a kind of vacuum in the mechanism of corporate governance and financial supervision. The state-based model was abolished but neither a bank-based nor a capital market-based model was introduced in its place.

As industrial policy, which had strictly regulated industrial entry, was abolished in the early 1990s, many *chaebol* firms expanded and diversified. This resulted in a sudden rise in the number of companies and in production capacity in the major industries between 1993 and 1996. A massive flow of foreign capital into Korea financed this excessive investment. Financial deregulation allowed NBFIs and offshore branches of commercial banks to mediate between global capital and the *chaebol*. The problem was compounded by the *chaebol*'s direct access to international financial institutions, via their offshore subsidiaries. According to our own calculations, a total of more than US$120 billion of international capital was supplied to the *chaebol* sector through these three channels between 1993 and 1996.

The absence of regulation and supervision of borrowing nurtured the moral hazard of the too-big-to-fail mentality among financial institutions and *chaebol* firms. Furthermore, foreign borrowings, particularly short-term ones, made the Korean economy vulnerable to external shock.

Excessive investment resulted in a recession beginning in late 1996. Several small and middle-sized *chaebol* groups subsequently collapsed before the outbreak of the crisis proper. This by itself, although serious, constituted nothing more than an economic downturn; it was the panic caused by international banks that magnified the downturn into a full-blown financial catastrophe. Panicked by foreign exchange crises in Southeast Asia, international banks ran on Korean banks, NBFIs and *chaebol* groups and collected their short-term credits. In the five months from November 1997 to March 1998, in the midst of the Asian financial crash, US$60 billion of foreign capital withdrew from Korea, causing the abrupt collapse of Korea's financial and corporate system.

In summary, liberalization and globalization were linked to the boom and crash in the Korean economy in various ways. First, they allowed and fostered the excessive flow of global capital into Korea's corporate sector, which induced the *chaebol*'s risky investments. Second, they created a situation of *laissez-faire* in corporate governance and financial supervision, and hence created moral hazard problems. Third, they allowed global capital to be rapidly withdrawn, causing a financial crash.

4
The *Chaebol*'s Corporate Governance and the Crisis

The *chaebol* have dominated the Korean economy. In particular, the five largest *chaebol* groups – Hyundai, Samsung, Daewoo, LG and SK – have symbolized the successful industrialization of the country. However, successive collapses of many large *chaebol* groups in 1997–9 raise the question of why they failed so suddenly and on such a large scale? The answer, according to the 'finally collapsed' view, is that failure was due to a significant weakness in the *chaebol*'s governance mechanism. Shareholder value literature has especially criticized the *chaebol*'s ownership and control structure for the low protection of minority shareholders and low transparency (see, e.g., Black *et al.* 2000; Jang 2001). Shareholder value advocates argue that the main cause of the 1997 crisis was a corporate sector crisis arising from a 'distorted' and 'abnormal' ownership and control structure, and that strengthening shareholder rights and corporate transparency is essential in order to enhance the efficiency of the Korean corporate – and economic – system (Kim K.-W. 1999; Jang 2001).

In this chapter, we will examine the question of whether the ownership and control structure of the *chaebol* was the main cause of the crisis. Section 4.1 will first outline the predominant position of the *chaebol* in the Korean economy and show the magnitude of the corporate sector crisis that struck the *chaebol* system. In section 4.2, we will look at the ownership and control structure of the *chaebol* and then make use of international comparative studies to address the question of whether the ownership and control structure of the *chaebol* prior to 1997 was responsible for the crisis. In section 4.3, we will argue that 'corporate governance' includes not only the firm level but also the national level system, and that the failures of the *chaebol*'s corporate governance prior to the crisis may be explained by failures in Korea's national laws and regulations regarding corporate governance, rather than the *chaebol*'s intragroup ownership and control structure. Finally, section 4.4 will investigate the argument that product market pressure may act as a substitute for corporate governance mechanism. We will emphasize the need to take an evolutionary view of market competition among firms in order to understand how and why individual *chaebol* firms have succeeded or failed in the long run.

4.1 The *chaebol*'s predominance and the crisis

Etymologically, *chaebol* means 'big wealth', but the term is used to describe the large family-controlled conglomerates in Korea. Because of their importance, the Fair Trade Commission (FTC) of Korea specifically defines and monitors the 30 largest *chaebol*. According to FTC data, these accounted for 41–46 per cent of national corporate assets during 1992–7 (see Table 4.1). The dominance of the top five – Hyundai, Samsung, Daewoo, LG and SK – was even more striking; their assets were about twice as large as the sixth to thirtieth-ranked added together.

Moreover, the *chaebol* are usually concentrated in manufacturing industries. The 30 largest *chaebol* accounted for two-thirds of the domestic market for manufactured products. As shown in Table 4.2, the top five's market share was increasing in the 1990s, while the share of the rest

Table 4.1 The *chaebol*'s share in national corporate assets, 1992–97 (%)

	1992	1993	1994	1995	1996	1997
Top 1–5	24.91	24.04	23.39	25.42	26.98	29.22
Top 6–30	20.05	19.17	18.17	19.45	19.63	17.03
Top 1–30	44.96	43.21	41.56	44.86	46.61	46.25

Source: Fair Trade Commission, *The Designation of Big Business Groups*, yearly.

Table 4.2 The *chaebol*'s share in gross manufactured product, 1995–99 (%)

	1995	1996	1997	1998	1999
Top 5	34.8	35.7	41.6	39.8	45.0
Top 6–30	29.7	28.6	28.9	26.6	22.4
Top 1–30	64.5	64.3	70.5	66.4	67.4

Source: Fair Trade Commission, *The Designation of Big Business Groups*, yearly.

was decreasing. This tendency intensified through the crisis between 1997 and 1999, when collapses were more frequent among smaller *chaebol*.

This predominant position in the national economy means that the collapse of a *chaebol* group immediately causes distress in the economic system. A remarkable aspect of the financial crisis and aftershocks during 1997–9 was the widespread collapse and radical reorganization of the *chaebol*. All through the period, the *chaebol* groups were under a cloud of impending insolvencies. Many of them failed to improve cash flow and collapsed. As shown in Table 4.3, as early as 1997 there had already been eleven defaults and near-defaults among the 30 largest *chaebol*. In addition, seven other *chaebol* were facing severe financial and operational difficulties in the same year. In early 1998, when interests rates soared to over 20 per cent and the Korean financial market collapsed, the number of troubled *chaebol* amongst the largest 30 increased to 21. Daewoo (ranked third in 1998) hit significant financial troubles, and 20 of the sixth to thirtieth largest *chaebol* were either struggling with impending insolvencies or went into bankruptcy. In 1999, even though the worst was over, Daewoo finally defaulted. This was the biggest bankruptcy with a debt of US$60 billion. In the same year, Hyundai (the largest *chaebol*) faced cash-flow problems and 15 of the sixth to thirtieth largest *chaebol* were still either radically restructuring or in the process of dismantling.

Table 4.3 shows that during three years between 1997 and 1999 one-third of the 30 largest *chaebol* – including Daewoo (ranked second in 1999) and Kia (seventh in 1997) – were dismantled. Under creditor banks' restructuring programmes and court receivership, their subsidiaries were sold, liquidated or transformed into independent companies. In some cases, there remains merely one company with the former *chaebol* name.[1]

Another one-third of the 30 largest *chaebol* have drastically reduced their assets. For instance, Ssangyong (ranked seventh in 1999) reduced the number of its subsidiaries from 27 to six, mainly by selling to foreign companies, and partly by liquidation. By the end of 1999 only about one-third of the 30 largest *chaebol* – Samsung, LG and SK included – had survived without such radical downsizing.

In sum, the Korean *chaebol* underwent a far-reaching and drastic crisis, followed by a corporate restructuring including forcible divestitures and ownership transfer which was comparable to the dissolution of the Japanese *zaibatsu* after the Second World War.

Table 4.3 The chaebol's crisis and restructuring, 1996–99 (%)

Size[a]	1996			1997			1998			1999		
	Chaebol	D/E[b]	State[c]	Chaebol	D/E[b]	State[c]	Chaebol	D/E[b]	State[c]	Chaebol	D/E[b]	State[c]
1	Hyundai	376		Hyundai	437		Hyundai	579		Hyundai	483	T
2	Samsung	206		Samsung	267		Samsung	371		Daewoo	355	A,W,D
3	LG	313		LG	347		Daewoo	472	T	Samsung	252	
4	Daewoo	337		Daewoo	338		LG	506		LG	315	
5	SK	343		SK	384		SK	468		SK	240	
6	Ssangyong	298		Ssangyong	409	T	Hanjin	908	T	Hanjin	458	A,R
7	Hanjin	622		Kia	517	A,I,D	Ssangyong	400	I,W	Ssangyong	1,403	W,R
8	Kia	417	T	Hanjin	557		Hanwha	1,215	B,I	Hanwha	333	B,R
9	Hanwha	620		Hanwha	751	B,I	Kumho	944	T	Kumho	558	T
10	Lotte	176		Lotte	192		Donga	360	A,I,W	Lotte	118	
11	Kumho	464		Kumho	478	T	Lotte	217		Donga	899	W,D
12	Doosan	622	T	Halla	2,066	I,C	Halla	N		Hansol	346	R
13	Daelim	385		Donga	355	I,W	Daelim	514	T	Doosan	332	R
14	Hanbo	675	T	Hanbo	675	A,I,D	Doosan	590	T,R	Daelim	346	
15	Donga	322		Doosan	688	T,R	Hansol	400	T	Dongkuk	198	
16	Halla	2,855		Daelim	423	T	Hyosung	465	T,R	Dongbu	266	
17	Hyosung	315		Hansol	292		Kohab	472	C,W	Halla	N	C,W,D
18	Dongkuk	190		Hyosung	370	T	Kolon	434	T	Kohab	N	C,W,R
19	Jinro	2,441	T	Jinro	3,765	I,C	Dongkuk	324		Hyosung	281	R
20	Kolon	328		Dongkuk	219		Dongbu	338		Kolon	335	
21	Tongyang	279		Kolon	318		Anam	1,499	I,W	Tongyang	303	
22	Hansol	313		Kohab	591	I	Jinro	N	I,C,D	Jinro	N	D
23	Dongbu	328		Dongbu	262		Tongyang	404		Anam	8,354	C,W,R
24	Kohab	572	T	Haitai	659	I,C	Haitai	1,501	I,C,D	Haitai	N	D

Table 4.3 (Continued)

Size[a]	1996			1997			1998			1999		
	Chaebol	D/E[b]	State[c]	Chaebol	D/E[b]	State[c]	Chaebol	D/E[b]	State[c]	Chaebol	D/E[b]	State[c]
25	Haitai	506	T	Sammi	3,245	D	Shinho	677	C,W	Saehan	277	
26	Sammi	3,245	I,C	Tongyang	307		Daesang	648	T,R	Kangwon	442	W,R
27	Hanil	936	T	Anam	479	T	New Core	1,784	I,C,D	Daesang	268	R
28	Kukdong	471	I,C	New Core	1,226	I,C	Keopyong	438	I,W,R	Cheiljedang	133	
29	New Core	924	T	Hanil	577	I,C,D	Kangwon	375	I,W	Shinho	N	C,W,R
30	Byucksan	486	I,W,D	Keopyong	348	T	Saehan	419		Samyang	207	

[a] Size is according to the asset value.

[b] D/E refers to ratio of debt to equity capital; N means that equity capital is zero.

[c] A (accused): the *chaebol* group Chief Executive Officer is accused of illegalities in business

B (bailout): one or more companies have bailout loans

C (court receivership): one or more companies under court receivership

D (dismantled): only one company remains or there exists no company any more

I (insolvency): one or more companies are unable to service debts

R (reduced): number of companies radically reduced (e.g. from 20 to 3)

T (trouble): one or more companies having significant trouble with cash flow

W (workout): one or more companies are under bank control for restructuring excessive debts.

Source: Various reports of Fair Trade Commission and other reports.

4.2 Concentrated ownership and control of the *chaebol*

According to the 'finally collapsed' argument (see Chapters 2 and 3), Korea's specific national institutions are responsible for the financial and corporate collapse of 1997, and moral hazard is the common character of the institutions. In the same context, given that an effective governance system is able to check and control moral hazard problems (Jensen and Meckling 1976), it is argued that Korea's governance institutions at the firm, financial and national levels totally failed (Corsetti, Pesenti and Roubini 1998b; Yoo 1999). Critics focus on so-called 'distortions' of the corporate governance of the *chaebol* firms. For instance, Frankel (1998) maintains that the corporate governance of Korea tends towards empire building rather than profitability or maximization of the company's stock price.

In the previous chapters, we examined the national and financial level corporate control mechanisms of developmental state capitalism. This chapter will look at firm level governance (i.e., the ownership and control structure of the *chaebol*).

Concentrated intragroup ownership and control

According to the principal-agent view, the unique features of the *chaebol's* firm level governance can be summarized as follows (see Lee and Lim 1998):

1 *Chaebol* firms are owned, controlled and managed by a principal shareholder (called *chongsu* in Korean) and sometimes by other close family members. In contrast, ownership, control and management are typically separated in big business firms of industrialized countries.
2 Firms belonging to a *chaebol* form a single and tight network through extensive intersubsidiary shareholdings. Control rights of the owner-manager family over subsidiaries are ensured by the intersubsidiary shareholdings.
3 There exists a strong interest conflict or agency problem between the controlling *chaebol* family and outsider shareholders as the absolute power of the family creates incentive distortion.
4 In addition, the high concentration of ownership-control has led to an organizational structure in which the controlling family members make key decisions, and members of directorial board are almost entirely under their control.

According to Chandler (1990), the decline of family capitalism in the USA, Germany and Japan was due to the limitations of family ownership and the managerial incapability of family members. Therefore, family capitalism is viewed as unsuitable for large-scale corporations in capital-intensive industries. In this light, the rapid growth of the Korean *chaebol* in capital-intensive industries such as cars, shipbuilding, semi-conductors and so on raised the question of how they could overcome these limitations.

The *chaebol* have overcome the limitation of family ownership through intersubsidiary shareholding (Park 1999). The *chaebol* have a highly concentrated structure of ownership and control, which ensures that the controlling family has exclusive power over subsidiaries.

Table 4.4 shows the intragroup shareholding of the *chaebol* as a measurement of the ownership concentration. In 1997 the share of stocks controlled by the *chaebol* families, which is equal to the intragroup shareholding (the sum of family shareholding plus intersubsidiary shareholding), amounted to 43 per cent of the total stock for the top 30 *chaebol*. The intersubsidiary shareholdings represented 34.5 per cent, while the *chaebol* families' direct holding amounted to only 8.5 per cent. This means that an average *chaebol* family controls the majority of total shares by owning only small shares, leveraged by intersubsidiary share-holding. The table also shows that ownership is more concentrated for the five largest *chaebol* because more intersubsidiary shareholdings are put in place in order to ensure majority control in spite of increased total shares outstanding. For instance, the dominant shareholder family of the Samsung Group, one of the largest *chaebol* in Korea, controls more than 46 per cent of the total outstanding shares of the group companies, even though the family owns only around 4 per cent.

The intragroup shareholding rose from 43 to 50.5 per cent during the crisis period between 1997 and 1999, when intersubsidiary shareholding

Table 4.4   Intragroup ownership of the top *chaebol*, 1983–97 (%)

	1983	1987	1989	1991	1993	1995	1997
Top 30 *chaebol*	57.2	56.2	46.2	46.9	43.4	43.3	43.0
Family	17.2	15.8	14.7	13.9	10.3	10.5	8.5
Subsidiaries	40.0	40.4	31.5	33	33.1	32.8	34.5
Top 5 *chaebol*	n.a.	60.3	49.4	51.6	49.0	n.a.	45.2
Family	n.a.	15.6	13.7	13.2	11.8	n.a.	8.6
Subsidiaries	n.a.	44.7	35.7	38.4	37.2	n.a.	36.6

n.a. = not available
Source: Fair Trade Commission, *The Designation of Big Business Groups*, yearly.

soared from 34.5 to 45.1 per cent. At the same time the *chaebol* families' shareholdings decreased from 8.5 to 5.4 per cent. The sudden rise of intragroup and of intersubsidiary shareholdings was a reaction by the controlling families against the danger of hostile mergers and acquisitions which became a possibility because of the IMF-led reform of corporate governance. This clearly shows the vital importance of the intersubsidiary holdings as a means of protecting family control.

The steady decline in family shareholding prior to 1997 can be explained by the increase in total shares outstanding for large corporations on the capital market and hence by the increasing dependence on equity financing for their large-scale investments, in spite of excessive reliance on debt financing (Park 1999: pp. 99, 132).

This high degree of ownership concentration shows a similarity to that of the pre-war Japanese *zaibatsu* which had a closed ownership structure. The concentration ratios of the top ten *zaibatsu* were on average 51.6 per cent in 1946 (Morikawa 1992).

If we regard a *chaebol* group as a single corporation, the degree of family control does not appear remarkable. But if individual subsidiaries are treated as legally independent units, it can be argued that the rights of outsider shareholders are infringed. Therefore, advocates of shareholder value vehemently criticize the ownership-control structure of the *chaebol* families because they control subsidiaries surreptitiously through inter-subsidiary shareholding (Kang C.-K., Choe and Chang 1991; People's Solidarity for Participatory Democracy 1999; Jang 2001).

Pyramid shareholding and its evolution

There are various types of intersubsidiary shareholdings: (a) cross-shareholding, where two firms hold each other's stocks; (b) circular shareholding, where a firm owns the stocks of the next firm in a chain and the last firm in the chain owns stocks of the first firm; (c) pyramid (radiant) shareholding, where a firm in a higher position of hierarchy holds stocks of firms in a lower position.

While horizontal cross-shareholding prevails in the post-war Japanese *keiretsu* that are formed as a federation of independent firms, the hierarchical pyramid shareholding is mainly used in the *chaebol* (as they were in the pre-war Japanese *zaibatsu*). Korea's corporate laws have not limited pyramid shareholding but cross-shareholding has been forbidden.

The strata in the pyramid ownership-control structure of the *chaebol* may be summarized as follows. First, *chaebol* family members directly own stocks of level A subsidiaries. Second, these companies own stocks of B level subsidiaries in the second stratum. The A level companies can be called quasi-holding companies because they run their own business, in contrast to pure holding companies. Third, B level companies own stocks of companies in level C. In the same way, the hierarchy can be extended further. Through the hierarchical structure, the *chaebol* families can control every subsidiary just by owning stocks of the quasi-holding companies.

Hattori (1989) classified the ownership structure of individual *chaebol* groups into three types, but Park (1999) regards the various types as the result of different evolutionary phases. According to him, four phases can be identified which correspond to four types (see Figure 4.1). In the first phase, only one stratum exists and the owner-manager directly owns the stocks of his companies. In the second phase, as the *chaebol* develops, a core company appears as it owns stocks of new subsidiaries that form the second stratum. The core company is usually the founding company or the largest company of the *chaebol*.

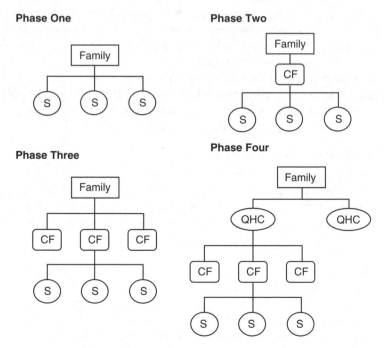

Figure 4.1   Evolution of ownership structure of the *chaebol*
S = subsidiary
CF = core firm
QHC = quasi-holding company
Source: Park (1999: p. 115).

In the third phase, which is usually associated with the Big Push in the 1970s, the number of core subsidiaries increases as more subsidiaries accomplish good business in key manufacturing industries and sectors. Financial subsidiaries with large assets could also be excellent candidates for the position of core firm because the *chaebol* groups could internalize the financial assets to invest in subsidiaries, as seen in Chapter 3. At the same time, as core business prospers, the subsidiaries make efforts to diversify business lines, which increases the number of subsidiaries further. The fourth phase adds further strata as one or two of the core firms take on the role of quasi-holding company by holding stocks of other core firms. In 1997, the largest three *chaebol* (Hyundai, Samsung and Daewoo) were in the fourth phase, while the fourth and fifth *chaebol* (LG and SK) and some smaller *chaebol* stayed in the third phase. Other *chaebol* were in the second or first phase (Park 1999).

4.3   Aspects of corporate governance

Firm-level governance, moral hazard and the crisis

Since Berle and Means's classic work, *The Modern Corporation and Private Property* (1932), the model of the large listed corporation in which ownership of capital is dispersed among numerous small shareholders, while control is concentrated in the hands of professional management, has been taken for granted in the industrialized countries. On the assumption that ownership and control are separate, 'managerialist' literature – such as Penrose (1959) and Galbraith (1967) – on the role of professional managers in such corporations has been written. More recently, shareholder value literature – Jensen and Meckling (1976), among others – has developed on the same assumption.

In the belief that Berle and Means' model of the modern corporation is a universal practice in the industrialized countries, much Korean literature criticizes the firm-level governance structure of the *chaebol* as 'pre-modern' and 'abnormal'. At the same time, it is argued that such a governance structure prevents Korea's large corporations from evolving into 'modern' and 'normal' ones (see, for instance, Kang C.-K., Choe and Chang 1991; Choe J.-P. 1999; Kim K.-W. 1999). Because they believe also that the 1997 crisis was an inevitable outcome of managerial misbehaviours (moral hazard) specific to the pre-modern and abnormal *chaebol* system, they share the 'finally collapsed' view that the crisis was primarily homegrown.

However, if we accept the idea that the *chaebol* system arose in the 'modernization' process of Korea, the definition of the *chaebol* as a 'pre-modern' business organization seems strange. Furthermore, as Park (1999) points out, why should the 'normality' of firm organization be defined with reference to the institutional norms prevailing in Anglo-American countries? Indeed, there are many industrialized countries whose institutional features do not conform to the Anglo-American norm, as many studies of the Japanese and German economy in the 1970–90s have shown (see, for instance, Jürgens, Malsch and Dohse 1989; Aoki and Patrick 1994; Lazonick and O'Sullivan 1997a, 1997b; Dietl 1998). Chandler (1990) and Chandler, Amatori and Hikino (1997) show that international differences in firm organization have been an essential feature in the development of capitalism during the last century.

In recent years, in addition, several studies have also questioned the empirical validity of the concept of large modern corporations presented by Berle and Means. Even in the United States, where this idea originated and developed, ownership is not completely dispersed, and majority shareholdings by families and wealthy investors are more common than is often believed (Demsetz 1983; Shleifer and Vishny 1986, 1997; Holderness and Sheehan 1988; Holderness, Kroszner and Sheehan 1999).

Moreover, heavily concentrated shareholdings and the predominance of controlling ownership seem to be the rule in the rest of the world (La Porta, Lopez-De-Silanes and Shleifer 1999). Studies of other advanced countries reveal significant ownership concentration in Germany (Edwards and Fischer 1994), Japan (Berglof and Perotti 1994), and other OECD countries (European Corporate Governance Network 1997).

La Porta, Lopez-De-Silanes and Shleifer (1999) discovered, by using data on ownership structures of large corporations in 27 wealthy economies to identify the controlling shareholders of these firms, that relatively few of these firms are widely owned. Rather, families or the state typically control these firms and the controlling shareholders often have power over firms significantly in excess of their cash-flow rights, primarily through the use of pyramids. La Porta, Lopez-De-Silanes and Shleifer also conclude that these families usually participate in the management of the firms they control. Therefore, the *chaebol*'s ownership-control structure is not a deviation from the typical case in the world, even if it differs from Berle and Means' model. This observation is further confirmed by studies of carmakers around the world (see, e.g., Jürgens *et al.* 2002). Hence the view that the crisis of 1997 in Korea resulted from 'abnormal' and 'distorted' governance does not seem valid since most of the countries with similarly concentrated ownership-control and family management did not experience such a disastrous financial crisis.[2]

Corporate financing and corporate governance

According to Shleifer and Vishny (1997), corporate governance has to do with the ways in which outside suppliers of finance to corporations ensure a return on their investment. This view rests on the assumptions that (a) the corporate sector needs external funds for investment, (b) the financial system channels such funds to the corporate sector from the household sector, and (c) in this system the interests of external providers of funds should be safeguarded through control rights giving them scope for intervention in management (Hellwig 2000).

These assumptions are not uncontroversial. First, the dependence of companies on external funds varies among countries and periods and, in some cases, little external finance is provided. Mayer's survey (1988), of the flow of funds from stock and other securities market and banking systems to the non-financial corporate sector in five countries over the period 1970 to 1985, showed that firms in the USA and the UK financed nearly all investment funds internally from retained earnings. In contrast, firms in France, Germany and Japan financed one-third of investment externally in the period.[3]

In particular, contrary to the neoclassical conception of the financial system, the stock market in the UK and USA made a negative contribution to the financing of equity capital formation in the period 1970–85, due to buying back shares in the process of cash financed acquisition. In Germany, France and Japan, in contrast, despite relatively underdeveloped stock markets and relatively ill-protected property rights, new equity made a larger contribution to domestic investment than in the USA or UK.[4]

This shows that the assumptions mentioned above in relation to corporate governance and corporate financing do not reflect the reality. The mechanism of the market for corporate control worked in the USA in the 1980s, for instance, even though the New York stock market provided little new equity capital for major corporations. So corporate governance and corporate financing are separable in reality, in contrast to the shareholder value theory of Shleifer and Vishny.[5] Corporate financing has to do with capital flow and corporate governance is related to capital stock.

Therefore, because majority shareholders of large corporations around the world are typically families, there are many cases in which external providers of funds to family-controlled firms are not safeguarded by control rights. There are typically conflicts – agency problems – between insider families and outside providers of investment funds around control rights. This shows that corporate governance involves more than firm level governance. Firm level governance is inseparably integrated with financial and national institutions because these are the organizers and providers of external financing.[6]

Thus, the finding of La Porta, Lopez-De-Silanes and Shleifer (1999) about the ultimate ownership of large corporations around the world has a limited significance for our understanding of the corporate governance mechanism of a country, as it refers only to firm level governance. Likewise, the criticisms of family ownership-control in the Korean *chaebol* are not satisfactory since they do not consider *national level* governance.

The primary function of corporate governance is to discipline the management (or corporate insider in general). Within the *chaebol*'s firm level organization, then, there is no governance mechanism. During the 1960s–80s, however, it was the government that disciplined the *chaebol* owner-managers by means of its industrial policy and credit control.

State-based model of corporate governance

In the international discussion over the corporate governance, two archetypes are usually referred to: the capital market-based model found in the USA and UK, and the bank-based model of Japan and Germany.

It has been argued that in the United States 'the market for corporate control' via mergers and acquisitions, based on the highest priority of shareholder rights, works as an effective corporate governance mechanism (Jensen and Ruback 1983; Jensen 1988). In Japan, which has not had a well-developed capital market, the main bank system played an important role in corporate control as a main bank monitors, both as creditor and equity holder (Aoki and Patrick 1994). In the German supervisory board system, the diverse interests of stakeholders, including *Hausbanks* and employees, are represented, and the supervisory board directors are powerful outsiders who are fully responsible for controlling and disciplining the management (Pfeiffer 1993; Schmidt and Drukarczyk 1997; Brendel 2001).[7]

In Korea, however, American-style mergers and acquisitions in the capital market were impossible because the relevant commercial codes and securities acts prohibited it.[8] Furthermore, the Japanese style main bank system did not exist, as Korean banks were not allowed to own shares of corporations worth more than 10 per cent of bank's equity. In addition, banks had no role in controlling the management of borrower companies since this was the task of the government in the developmental system.

Even following the financial reforms in the 1990s, Korean banks were not allowed any controlling role because the reform followed the model of the American banking system.[9] While Japan's main banking system has been in the *keiretsu* tradition, where a main bank is the holding company for the group's companies, Korea's institutional frameworks require separation of commercial banks and industrial enterprises, as in the Anglo-American banking system (Cho and Kim 1997; Koo 1998). Therefore, a German style of bank intervention in corporate governance has been impossible, too.

In Korea, however, instead of capital market control and bank-based control, the government played the key role in corporate governance as it organized external fund-raising for the *chaebol*. The case of Korea during the 1960s–1980s is similar to that of France in that the government provided external funds to family-controlled firms through commercial banks. Nominally, the *chaebol* families were the owner-controllers of their firms but, in reality, the developmental state governed them. Therefore, in view of the crucial role of the state in corporate governance and financing in a developmental system, a third archetype of corporate governance can be suggested: a state-based model.

In the agency approach to corporate governance, the principals of publicly-owned companies are presumed to be shareholders, based on the property rights theories of Coase (1960), Demsetz (1967) and Alchian and Demsetz (1972). Following the liberal dogma that 'the individual is the best judge of his own welfare', the shareholder value theory claims that there is no room for state intervention in the private corporate sector.

However, governments in late industrializing countries have participated widely in corporate control in direct and indirect ways. In the case of post-war Japan and France, the governments exerted a powerful influence on the financial and corporate sectors. In the strong and centralized banking and credit system designed for post-war recovery, Japanese banks, although nominally owned by the private sector, were subject to careful and tight regulation by the Ministry of Finance (MOF) and the Bank of Japan until the late 1970s (Walter 2000). In principle, government regulators had access to the details of loans to every industrial company, as well as to the daily cash flows and the problem credits of all the banks. Using the *keiretsu* relationship between banks and industrial companies, the government could intervene in the corporate governance of industrial firms in indirect ways.

In the French financial and industrial system also, the government was the dominating power for more than 30 years until the 1970s

(Walter 2000). The system was highly *dirigiste* to ensure that investment funds were directed to projects given priority in the 'indicative planning' of the industrial policy. Until 1985, the French government effectively controlled bank lending to industrial companies through the so-called *barème* system, whereby the state-owned largest commercial banks shared out corporate business according to fixed percentages. In the French system, as in the developmental system of Korea, the commercial banking system was viewed more as an instrument of industrial policy than as an independent sector with profitability targets and market principles. Furthermore, France has traditionally had the highest level of corporate shareholding by banks in Europe. These industrial holdings could be viewed as indirect state ownership of industrial firms. Therefore, in the French model, until the mid-1980s, the role of corporate governance of industrial firms fell much more upon the state than on banks. State domination was significantly eroded when the *barème* system was abandoned in 1985 and Jacques Chirac undertook the privatization of the largest state banks in the late 1980s. Nevertheless, the influence of the state in the financial and corporate sector remained much greater than in either the Anglo-American or the German model.

The relationship between the government and business in the developmental system of Korea until the 1980s was similar to that in France. As seen in Chapter 3 the government, as an insurer and financier providing policy loans through state-controlled commercial banks, monitored and controlled the performance of the *chaebol* through its industrial policy, trade policy and various financial control policies. The most important aspect of the government's role in corporate governance was the *ex ante* investment coordination involving restrictions on entry and capacity expansion and *ex post* restructuring of overinvestment (including government mediation) and sometimes the imposition of takeovers, mergers, forced exits and business swaps. Another important aspect of government policy affecting the governance of the *chaebol* was export promotion policy. Export targets fostered competition among the owner-managers for policy loans and other subsidies.

Abolition of the state-based model and *laissez-faire* in corporate governance

However, as liberalization and deregulation started, the government's controlling power disappeared rapidly. As mentioned in Chapter 3, industry policy and credit control were abandoned during 1993–7. The government gave up its role in corporate and financial governance without introducing alternative national and financial institutions for corporate control. Because bank reform in the period followed the Anglo-American model, commercial banks continued to play a passive role even in the 1990s. NBFIs, which now became the most important providers of external funds for the *chaebol*, were mainly under the *chaebol*'s direct control. Consequently, liberalization and deregulation created a *laissez-faire* environment for the *chaebol*.

The absence of a functioning national system of corporate governance characterizes the period preceding the 1997 crisis. Liberalization had abolished the state-based model in Korea. Nonetheless, it introduced neither a capital market-based model nor a bank-based model as an alternative.[10] In this vacuum, the *chaebol* enjoyed full freedom of business. Lax liberalization and imprudent deregulation in the period created an institutional failure. This resulted in overinvestment by the *chaebol*, based upon excessive capital and credit supply by domestic and foreign financial markets.

4.4   Corporate governance and product market pressure

Corporate governance and economic governance

In traditional neoclassical economics – and also in Marxist analysis of the capitalist market economy – product market competition is enough to solve efficiency problems in a market economy. As seen in Chapter 1, neoclassical economists argued that Korea and other East Asian NICs grew fast by introducing an export promotion policy (Krueger 1980, 1990; Balassa 1981, 1991). This policy forced private firms to be exposed to fierce competition in the world market, which disciplined their misbehaviour. 'Product market pressure' is the ultimate solution for problems in the economic governance of a capitalist market economy.

In this regard, it has been argued that product market competition may act as a substitute for the corporate governance mechanism or, at least, that in competitive markets corporate governance loses importance in terms of enhancing economic efficiency (see, for instance, Alchian 1950).

Agency theory is sceptical about whether product market pressure alone can solve the problem of corporate governance in big business corporations, and it argues that agency problems, which are caused by managerial opportunism and expropriation, require something more than product market competition (Shleifer and Vishny 1997).[11] As we have seen, DS literature also, in its critique of the neoclassical explanation of East Asian success, emphasizes the governance problems (rent-seeking activities) in late industrializing countries and appreciates the government's role in corporate disciplining (Amsden 1989; Wade 1990).

Nonetheless, Allen and Gale (2000) question the agency approach, particularly in its treatment of moral hazard and managerial misbehaviour (see also Vives 2000a). They favour an 'evolutionary approach' according to which product market competition will eliminate inefficient firms: if managers waste resources, the firm will not be able to survive in the long run. According to this view, competitive market pressure is particularly important for efficiency when corporate governance is weak. Even if there exists a weak governance system or none at all, product market competition would force firms to become fit in order to survive (see also Vitols 2000).

This view surely ignores the reality that in an imperfect market economy there is an oligopoly of big business firms and hence, when individual big business firms fail, the national economy cannot allow them to go bankrupt and be liquidated. Because the social and economic costs of the liquidation of large corporations are too high, the logic of 'too-big-to-fail' is not an empty idea but a reality. Therefore, in order to avoid the moral hazard problem of 'too-big-to-fail' logic among controlling shareholders or management of big business firms, and effectively to organize *ex ante* and *ex post* replacement of the insiders, it is necessary for big corporations to have good governance at firm and economic levels.

Market competition among firms and business dynamics

At the same time, however, the view that product market pressure is particularly important when corporate governance is weak, as in the Korean economy in the 1990s, has significance if we want to explain how and why individual *chaebol* firms have succeeded or failed *in the long run*.

According to Allen and Gale (2000), product market competition among companies has two functions; it disciplines managements and at the same time reveals which managements are the strongest. 'The company with strongest management will develop the best products, produce the highest earnings and growth and drive companies with weaker management out of business or, at least, leave them with a much smaller share of the market' (p. 65). Thus, the fundamental question for individual firms is how they achieve and sustain competitive advantages.

Up to this point, we have examined the institutional problems of the Korean economy; but this is not enough to explain Korea's industrial dynamics in the 1990s. For instance, if we are to understand why and how in the Korean automotive industry one *chaebol* carmaker survived and the others collapsed in the 1990s, we need to look at the strategies and capabilities of *chaebol* groups for product market competition.

4.5 Conclusion

The intragroup governance structure of the *chaebol* is characterized by highly concentrated ownership and control. This causes agency problems for outsider shareholders. The shareholder value theory criticizes the agency problems for causing moral hazard – misbehaviour among controlling *chaebol* families – and attributes the 1997 crisis to the problem.

Opposing this argument, we insisted that the 1997 crisis was not caused by agency problems. Shareholder value theory's critique depends on supposed Anglo-American 'norms', in which ownership is dispersed among numerous shareholders, yet control is concentrated in the hands of professional management. But international comparative studies show that highly concentrated ownership and control and controlling families' participation in management are common in many industrialized economies; low protection of shareholder value is not a special feature of Korean capitalism. More importantly, 'abnormal' corporate governance did not lead to a serious financial crisis in those other economies.

We also criticized shareholder value theory's concentration on the *chaebol*'s firm-level governance (i.e., intragroup ownership and control). We stressed that the weakness of the *chaebol*'s corporate governance prior to the crisis was at the national system level: Korea's state-based model of corporate governance was abolished, but no alternative corporate governance mechanism was set in its place. This national institutional vacuum was the primary problem. The fact that many *chaebol* groups recovered from the crisis even though they strengthened the intragroup ownership and control suggests that intragroup governance problems were not the major cause of the crisis.

We also discussed the argument which states that, even when corporate governance is weak, as it was in Korea in the 1990s, (product) market pressure can operate as an effective governance mechanism. According to traditional neoclassical as well as Marxist analyses of the capitalist market economy, market competition resolves questions of corporate efficiency. Hence, it is necessary to study market competition among firms in order to explain the real causes of *chaebol* firms' failures. This is the task of the next chapters.

5
Korea's Automotive Industry: The 1960s–90s

In this chapter, we will take the Korean automotive industry as a case study of the growth and crisis of the *chaebol* and the Korean economy.

Developmental state literature emphasizes that in developing countries government policy is important in shaping the development of industries. In Korea, industry policy was the main institution that determined the relationship between the government and *chaebol* carmakers up to the late 1980s. Section 5.1 will examine that industry policy closely in order to identify the government's promotional role in the development of the Korean automobile industry. However, we will also stress that not all manufacturers conformed to government requirements. In section 5.2, we will see the effects on this sector of the abolition of industry policy, which occurred within the general context of liberalization and globalization in the 1990s. The entry of Samsung and Ssangyong, and capacity expansion by the three existing carmakers, will be briefly analysed.

Section 5.3 will focus on the industry's expansion and then crisis in the 1990s. We will see that the vigorous capacity expansion from 1991 to 1997, associated with industrial deregulation, led to falling capacity utilization rates from late 1996 which, in turn, resulted in an industry-wide recession. In addition, we will compare the Korean car industry's profitability in the 1980s and 1990s in order to test the validity of the 'finally collapsed' argument which asserts that the chronic low profitability of Korea's industries was a primary cause of the 1997 crisis.

5.1 The developmental state and the automotive industry: the 1960s–1980s

Beginnings of foreign model assembly in the 1960s

The government's industry policy drove development of Korea's automobile industry from the earliest days. The automotive industry in Korea dates from 1962, when Park Chung-Hee's military government, established in 1961, enacted the Law for the Protection of the Automobile Industry. This law was modelled on Japan's 1936 Automobile Industry Act and was part of the first Five-Year Economic Development Plan for 1962–66. The law provided the Ministry of Commerce and Industry with legal grounds for directing, or at least significantly influencing, industrial structure by controlling exit and entry on the basis of a licensing system (Kim H.-J. 2001). The import of finished cars was completely prohibited, and a favourable tariff was applied to imported components and machinery for assembly.

As a result of this promotion policy, the Saenara Auto Company established the first modern assembly plant with technical assistance from Nissan of Japan. It was a small plant with a capacity for assembling 6,000 passenger cars a year from imported semi-knocked down kits. However, a big corruption scandal involving the company's owner and high-level politicians soon stopped production. The scandal prompted the military government to put a curb on corrupt links between businessmen and the politicians.

In 1966, the Shinjin Motor Vehicle Industrial Company, Saenara's successor, started assembling the Corona, a Toyota car model, under a licensing arrangement. The modern automobile industry in Korea started with assembling cars from imported SKD (semi-knocked down) parts.

Government's push towards content localization

At first, the car industry was not among the top priorities in government planning for industrialization, so that an import substitution policy could not be strongly pursued. However, from the end of the 1960s, the Korean government started serious planning for the industry. From 1968, the government began strongly to urge the car industry to turn to import-substitution by introducing an obligatory level of component localization.

The three licensed knocked down (KD) assemblers, Shinjin, Hyundai and Asia, did not have any incentive to make efforts to increase local content rates (Oh and Cho 1997; Kim H.-J. 2001). Since assembling imported KD components was exempted from tariffs, and selling automobiles at a high monopoly price (nearly double their price in the original countries) was an extremely lucrative business, the companies were competing only on the assembly of imported cars under KD licence.[1] As a result, in 1970, the number of car models in the Korean car market exceeded 20, while total domestic production of cars amounted to merely 30,000 units. This made the standardization and mass production of local parts literally impossible.

This structural problem could not be removed within a framework of free market competition among carmakers. Having recognized the 'market failure' in industrial promotion, the Korean government intervened in a dramatic manner (Kim H.-J. 2001). It announced the 'Plan for the Comprehensive Promotion of the Auto-Industry' in 1969 to urge firms to quit assembling and push them towards full-blown import substitution. According to this plan, each of the three automakers had gradually to raise local content until localization was complete. To this end they were required to concentrate on a single car model and establish mass production. If an automaker failed to achieve the compulsory level of localization, the business licence could be withdrawn as punishment. In order to ensure a minimum economy of scale in the industry, the government limited the number of automakers.

In spite of these policies, however, the share of locally produced parts in total value added was still less than 50 per cent by the end of 1971. Furthermore, the number of automakers also increased. In 1967 the Hyundai Motor Company was established and began to assemble the Cortina, a British Ford subcompact model, and in 1970 the Asia Motor Company began to assemble the Fiat 124 model. In the same year, the Kia Industrial Company (established as a bicycle manufacturer in the 1940s) started assembling small trucks under licence from Toyogogio (later Mazda). The government allowed Kia to start passenger car production in 1971 since it acknowledged the company's effort to localize engine manufacturing (Oh and Cho 1997). By the end of 1971, there were five automakers: Shinjin, Hyundai, Kia, Asia and Hadonghwan (later Ssangyong), all of which were engaged in assembling cars from imported CKD (completely knocked-down) parts. The government policy did not succeed in its goal of taking the industry to a higher level.

Big Push towards national car development in the 1970s

In the early 1970s, the Korean economy was facing difficulties arising from the collapse of the Bretton Woods System and a worsening current account deficit. Under these circumstances, the Korean government was determined to move to import substitution and export of products in the heavy industries, such as heavy machinery, electronics, transport equipment, petrochemicals and steel. As a result, the 'Plan for Heavy and Chemical Industrialization' (the so-called 'Big Push' policy) was put forward in 1973. It was this policy which laid the foundations of Korea's present industrial structure. With the proclamation of a state of national emergency, creating a dictatorship under President Park Chung-Hee, the government directed almost all public and private resources toward heavy, chemical and military industrialization.

The government selected automobile manufacturing as a strategic industry with the aim of developing it as an export industry. A promotional policy guideline was formulated in early 1973. It was announced as the 'Long-term Plan for the Promotion of the Automobile Industry'. Indeed, the Long-term Plan was an epoch-making initiative in the history of developing countries' automobile industry (Jenkins 1984), and was a quantum leap for Korea's automobile industry.

The government pressed the automakers to develop indigenous car models because otherwise export was impossible, since foreign-licensing automakers would not agree to the re-export of their models. And without exports, further increases in localization would be difficult, as the small domestic market did not offer the minimum economies of scale. Hence, the development of an indigenous car model was of the utmost importance for the industry's upgrading. At the same time, greater emphasis was placed on scale economies to enable standardization of components, cut costs, improve quality and increase exportability.

According to the Plan, three major automakers selected by the government – GM-Korea, Hyundai and Kia – were to produce a 'People's Car' following the model of the German Volkswagen in the 1930s. The car was required to be small and low-priced enough for average Koreans to purchase. In addition, in view of the export ban imposed by the foreign carmakers based on intellectual property rights, the car was required to have a national proprietary design for the purpose of free export. The plan anticipated an export figure of 75,000 cars by the end of 1981. The localization of parts and components had to increase to 100 per cent by 1981. The government promised its full support to successful companies.

Hyundai Motor Company (HMC) was the most enthusiastic follower of the government policy. It ended its licence arrangement with Ford in 1972 and made strong efforts to develop its own car model, with technical assistance from ItalDesign, an Italian car design company, and Mitsubishi of Japan. It succeeded in launching Korea's first indigenous car model, the subcompact Pony in October 1975. The Pony was exported to the Middle East and Latin America, and Hyundai immediately took 57 per cent of the domestic passenger car market. The local content ratio of the Pony amounted to 85 per cent in 1976 and increased steadily. Exports increased to about 20,000 units in 1979.

It was during the 1970s that the Korean government promoted specialization between automakers and component suppliers. The government gradually raised the obligatory rate of content localization and 85 per cent on average was achieved during the 1970s.

However, there was wide variation among automakers. Hyundai achieved nearly complete localization with its own model but other automakers were less ambitious, and continued licensing foreign designs for the domestic market. Kia produced the Brisa, a Mazda model, and also assembled imported KD kits for the Peugeot 604 and the Fiat 132. With the Brisa, Kia immediately captured 55 per cent of the Korean car market in 1975, but its design was not original and hence it could not be exported. This disappointed the government. Nonetheless, Kia maintained the strategy of licensing car design until the late 1980s.

GM-Korea made even less effort to be innovative. While Hyundai and Kia shifted to full localization, GM-Korea maintained KD production. GM-Korea (the forerunner of the Daewoo Motor Company) was established in 1972 as a 50:50 joint venture between Shinjin and General Motors, and produced Korean variants of subcompact car models originally developed by Adam Opel, a GM subsidiary in Germany. It did not try to reach the localization target. The government could not intervene because GM-Korea was a subsidiary of the world's biggest transnational company and so was outside the government's industry policy.

As for the Asia Motor Company, however, the government withdrew its business licence as it failed to meet the localization requirement. The government stopped providing policy loans to the company and forced it to merge with Kia in 1975.

In the latter half of the 1970s, Hyundai became the domestic market leader with the Pony because the design of the car was the most suited to the demands of Korean drivers. In contrast, GM-Korea's models were extremely unpopular in Korea because they ignored those demands. GM-Korea suffered losses and eventually fell into court receivership in 1976. In 1978, the Daewoo Group acquired its local share.

Further restructuring: 1980–1

The Korean government exerted decisive influence over the entry of *chaebol* groups into the automobile industry, and also over the scale of operations. The market structure was the outcome of such government decisions.

However, the relationship between the government and business was not unilateral. We have already seen that Kia and GM-Korea resisted the government's Big Push in both passive and active ways. In the framework of state-led capitalism, there existed interaction between bureaucrats and businessmen. Samuels (1987), in his study of the Japanese business–state relationship, called this 'reciprocal consent': firms gave the state jurisdiction over the market and, in return, their own domination of the market was guaranteed. The restructuring to the Korean auto industry in 1980–1 demonstrated both the government's controlling power over the automakers and the process of reciprocal consent building.

Guided by the 1973 Long-term Plan, the Korean auto industry entered the take-off phase in the latter half of the 1970s. Annual car production volumes increased rapidly from 37,000 to 204,000 between 1975 and 1979. The industry's capacity utilization rate averaged 76 per cent in 1979, despite GM-Korea's extremely low rate. But at the end of 1979, the economic situation abruptly changed. The Second Oil Shock hit the economy. In 1980, domestic car sales fell sharply and the capacity utilization rate fell below 40 per cent. In a time of political uncertainty (President Park was assassinated in October 1979) and economic recession, the new military government – established in May 1980 through a military coup – took the initiative to rationalize the industry.

To solve the overcapacity problem, the government tried to consolidate the existing four automakers into two companies. Hyundai and GM-Daewoo were to be merged into a single passenger car manufacturer, and Kia and Donga (Hadonghwan's successor) transformed into a single commercial vehicle manufacturer. But both Hyundai and GM wanted controlling power in the consolidated firm and could not reach an agreement. Kia and Donga also strongly resisted the merger plan.

Faced with these difficulties, the government abandoned the original merger plans. The final outcome of negotiations was that both Hyundai and GM-Daewoo were permitted to remain in passenger car production while Kia was required to withdraw from the sector. In return, the government forced Hyundai and GM-Daewoo to vacate the light commercial vehicle sector, and allowed Kia a monopolistic position there. This specialization policy was to have legal force until the end of 1986 when competition was reintroduced to both sectors.

Hyundai's success with Pony II and Pony Excel

In 1982, the Korean economy emerged from recession. In 1983, total vehicle production reached 220,000 units, a record-breaking number. Hyundai's successful export of the Pony II to the Canadian market in 1983 was the second turning point in Korea's car industry.

Based on the success of the Pony and Pony II, Hyundai launched the more ambitious Pony Excel Project. The model was designed for the US market and a new plant was built with an annual production capacity of 300,000 cars. Hyundai's entry into the US market with the Excel in 1986 was again a great success. As a result, the company's annual car production capacity expanded from 70,000 units in 1981 to 700,000 units by the end of 1987. The success of Hyundai Motors was regarded as a result of the government's policy of forcing the car industry away from import substitution and into exports.

Shift of industrial policy in the mid-1980s and increases in car exports

In the first half of the 1980s there was a dramatic improvement in the auto industry's performance, and therefore, as envisaged in the restructuring measures of 1980, the government relaxed its specialization requirements. In 1987, it allowed Kia to re-enter the passenger car sector, and Hyundai and GM-Daewoo to re-enter light commercial vehicle production. Nonetheless, the government continued to prohibit new entry into the automobile industry. Ssangyong could enter the industry (commercial vehicle) in 1986 only by acquiring Donga, an existing automaker.

With the relaxation of restrictions, the three main automakers began to compete intensely by investing in car model development and capacity expansion. As a result, Korea's vehicle production grew by 11 per cent each year on average between 1987 and 1991, despite serious labour disputes during the period.[2] In 1991, it reached 1.5 million units. Passenger cars and jeeps accounted for three-quarters of this total production. In 1993, it exceeded 2 million units and Korea became the sixth largest car production site in the world.

The main mover of the capacity increase was Hyundai Motors. Its vehicle production grew from 610,000 to 960,000 units between 1987 and 1993, as it continued to succeed at home and abroad with its indigenous car models.

In parallel with Hyundai's success in car export to the North American markets, Kia and GM-Daewoo also made efforts to exploit export opportunities. Kia built an international business network with Mazda and Ford. In 1986, Ford and Mazda became partners of Kia with 10 per cent and 8 per cent ownership respectively. Kia produced Mazda-designed cars which were exported to the US market where Ford distributed them with the Festiva brand. With the favourable sales performance of the Festiva at home and abroad during 1987–91, Kia became the second largest carmaker in Korea, surpassing GM-Daewoo.

GM-Daewoo, whose operation had been limited to the domestic market until 1986, began to produce GM's world car, the LeMan, a minor variation of the Opel-designed Kadett, in 1987. It was exported to the US market, and distributed by the Pontiac division of GM. With the LeMan, GM-Daewoo's car production capacity jumped from 40,000 to 400,000 units. However, the LeMan project did not improve GM-Daewoo's business figures. Only an average of 170,000 units a year were produced during 1987–92, keeping the company's average capacity utilization rate below 60 per cent. This resulted in chronic losses and the company was on the verge of bankruptcy at the end of 1992.

5.2 Deregulation and industrial expansion in the 1990s

Abolition of industrial policy and new entrants

In 1986, the government integrated various industry-specific promotion laws into a single law, the Industrial Development Law (see also Chapter 3). The law shifted the government's industry policy towards function-oriented industrial support, such as support for R&D. In addition, the law offered troubled industries rationalization programmes with limited lifetimes, usually 2–3 years. The automobile industry was designated by the Ministry of Commerce and Industry for the programme during 1986–89, and was supported by the law in various ways, such as entry restriction, control of capacity expansion and product price control.

The government legally controlled entry and capacity expansion until 1989. From 1990 on there were no legal restrictions on entry and capacity expansion. In reality, however, the habitual practice of banning entry continued implicitly until 1994, when Samsung succeed in breaking the taboo.

The early 1990s saw the collapse of state socialism in the former Soviet Union and Eastern Europe. In Korea also, the triumphant spirit of free market economics seized economic and political policy-makers. The year 1993 saw the abolition of industrial policy and this opened the door to diversification by the *chaebol*. Since all of the *chaebol* groups wanted to diversify into similar business lines, the abolition immediately resulted in fierce competition between the existing companies, and between existing companies and new entrants in almost all industries, leading to overinvestment and overcapacity building.

In the case of the car industry, Ssangyong began to produce cars on a small scale in 1991. More importantly, Samsung – the second largest *chaebol* group – entered the industry in 1994 but only started commercial production in early 1998. Hence, the entry itself could not have

Table 5.1 Increase in domestic vehicle production capacity, 1990–9[a] (thousand vehicles)

	1990	1991	1992	1993	1994	1995	1996	1997	1998	1999
Hyundai[b]	920	1,120	1,150	1,150	1,270	1,350	1,450	1,800	1,800	1,890
Hyundai Pr.[b]	0	76	76	76	81	136	136	136	136	0
Kia-Asia	490	490	510	697	793	937	937	937	937	830
Daewoo[c]	373	423	581	600	600	600	610	833	863	863
Ssangyong	39	39	39	39	59	112	120	154	154	154
Samsung[d]	0	0	0	0	5	5	5	5	130	130
Total sum	1,822	2,148	2,356	2,562	2,808	3,140	3,258	3,865	4,020	3,867

[a] Uniform production capacity is calculated on 16 hours × 265 days = 4,240 hours a year.
[b] Hyundai is Hyundai Motors. Hyundai Precision was merged with Hyundai Motors in 1999.
[c] Daewoo includes both Daewoo Motors and Daewoo Heavy Industry.
[d] Samsung includes Samsung Commercial Vehicle Company and Samsung Motors.
Source: KARI, *Korean Automotive Industry*, yearly.

contributed to the overcapacity building that caused the sector's recession from late 1996. The more serious effect of Samsung's entry was, however, that it induced the existing companies excessively to expand production capacity as they sought to suffocate the new company before it attained a minimum size of scale economy.

Competition for capacity expansion

A change in the market structure that was more significant than Samsung's entry occurred in late 1992, when GM separated from Daewoo and withdrew from the Korean market. In early 1993, Daewoo announced its 'global management' plan, and began aggressively to expand its range of models and production capacity at home and abroad. Daewoo's new positioning strategy, in turn, forced Hyundai and Kia also to expand output. In the 1990s, about 75 per cent of investment funds were allocated to capacity expansion (O'Brien 1998). In 1990, domestic production capacity had reached 1.8 million units, but by 1998, this had grown to about 4 million units, as seen in Table 5.1.

Financial opening and Daewoo's overseas expansion

The increase in overseas car production between 1993 and 1997 is also noteworthy. Encouraged by the globalization motto of the Kim Young-Sam government, Korean automakers made strong efforts to build international business empires. Korean automakers' manufacturing capacity abroad grew by 1.4 million units between 1993 and 1998. Daewoo led the investment in globalized manufacturing. While Hyundai built an overseas capacity of 0.4 million units during 1993–8, Daewoo planned to build more than 1 million units in the same period. After its bad experience in North America in the late 1980s, Hyundai became cautious in its development of overseas manufacturing.[3] Therefore, most of its overseas projects in the 1990s were limited to low-volume CKD operations with minor equity participation. Table 5.2 shows that CKD assembly plants amounted to 70 per cent of Hyundai's overseas production capacity. The only exception was in India where Hyundai set up a 120,000 unit manufacturing plant under full ownership in October 1998.

Daewoo was far more ambitious in developing a global manufacturing strategy.[4] Daewoo built internationally networked manufacturing sites with a capacity of 1 million in emerging market countries. Most of the new capacity was made up of high-volume plants that started operation in India, Uzbekistan, Romania and Poland between 1995 and 1996.

Daewoo made the most use of the financial opening of Korea in the 1990s. In 1993, government policy was changed to allow overseas subsidiaries of Korean non-financial firms to borrow directly from foreign financial institutions (see also Chapter 3). Without liberalization and financial opening, Daewoo could never have made such aggressive ventures overseas. In contrast with Hyundai and Kia, which had been passive in global fund raising, Daewoo financed its overseas projects worth

Table 5.2 Expansion of overseas vehicle production capacity by Hyundai and Daewoo, 1993–8

Hyundai			Daewoo		
Start date	Country	Capacity	Start date	Country	Capacity
May '93	Botswana	40,000	Mar.'94	Vietnam	22,000
Aug. '94	Egypt	10,000	Aug. '94	China	5,000
Feb. '95	Thailand	10,000	Oct. '94	Philippines	10,000
May '95	Philippines	10,000	Feb. '95	Iran	50,000
Feb. '96	Venezuela	20,000	July '95	Indonesia	50,000
May '97	Brazil	30,000	July '95	India	180,000
July '97	Taiwan	20,000	Mar. '96	Uzbekistan	200,000
Sept. '97	Turkey	100,000	Mar. '96	Romania	200,000
July '98	Pakistan	10,000	Nov. '96	Poland	170,000
Aug. '98	Malaysia	20,000	Dec. '96	Poland	400,000
Oct. '98	India	120,000	Dec. '96	Czech	25,000

Source: O'Brien (1998: p. 122) and company reports of Hyundai and Daewoo.

total US$20 billion mostly by borrowing directly from international financial institutions.

With the increase in capacity at home and abroad, Korea more than doubled its share of world car output, from 2.7 per cent to 5.8 per cent, during 1990–7. According to O'Brien (1998: p. 45), Korea accounted for about 50 per cent of the increase in global car supply over the decade.

The basic reason of the industrial collapse in 1998 was this rapid expansion of production capacity at home and abroad between 1993 and 1997. Korean automakers, particularly Daewoo, operated on the assumption that sales and export opportunities would continue to expand and that international financial markets would continue to supply investment funds.

5.3   Financial crisis and industrial crisis

Growth, recession and industrial crisis

The Korean car industry in the period preceding the crisis presents a picture of steady growth. Vehicle ownership in Korea expanded rapidly from 1987. By 1997, there were more than 10 million cars, or one per 4.5 Koreans.

Between 1993 and 1996, the industry experienced a boom in sales, production and investment. But after peaking in 1996, the growth of production stagnated. As seen in Figure 5.1, the year 1997 saw barely any

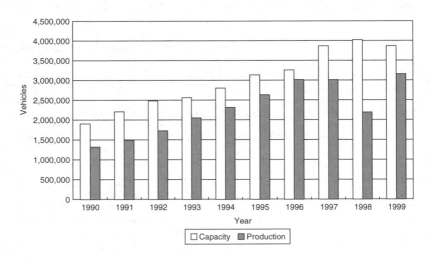

Figure 5.1   Domestic vehicle production in Korea, 1990–8[a]
[a] Production for CKD exports is included. Capacity utilization rate is calculated on the basis of the uniform production capacity with 16 hours × 265 days = 4,240 hours a year.
Source: KARI, *Korean Automotive Industry*, yearly.

increase in production. At the same time, operations started up at new plants owned by Daewoo and Hyundai at home and abroad and many new models were introduced during 1996–7. The result of stagnating sales on the one hand and increasing capacity on the other was falling capacity utilization, as shown in Figure 5.1 and in the percentage chart for the capacity utilization rate of the automotive industry for 1997:

1990	1991	1992	1993	1994	1995	1996	1997	1998	1999
69%	68%	70%	80%	83%	84%	92%	78%	54%	82%

Source: KARI, *Korean Automotive Industry*, yearly.

Nonetheless, these figures show that, when compared with the years 1990–5, the industry's capacity utilization rate in 1997 did not drop dramatically. As we have already seen in Chapter 3, the declining tendency of the Korean economy between late 1996 and October 1997 was not a crisis but a recession, even though it was a severe one.

In 1998, however, the industry's sales and production collapsed. The financial market panic and soaring interest rates brought about sudden collapse of Korea's financial and corporate system, as mentioned in Chapter 3. This in turn led to a dramatic deterioration in consumer confidence. The capacity utilization rate of the industry fell to 50 per cent. Kia, which had already filed for insolvency and was under a bank bailout programme, went into court receivership in 1998. Ssangyong, which was sold to Daewoo in December 1997, made record losses in 1998. Samsung Motor Company, which started operations in March 1998, had to stop production in December of the same year because of sluggish sales and soaring losses. In 1999, the Korean economy and the industry had to some extent recovered from the effects of the crisis. In August 1999, however, Daewoo Group and all of its subsidiaries, including the Daewoo Motor Company, collapsed due to rising debts and losses. By the end of 1999, all automakers except Hyundai had collapsed.

Inefficiency of Korean carmakers and its causes

During and after the 1997 crisis, Korea's state-led capitalism was widely regarded as the main institutional failure that caused the chronic inefficiencies which led eventually to the crisis. For example, Krugman (1998a) insisted that state intervention had created 'moral hazard' among the Korean corporations which resulted in 'reckless investments and low efficiency', as reflected in low corporate profitability.

However, Chang, Park and Yoo (1998) and Chang and Park (2000) indicate that the low corporate profitability in Korea was mainly due to high interest payments rather than to inefficiency. Table 5.3 shows that Korea's post-interest-payments profitability (the ratio of 'ordinary income' to sales) was really low owing to high financial costs: 2.8 per cent (1973–96) as opposed to 7.9 per cent in the US (1995), 5.1 per cent in Taiwan (1995), 4.3 per cent in Japan (1955–73) and 2.9 per cent in Japan (1995). However, this should not be interpreted as showing Korea's low corporate efficiency because profitability before interest payment (measured by the ratio of 'operating income' to sales) was not low by international standards. Between 1973 and 1996, Korea averaged 7.4 per cent. The USA recorded 7.7 per cent in 1995.

The figures for the Korean automobile industry from 1978 to 1998 provide further evidence against Krugman's argument (see Table 5.4). The industry's balance sheets for 1978–89, except for the three years of industrial restructuring between 1980 and 1982, look relatively better than those for 1990–8. This is to say that the performance of the industry in terms of operational income and ordinary income was largely better in the 1980s than in the 1990s. This partly reflects the intensified competition among automakers in the 1990s because of new entries and capacity expansions. This also suggests that it was not state intervention but industrial deregulation in the 1990s that resulted in 'reckless investments and low efficiency'.

It was in the 1990s that the Korean automobile industry experienced a chronic deterioration in overall profitability. Between 1991 and 1997, the industry's ratios of operating income to sales stayed at 4.9 per cent on average, down from 6.1 per cent in 1981–90. The lowered operating

Table 5.3   International comparison of corporate profitability[a] (%)

	Korea		Japan		USA	Taiwan
	1973–96	1996	1955–73	1995	1995	1995
Operating income/sales	7.4	6.5	7.2[b]	3.3	7.7	7.3
Financial expenses/sales	5.5	5.8	3.4	1.3	n.a	n.a.
Ordinary income/sales	2.8	1.0	4.3	2.9	7.9	5.1

n.a = not available

[a] Operating income is defined as gross profit minus selling and general administration expenses. Ordinary income is defined as operating income minus net non-operating expenses. Net non-operating expenses include interest payments, loss on foreign currency transactions and translation, loss on valuation of marketable securities, loss and disposition of investments or tangible assets, and so on.

[b] For 1961–73.

Source: Chang, Park and Yoo (1998).

income rate was a result of increased competition. Furthermore, the ratios of ordinary income to sales in the same period were squeezed to nearly zero. This was because of increasing financial expenses, as shown in Table 5.4.

It was in the 1990s, the period of liberalization and financial opening, that Korea's automakers borrowed excessively. Table 5.4 shows that the industry's debt/equity ratio during the 1980s remained largely under 400 per cent, except for the years of recession and restructuring in the early 1980s. By contrast, it rose to an average of 520 per cent during the period 1991 and 1997 although the industry was not in crisis in the period. Furthermore, Table 5.4 includes only the domestic debts of the industry. If the overseas debt of Daewoo's overseas auto business is included, the ratios are actually more than 700–800 per cent.

This rapid growth in debts resulted in the increase in financial expenses in the period, which in turn reduced the industry's income to

Table 5.4 Profitability of the Korean automotive industry, 1978–98[a] (%)

	Sales increase	Operational income/sales	Ordinary income/sales	Financial costs/sales	Debt/equity
1978	88.12	4.56	3.89	3.73	342.60
1979	31.14	5.02	3.51	4.98	415.50
1980	−10.77	1.54	−13.00	12.81	853.90
1981	22.94	1.67	−10.44	13.71	740.60
1982	30.85	7.61	−0.53	9.76	622.70
1983	36.37	9.55	5.12	5.90	440.20
1984	14.23	9.18	5.61	5.71	377.20
1985	25.58	9.18	5.09	4.34	263.30
1986	52.28	6.25	3.98	2.97	327.70
1987	56.92	5.22	3.83	3.23	390.30
1988	21.74	3.85	3.33	3.44	348.40
1989	18.41	3.73	1.55	4.18	315.00
1990	31.66	5.06	1.95	4.25	398.80
1991	13.47	3.35	−0.50	6.43	484.90
1992	9.46	3.56	−0.17	7.66	530.50
1993	19.98	3.89	−0.67	6.73	415.66
1994	26.32	5.34	0.20	6.45	462.96
1995	17.87	5.82	0.41	6.37	460.87
1996	14.88	6.78	0.80	6.18	490.97
1997	3.89	5.85	−2.33	7.80	826.40
1998	−23.48	−5.44	−21.70	17.01	630.36

[a] Financial expenses primarily refer to interest payments and principal repayments, and also to loss on foreign currency transactions and translation.
Source: Bank of Korea, *Analysis of Corporate Operation*, yearly.

Table 5.5 Net profit of Korean carmakers, 1989–99[a] (hundred million won)

	1989	1990	1991	1992	1993	1994	1995	1996	1997	1998	1999	Total
Hyundai	452	675	538	416	582	1,368	1,567	530	464	-331	4,143	10,404
Kia[b]	256	423	158	150	187	-696	115	70	-3,829	-66,496	1,357	-68,305
Asia[b]	77	130	104	74	81	73	73	-294	-4,083			-3,765
Daewoo[c]	-163	102	-1,467	-956	-847	-91	105	229	2,512	176	-46,402	-46,802
Ssangyong[d]	27	58	94	-88	-621	-793	-1,262	-2,285	-3,133	-4,998	-10,746	-23,747
Samsung[e]							-7	-216	6	-6,771		-6,988
Total sum	649	1,388	-573	-404	-618	-139	591	-1,966	-8,063	-78,420	-67,700	

[a] Net profit refers to net income. Net income is defined as ordinary income + (one-time gain – one-time loss) – corporate income tax.
[b] Kia Group collapsed in mid-1997. Asia Motor Company was merged with Kia Motors in 1998. Then, Kia Motor Company was merged with the Hyundai Motor Group in 1999.
[c] Daewoo Group, including Daewoo Motor Company, collapsed in mid-1999.
[d] Ssangyong Motor Company was merged with Daewoo Motor Company in 1998.
[e] Samsung Motor Company began production in March 1998 and stopped in December 1998.
Source: Each company, *Annual Report*, yearly.

nearly zero. Table 5.5 shows that except for Hyundai, all automakers made negative net incomes during the period 1991–7. Hyundai was the sole Korean automaker whose total sum of added net profits between 1991 and 1997 was positive. In contrast, it was minus 782 billion won for Kia-Asia, minus 72 billion won for Daewoo (even before the revelation of a large scale fraud in the financial statements; see also Chapter 7), minus 809 billion won for Ssangyong, and minus 22 billion won for Samsung. It is certain that these chronic losses made most of the Korean automakers financially vulnerable and led them eventually to collapse between 1997 and 1999. The final consequence of the expansionist strategies of Korean automakers during 1991–7 was a series of defaults at Kia, Ssangyong, Samsung, and Daewoo. Only Hyundai Motors proved to be competent enough to survive the 1990s.

The huge losses of Kia and Daewoo in 1998 or 1999 were because of their one-time losses. Daewoo and Kia committed large-scale frauds in their financial statements from the mid-1990s up to the time of their collapse. After the defaults of Kia and Daewoo in July 1997 and August 1999, the Financial Supervisory Commission of Korea investigated the accounting frauds and re-evaluated financial statements in an extremely strict way. The result was the huge one-time losses in those years. Ssangyong Motor Company, which had been merged with Daewoo Motor Company in 1998, also showed a sudden rise in losses in 1999 due to the revaluation of financial statements.

5.4 Conclusion

Korea's automotive industry went through two stages: the first was the stage of the developmental system, embracing the period between the 1960s and the 1980s, and the second was the stage of deregulation in the 1990s.

In the first stage, the state in Korea played an active role in initiating and promoting the industry at both industrial and corporate levels. It protected the domestic market by limiting the number of automakers and transnational participation. It also pushed automakers to localize design and content, so that Korean cars could be exported. The government's 1973 Plan required carmakers to stop licensing foreign designs and instead to develop national cars. Due to the success of the plan, Korea has remained a unique case among developing countries, since transnational automakers have not played a leading role. In this light, the plan presents a strong case for DS literature.

However, we also saw that the plan's success was only partial. This was because Korea's carmakers responded to the policy with diverse strategies. Only Hyundai enthusiastically followed the policy. Kia resisted, and continued licensing foreign car designs. GM-Korea (later GM-Daewoo) ignored the policy from the outset, and kept assembling cars from imported KD kits.

Hyundai, the best-known Korean *chaebol* carmaker, has not grown by cronyism or other rent-seeking activities, but rather by successful use of industrial policy and a strategic determination to become technologically independent. By contrast, Kia and GM-Daewoo rejected industrial policy more or less, and failed to catch up with Hyundai. It was not until the 1990s that Kia and Daewoo followed Hyundai's strategy. This presents a strong case against the neoclassical argument of 'crony Asian (Korean) capitalism'.

In the second stage, which started during the 1990s, the industry was deregulated. With the abolition of industrial policy, Ssangyong and Samsung entered the automotive business while existing carmakers – Hyundai, Kia, and Daewoo – vigorously invested in capacity expansion. Deregulated financial sectors supplied funds for the risky investments. But excessive investment in capacity, combined with increasing costs of debt repayments, brought incomes down to their lowest level. This, in turn, made them vulnerable to external shock. Kia, Ssangyong, Samsung and Daewoo collapsed between July 1997 and August 1999. Only Hyundai survived the crisis of 1997–99 more or less intact. From this, we conclude that industrial deregulation, combined with financial liberalization, caused the industry's inefficiencies in the 1990s, which resulted in the corporate collapses during the crisis.

In the next three chapters, we will look at the cases of Hyundai, GM-Daewoo and Daewoo in greater detail to see why they chose different paths of development despite being in the same institutional environment. This will make clear the importance of both corporate control and the strategic determination of top management.

6
Hyundai Motor Company

Founded in 1967, the Hyundai Motor Company (HMC) is today Korea's largest carmaker. Now merged with Kia, the company is one of the ten largest carmakers in the world. The Hyundai Automobile Group (HMC and Kia) produced 2.8 million cars in 2001.

HMC, the most efficient carmaker in Korea, was a star pupil of the developmental state system. In contrast with GM-Daewoo and Kia, both of which rejected or hesitated to follow industrial policy, HMC actively cooperated with the government and used the industrial policy to learn foreign technology and expand into export markets. Together with Samsung Electronics, the company throughout the 1980s and 1990s has been synonymous with Korea's success in catching up industrially, in spite of allegedly 'distorted' corporate governance. Furthermore, HMC was the only Korean carmaker to survive the 1997 crisis.

This chapter will investigate the strategies and capabilities of HMC from the company's birth to recovery from the 1997 crisis. To explain how HMC has gained and held competitive advantages, we will apply the 'dynamic capabilities approach'. In section 6.1, we will first look at the business structure and corporate governance structure of the Hyundai Group and HMC. In section 6.2, we will see how HMC, with the encouragement of the government, was determined to retain full corporate control in the face of transnational carmakers. The determination of HMC's top management to stick with its vision of developing its Hyundai-designed cars and expand into the world market will be illuminated in the context of HMC's confrontation with transnational carmakers. Section 6.3 will investigate the ways that HMC built its own capabilities in technology. In long-term projects, HMC has actively and intentionally used a variety of ways of technological learning and technology transfer, in order to become independent of foreign technologies. In section 6.4, we will look at the business of HMC in the 1990s and up to the present day. The company's survival and then further growth after the crisis may be attributed to its fidelity to the notion of dynamic capabilities building, as described by Alfred D. Chandler.

6.1   Hyundai Group and Hyundai Motor Company

History and business

Hyundai Motor Company (HMC) was one of the key business units of the Hyundai Group, Korea's largest conglomerate. The history of Hyundai Group began in 1940 when the founder, Chung Ju-Young, took over a small car repair shop.[1] During the Second World War, the repair shop became a victim of Japanese repression. After the liberation, Chung re-entered the vehicle repair business in 1946. He named his new firm Hyundai Auto Service ('Hyundai' means 'modern' in Korean). His business soon became successful, and he noticed in 1947 that the construction business made far more money than the repair side, so he established the Hyundai Civil Works Company. In 1950, Hyundai Engineering & Construction Company (HECC), the cornerstone of the current Hyundai business group, was established by merging Hyundai Auto Service and the Hyundai Civil Works Company. In the 1950s, HECC enjoyed continued growth through military demand for construction and post-war reconstruction works.

In the early 1960s, however, the post-war demand for reconstruction diminished. HECC turned to overseas construction markets. The company participated in highway construction in Thailand in 1965 and stepped into the South Vietnamese market at the time of the Vietnam War, earning a good reputation as a construction company.

In the late 1960s, when the Korean government projected ambitious plans for promoting heavy industries, HECC began to diversify. Hyundai concentrated on its investments in shipbuilding, automobile, steel and machine industries, laying the foundations of the Group. The first diversification target of Hyundai was an area already familiar to Chung: the automobile business. In 1967, Chung established the Hyundai Motor Company, realizing a dream he had had since his experience in the car repair shop in the 1940s.[2]

In the 1980s, the Hyundai Group made a series of diversifications into electronics, petrochemicals, finance and service. With the establishment of Hyundai Electronics in 1983, the Group's efforts focused on semiconductors, particularly on D-RAM production. As of 1998, the group consisted of 53 subsidiaries in the automobile, shipbuilding, engineering and construction, machinery, iron and steel, petrochemicals and energy, electronics and telecommunication sectors as well as finance, trade and other service sectors (see Figure 6.1).

Automobiles and Machinery	Metal
Hyundai Motor Company	Inchon Iron & Steel Co.
Hyundai Precision & Industry Co.	Aluminium of Korea Ltd
Hyundai Auto Service Co.	4 other companies
Korean Flange Co.	**Electronics**
KEPICO Corporation	Hyundai Electronics Industries Co.
Shindaehan	Hyundai Information Technology Co.
Engineering and Construction	**Energy and Petrochemicals**
Hyundai Engineering & Construction Co.	Hyundai Oil Refinery Co
Hyundai Development & Construction Co.	Hyundai Oil Sales Co.
Korea Industrial Development Co.	Hyundai Energy Co.
Hyundai Engineering Co.	Hyundai Petrochemical Co.
Hyundai Construction Equipment Service Co.	**Trade and Finance**
Dongseo Industrial Co.	Hyundai Corporation
Hyundai Livart	Hyundai Merchant Marine Co.
Hyundai Construction Equipment	Hyundai Marine & Fire Insurance Co.
Hyundai Elevator	Hyundai International Merchant Bank
Hyundai Wood Industries Co.	Hyundai Securities Co.
Shipbuilding and Industrial Plants	**Service and other businesses**
Hyundai Heavy Industries Co.	Keumkang Development Industrial Co.
Hyundai-Mipo Dockyard Co.	Woolsan Broadcasting Co.
Sun-Eel Shipping	Munhwa Dairy Newspaper
2 other companies	12 other companies

Source: HMC, *Annual Report*, 1998.

Figure 6.1   Hyundai Group and its 53 subsidiaries, 1998

Ownership and control

The ownership and control structure of the group before 1999 was typically pyramidal. The founder, Chung, owned majority shares in HECC and Hyundai Heavy Industry (HHI).[3] These two companies in turn played the role of quasi-holding company for the other affiliates (see Chapter 4 for the role of quasi-holding companies of a *chaebol*). The pyramid structure of the group's ownership reflects its origin and diversification history (see Figure 6.2).

In the case of Hyundai Motor Company (HMC), HHI and HECC were principal shareholders owning 13.98 per cent and 5.36 per cent of shares respectively. A younger brother of the founder, Chung Se-Young, who had been the Chief Executive Officer (CEO) of HMC for 30 years, owned 6.07 per cent. Including other subsidiaries' shareholdings, the total intragroup shareholding in HMC, owned by the *chaebol* family and subsidiaries, amounted to 35.36 per cent in 1997 (People's Solidarity for Participatory Democracy 1999: p. 158).

Like the other subsidiaries of Hyundai, HMC was under the direct control of its founder even though he did not own any stock in the company. This is due to the pyramid structure of ownership via the quasi-holding companies. Besides, Chung's family is famous for its Confucianism: the younger members usually obey the older. Chung Se-Young, the younger brother and the nominal CEO of HMC, loyally followed the founder, his eldest brother. Thus, we can regard the shares of the younger brother as being also under the direct control of the founder.[4]

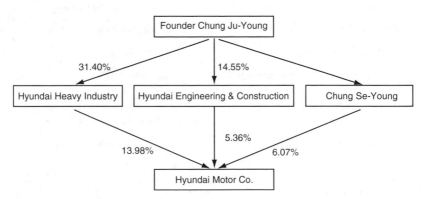

Figure 6.2   Ownership and control of Hyundai Motor Company, 1997
Source: HMC, *Annual Report*, 1997.

The founding chairman was not only the quasi-owner of HMC; even though he did not take an official position in the company, he was also the top decision-maker in strategic matters. He was the entrepreneur who created HMC's unique strategies and competences, while the role of Chung Se-Young, the official CEO, became increasingly important from the mid-1980s.

6.2 HMC's strategies and vision

The current competitive capabilities of HMC are the result of its persistent strategic efforts in the past decades, which continue today. The company's key strategies fall into two categories. The first concerns its relationship with foreign automakers, and the second refers to the ways that it accomplished technological learning.

Emphasis on full corporate control

Hyundai Group has always emphasized the importance of retaining full managerial control even when it cooperated with foreign business partners. Likewise, HMC has made efforts to minimize foreign influences on management. Without any technological or managerial know-how in the beginning, however, it had no choice but to rely on foreign assistance.

When HMC was founded in late 1967, Shinjin, the KD assembler of Toyota, was the dominant automaker in the Korean market. It seemed that its predominance would continue in the 1970s when it established a 50:50 joint venture with GM, the world's largest automobile producer, in 1972, while Hyundai failed to find a foreign partner. No industry experts thought that GM-Korea (originally Shinjin) could be challenged by the much smaller Korean firms, but by 1976, GM-Korea had sunk to third position after HMC and Kia Motors. Until 1992, when the joint venture agreement between GM and Daewoo finally ended, GM-Korea (renamed Daewoo Motors in 1983) never regained the market position that Shinjin had enjoyed in the 1960s. Up to now, Korea has remained the only developing country in which multinational automakers have not been able to predominate.

The differences in strategies and capabilities among the three main automakers became apparent as early as the 1970s. Hyundai's effort to export to the world market was a unique case at the time: Shinjin (assembler of GM) and Kia (assembler of Fiat, Mazda, etc.) did not attempt to be anything other than local manufacturers of foreign vehicles. Hyundai, in contrast, rejected any cooperation with foreign automakers that might constrain full managerial control. This strategic principle was already apparent in the early 1970s when Korea's first indigenous car, the Pony, was developed.

Hyundai and Ford in the early 1970s

As soon as Chung established Hyundai Motors in late 1967, he looked into the possibility of technology transfer from foreign automakers. At the time, GM and Ford were aiming to expand their Asian operation and looking for Korean partners. Ford dispatched a delegation to investigate the industrial capabilities of potential Korean automakers and interviewed industrialists who were interested in a partnership. The delegation chose Hyundai because of Chung's experience in the car business.

In the negotiations between Ford and Hyundai, however, there arose discords. Ford insisted on strong capital and management participation in the joint venture company, but Chung rejected any kind of intervention in management by Ford. His insistence on full management control was so strong that Ford finally gave up. However, Ford regarded it as pointless to pursue full participation in management and capital for the small Korean auto market: total yearly sales of vehicles were below 30,000 units at the time. In February 1968, Ford agreed to provide assembly technology and supply CKD kits for Hyundai. There was no capital participation but only a technical licensing agreement. The role of Ford in HMC was limited to technical assistance and quality control.

Full control of management gave Hyundai the possibility of selecting, from among Ford's various products, the most appropriate vehicle for the Korean market. Taking the bad road and driving conditions of Korea into consideration, Hyundai chose Cortina, a subcompact car designed by British Ford. Market surveys and product investigations helped the company build capabilities in marketing.

The licence agreement between Ford and Hyundai soon faced a significant change. In December 1969, the Korean government announced a plan for the promotion of the Korean automobile industry (see Chapter 5). The 1969 plan demanded that automakers fully localize major components by 1976. It was anticipated that only one automaker would produce car engines, in order to achieve economies of scale. As a result of his personal experience of car repair, Chung had long been interested in car engines. In line with the government's 1969 plan, Hyundai began to negotiate with Ford for an engine plant. This time, Hyundai accepted Ford's demand for 50 per cent equity participation. In 1970, HMC and Ford signed a provisional agreement for a 50:50 joint venture that was expected to produce 53,000 petrol and diesel engines a year.

Before long, however, both companies found it difficult to agree on a business strategy. Supported by the government policy of export promotion, the top management of HMC insisted on exporting cars containing engines manufactured by Ford's technology and capital through Ford's world dealer network, but Ford was not interested in exporting cars produced by the joint venture. Furthermore, Ford regarded the company as only a local part of its global component supply system, while Hyundai – and the Korean government too – wanted to localize fully all components. Ford did not want to compromise because its transnational strategy and structure were at stake, so it rejected Hyundai's proposal. Hyundai also refused Ford's counterproposal, according to which Hyundai would become a subcontractor of Ford's 'world car project'. Finally, the provisional joint venture agreement was annulled in January 1973. The partnership between the two companies was never restored, even though Hyundai continued to assemble the Ford Cortina until the late 1970s.

The first national car: the Pony

After the breakdown of negotiations with Ford, HMC's position seemed hopeless because it had no foreign automaker promising technology transfer. In the meantime, Shinjin contracted with GM to establish GM-Korea, and Kia acquired licensing agreements with Mazda, Peugeot and Fiat.

In early 1973, however, as a part of the Big Push Plan, the Korean government selected automobile manufacturing as one of the targeted industries that were to receive various preferential subsidies. A promotional policy guideline was announced as the Long-term Plan for the Promotion of the Automobile Industry (see Chapter 5 for this policy change).

The government requested that selected industries expand into the main exporting sectors. For the automobile industry, however, export was impossible so long as the Korean automakers did not have a proprietary product, since foreign licensing companies would not agree to re-export their models. Moreover, a further increase in localization would be difficult without export as the small domestic market could not offer the minimum economies of scale necessary for localization. Hence the development of an indigenous car was of the utmost importance for the expansion of the country's exports base, and the government pressured automakers to develop indigenous cars by 1975.

However, the automakers regarded the Plan as unrealistic as it appeared impossible to develop proprietary products without technology transfer from foreign automakers. They did not follow the government guidelines and continued licensing foreign designs for the domestic market. Kia simply localized the Brisa, a subcompact Mazda, and assembled the Peugeot 604 and Fiat 132. GM-Korea continued to produce only slightly changed variants of subcompact and compact cars originally developed by Opel.

Hyundai was the only company that voluntarily followed the government policy; but how could it overcome the technological barrier? A government officer who was in charge of the automobile industry in the Ministry of Commerce and Industry during 1972–74, and who participated in initiating and drafting the Plan, recounts:

> One day after I had sent an official notice to three automakers requesting them to present plans for developing proprietary cars, Hyundai's Chung visited me in the office and complained about the 'Plan'. He said that no foreign automaker would help his company develop an indigenous car. But I knew that there were other sources of technology transfer from my experiences of study and work in Germany in the 1950–60s. I advised Chung that there were specialized design-houses in Europe and they might help his company.[5]

Chung Se-Young, the younger brother, travelled to Europe with an engineer and collected information about other sources of technology transfer. They discovered that there were small car design-houses that would help Hyundai develop its own car.[6] On this basis, the elder Chung decided immediately to develop a national car.

In March 1973, Hyundai announced its plan to develop a subcompact car. Giorgetto Giugiaro's ItalDesign, car stylist for Alpha Romeo and Fiat and the designer of the Volkswagen Golf, took the job of designing both styling and body. However, another difficulty was that ItalDesign was not capable of developing a car platform. Hyundai asked Mitsubishi of Japan. At that time, HECC was diversifying into shipbuilding and acquired technological assistance from Mitsubishi Heavy Industries (MHI). Their agreement on technological cooperation was extended to other areas because, like Mitsubishi, Hyundai continued to diversify into other heavy industries including machinery, electrical equipment, turbines, energy facilities, plant engineering, and so on. Mitsubishi Motor Company (MMC), a spin-off of MHI, was under the control of MHI and, hence, it was easy to couple HMC and MMC. MMC, a small latecomer in auto manufacturing at the time, was trying to expand sales against larger Japanese and American automakers, and the royalty gains from licensing the technology were by no means negligible for the new entrant. Thus, Mitsubishi decided to offer platform designs for the Lancer, its first subcompact car. The offer was acceptable to HMC since MMC was not interested in participating in HMC's ownership and management.[7]

Consequently, Hyundai's first proprietary car, the Pony, was developed with a Mitsubishi platform and ItalDesign body and styling. Because the Pony was the only car designed with Korean conditions in mind (fuel economy, unpaved roads, etc.) the car was an immediate success in the Korean market, and made the company market leader. Moreover, as both foreign partners were not interested in corporate control and the business strategy of HMC, it could export the car, at first to developing countries in Latin America and the Middle East.

In contrast, GM-Korea failed to provide cars suited to Korean conditions. Its Chevrolet 1700 and Camina (smaller variant of the Chevrolet 1700) were too heavy and large, and did not have good fuel economy.[8] Nonetheless, GM-Korea did not want to develop a local model because it regarded the Korean market as being too small for product localization.

Hyundai and GM in confrontation, 1980–1

In late 1979, the Second Oil Crisis hit the Korean economy and interrupted the growth of the automobile industry. In 1980, auto production declined and the rate of capacity utilization dropped to 38 per cent overall. HMC's rate fell to 44 per cent and the decline continued in 1981. Its debts increased and the resulting high financial costs brought the company to the verge of insolvency.

Amid this economic depression, the new military government of Korea that came to the power in May 1980 aimed at a monopolization of car production. It wanted GM-Korea (renamed Saehan Motors in 1976) and HMC to merge to form a monopolist carmaker (see Chapter 5 for more about the 1980 restructuring policy), but GM and Hyundai clashed on every important point. GM wanted equal participation in ownership and management of the new monopoly carmaker and wanted the company to be positioned as a part of its world car strategy. HMC, however, wanted to exclude GM from ownership and management in order to ensure free access to the world market for its own cars. The differences between Hyundai and GM were not resolved and the government finally gave up the monopolization policy and allowed both HMC and GM-Korea to continue car production. Only Kia was required to withdraw from the car sector.

In October 1981, immediately after negotiations with GM broke off, Hyundai announced an ambitious plan to develop another subcompact car that would compete with GM's world car project.

Strategic alliance with Mitsubishi and the success of the Pony Excel

For its second proprietary car project, Hyundai built a new car plant with a 300,000 unit capacity that gave an international standard of scale economies. As a result, the company's annual production capacity soared from 70,000 to 370,000 units. In spite of its restricted credit condition due to the high level of corporate debts, HMC was able to raise funds for the project. The government supported the company with a preferential policy loan (see Chapter 3 for more about policy loans).

The project faced a technological problem, however. In the late 1970s, some world automakers (Volkswagen, for instance) developed front-wheel-drive technology. It was introduced to small car segments particularly because of gains in fuel economy. Hyundai also wanted front-wheel-drive for its new car but was not yet capable of developing it alone. It needed technology transfer once again.

In 1978, Hyundai contacted Volkswagen, which had just developed a successful front-wheel-drive car, the Golf. Volkswagen was planning to establish a local production site in Asia. Volkswagen's proposals were attractive: the lowest level of licensing royalty (only 1 per cent of the sale price for each car), and a guaranteed export of 100,000 cars from the licensee. In return for the benefits, however, Volkswagen wanted a share in the ownership and management of HMC. Hyundai would not compromise on the issue, and subsequently contacted Renault and Ford; but they also rejected cooperation without management participation.

In the meantime, Mitsubishi succeeded in developing a front-wheel-drive subcompact car, the Mirage, which was launched in 1979. Once again, Hyundai approached Mitsubishi for the transfer of technology, but Mitsubishi initially rejected licensing its newest technology. The negotiations continued over two further years before Mitsubishi finally agreed to license the platform design of the Mirage to HMC. But this time, cooperation between Hyundai and Mitsubishi was not limited to platform design;[9] they had established a strategic alliance that tied Mitsubishi and Hyundai in technology as well as capital. Mitsubishi participated in HMC's capital ownership with a 10 per cent shareholding (increased to 15 per cent in 1985) and dispatched two representatives to HMC's directorial board.[10] In spite of the equity participation, however, Mitsubishi did not acquire managerial control of HMC. Hence, HMC was able to continue expanding world market sales and learning technologies from other sources.

Once again, ItalDesign carried out the styling design of HMC's new car, but this time HMC's engineers, together with ItalDesign, designed the body. Chassis and power train designs were licensed.

At the same time, while the second proprietary car development was in hand, HMC launched an improved model of the Pony, the Pony II, in 1983. HMC brought the car to the Canadian market and succeeded in increasing sales. This encouraged HMC and showed that there was a niche market for the company in the subcompact low-price car segment. The Canadian experience was studied for the development of the new car.

HMC launched the Pony Excel, the second proprietary car, in 1985 and introduced it to the US market in 1986. American sales of the subcompact car were spectacularly successful. The Pony Excel broke the record for the best selling imported car in 1987, with sales of 260,000 units.

Difficulties in the late 1980s and growth in the 1990s

Despite its initial success in the US market, however, HMC's sales soon slumped. This was because of poor product quality and poor resale value. Sales of the Pony Excel remained static in 1988 at 263,000 units, and by 1989 total sales had dropped to 188,000 vehicles. The third proprietary product, the compact car Sonata, was launched in the North American market in December 1988. The car was partly supplied by a North American assembly plant in Bromont, Quebec, with a capacity of 100,000; but the Sonata made the problem worse.[11] By 1991, US sales had dropped to 120,000 units and again to 77,000 by 1992. Because of low operational activities, the Bromont plant was closed in October 1994:

> Hyundai's rush into the marketplace – perhaps before they were ready – cost them dearly in terms of brand image and corporate reputation. Poor-quality products, combined with poor marketing and after-sales service, tarnished the company's reputation in the U.S. marketplace for years to come. It would be a bitter lesson. (Steers 1999: p. 88)

In spite of the export slump from 1989, however, HMC's total car production increased again from 1991, as Figure 6.3 shows. First of all, HMC increased its domestic market sales steadily. Because of Korea's motorization in the late 1980s, the domestic market expanded rapidly, and HMC never lost the position of market leader. Second, HMC made efforts to diversify its export markets beyond North America and consequently, by 1995, car exports reached the level of 1988. At the same time, it endeavoured to improve product quality by reorganizing labour relationships, adopting Japanese management concepts, and introducing flexible automation (see Chung M.-K. 1998).

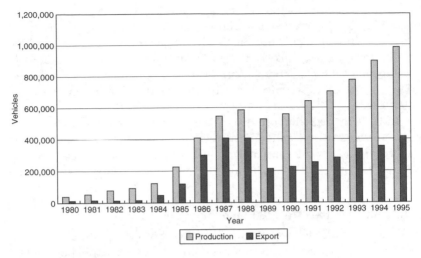

Figure 6.3   HMC's passenger car production, 1980–95[a]
[a] Export for overseas KD production is not included.
Source: KAMA, *Automobile Statistics*, yearly.

6.3   HMC's efforts to develop technological capability

As we have seen, Hyundai's strategy consisted of – and still consists of – three elements. The first was the emphasis on national and full management control. The second, secured by the first, was free access to the world market. The third, supported by the first and the second principle, was a determination to build its own technological and managerial capabilities. We will focus here on the third aspect.

Strategic efforts to keep full management control and unlimited access to export markets have enhanced Hyundai's ability to learn from various sources of technology transfer, unconstrained by multinational automakers. The founder Chung summarized his strategies as follows: 'we can upgrade our product quality and technology only when we find ourselves in competition with automakers of the industrialized countries. The world market pressure will strongly drive us to promote our technology and industry and make our national economy independent' (HMC 1992: p. 482).[12] He was one of the few industrialists in Korea who had personal technical experience in the auto business. In his view, learning technology at any cost was extremely important for companies in developing countries. Consequently, Hyundai's efforts to achieve technological capabilities, in manufacturing as well as R&D, have been much more persistent than those of Kia or Daewoo.

Hyundai's technological catch-up process can be characterized as follows. First, HMC searched for various foreign sources of technology and avoided dependence on any specific source. Second, it focused on training its engineers and technicians with long-term projects, sometimes as long as 10 years. Third, it appropriated foreign technology by incremental improvements for Korea-specific industrial and technical conditions.

Between 1973 and 1998, we can observe three phases in the history of new car development by HMC (see Table 6.1). The first was the period between the early 1970s and the mid-1980s when the Pony and the Pony Excel were developed. The company licensed or outsourced the designing of the platform (chassis layout and power train) and styling from Mitsubishi and ItalDesign. Design of the car bodies was also

Table 6.1   HMC's history, 1967–99

Year	Major events
1967	Hyundai Motor Company founded.
1968	HMC begins assembling Ford Cortina.
1973	HMC began with development of the first national car.
1975	The Pony, the first Korean proprietary model, launched.
1982	Pony II launched.
1983	Pony II exported to Canada and is successful.
1985	Pony Excel launched.
1986	Pony Excel exported to America.
1987	Pony Excel rated imported car of the year in America.
1988	Sonata, a compact car with Mitsubishi-designed platform, launched.
1989	Pony Excel reached 1 million in worldwide sales.
	North American assembly plant opens in Bromont, Canada.
1990	Lantra, a subcompact car, launched.
1991	HMC successfully develops its first proprietary engine, the Alpha.
1994	Accent, a subcompact car with the first in-house designed chassis and engine, launched. Bromont plant closed.
1995	Avante, a subcompact car with the second in-house designed chassis and engine, launched.
1997	Atoz, a mini car with the third in-house designed chassis and engine, launched.
1998	EF Sonata, a compact car with the fourth in-house designed chassis and engine, launched.
	HMC initiates a market campaign with the EF Sonata in the American market.
1999	Hyundai doubles US sales.
	Hyundai acquires Kia Motors.

contracted to ItalDesign. But at the same time, HMC invested in building its own capabilities in designing body and chassis components as well as prototype car building.

In the second phase, between the mid-1980s and the early 1990s, the company's investment in R&D increased rapidly. Various institutes and testing facilities were established: most notably, a long-term project for developing an in-house designed engine and platform was launched and executed. In addition, beginning with the Sonata, Hyundai carried out car styling design alone, while its development organization progressively replaced ItalDesign in designing body structure.

The third phase began in the early 1990s when it succeeded in launching its first proprietary engine. Throughout the 1990s, HMC replaced the existing Mitsubishi-designed platforms with its own, and launched completely new models successively. As of 1998, the company became fully capable of developing car engines. The focus of technological efforts was moving to more sophisticated areas such as electronic engine management, air bag, active suspension, automated braking system (ABS), and so on.

Licensing and using foreign technology: the 1970s

As we have seen, Hyundai developed the Pony by using a Mitsubishi-designed platform and an ItalDesign-designed body. The success of the Pony in the Korean market was no accident but a result of HMC's efforts to develop a product meeting Korean requirements at the time (roads were narrow and largely unpaved until the early 1980s). HMC demanded from ItalDesign a car with a higher chassis position, stronger body structure and lower weight. In addition, it consulted with Mitsubishi about possible variations of the Pony platform and chose a fuel-economic option. It took into consideration that the First Oil Shock would make car drivers of resource-poor Korea sensitive to fuel prices.

From the very beginning HMC made every effort to reduce its dependence on Mitsubishi and ItalDesign. The company established its first product development organization in January 1975. It was a small department consisting of four sections, which were responsible for the body, the chassis for commercial vehicles, the chassis for passenger cars, and vehicle testing respectively.[13]

It is noteworthy that the chief engineers of all four sections were foreigners. In 1974, HMC employed seven foreign experts, mostly from Europe, on three-year contracts. They were experts not only in product technology but manufacturing technology as well. This was inevitable since Hyundai had first to master manufacturing technology. The seven foreign experts were in charge of chassis, body, die, press, engine, transmission, and vehicle testing respectively. One of their most important duties was training HMC's technical engineers and technicians (HMC 1992: p. 387). The company also sent its engineers and technicians to England, Japan and the USA for training. They learned primarily manufacturing engineering, but also product development technology. In 1978 HMC established a manufacturing technology institute, the first one in Korea.

The first vehicle developed entirely in-house was a light truck. In June 1975, after having completed the manufacturing technological works for the pilot production of the Pony, a project team consisting of nine members from the above-mentioned department was organized. The team included an engineer who had been trained in a Ford design centre and three engineers who had been officially trained by ItalDesign for one year, during the Pony project. Relying on this experience and learning by failures, the small team successfully designed a light truck body. Reverse engineering studies on various Japanese models were particularly instructive (HMC 1992: p. 444).

In the latter half of the 1970s, after the Pony project had been completed, the R&D organization expanded to a division that included three departments in charge of passenger car development, commercial vehicle development and vehicle testing respectively. In addition, the division undertook prototype car building for the first time.

HMC's efforts to replace foreign technology with its own were now concentrated on designing body and chassis parts. As shown in Table 6.2, HMC steadily increased participation in developing body structure and body parts, from 20 per cent for the Pony to 60 per cent for the Pony Excel.

The increase in HMC's participation in body designing was achieved through its development of press dies for body parts. In 1975, the company sent some engineers to a Japanese die manufacturer where

Table 6.2 HMC's participation in new car development, 1974–84 (%)

Car	Pony	Pony II	Stellar	Pony Excel
Development period	Jan. 1974–Dec. 75	Jan. 1980–Dec. 81	Jan. 1981–May 83	Jan. 1982–Dec. 84
Styling design	0	0	0	0
Chassis design	30	35	30	10
Body design	20	45	50	60
Power train design	0	0	0	0

Source: Lee and Hyun (1985).

they were trained in press die design and manufacturing for 2½ years. Consequently, HMC became capable of developing press dies from the time of the Pony II.

Product market pressure in the world car market pushed HMC into technological learning. In contrast to Kia and Daewoo, who were not interested in car export, Hyundai was continually faced with unexpected technical and market difficulties in the export target countries: different climates, driver cultures, safety and emission regulations, to name but a few. For instance, in the Middle East and Latin America, many technical problems appeared in the Pony due to different climate and road conditions. HMC had to search for solutions and this was a good chance to upgrade technological and managerial capabilities. In another instance in 1978, the company made a long-term plan to enter the American market in the early 1980s. Hyundai had to face the strictest emission and safety regulations. HMC cooperated with America's specialized technical service companies for testing and modifying the regulation-related performances of the Pony. Olson and Calspan were contracted for car crashing tests and engine tuning for emission reduction. In this case also, Hyundai sent engineers for training and they participated in the modifications. Furthermore, it employed foreign experts in crash testing and emission control. In this way, HMC's engineers and technicians were able to gain valuable expertise (HMC 1992: p. 484). Through crash testing in particular, HMC's engineers began to acquire the basic mechanical know-how to design body and chassis structure.

Developing proprietary technology: the 1980s

The year 1983 was a turning point in HMC's R&D investment. The ratio of R&D expenditure to total sales remained around 1 per cent until 1981, then began to soar from 1982. Since the mid-1980s, it has stayed around 4 per cent, falling to 3 per cent between 1996 and 1997 (see Figure 6.4). The increase in R&D expenditure in the early 1980s was due to investment in vehicle testing facilities. HMC built a vehicle-testing track in 1984, the first one in Korea. Until then, HMC had had a small testing ground on which only limited testing was possible. For major vehicle testing HMC sent prototype cars to foreign specialized testing firms. With its own testing track, HMC was able to save time and costs. For this project, HMC licensed technical data from various sources: from specialized car testing firms such as MIRA, Calspan and Olson and also from Mercedes-Benz and MMC. At the same time, HMC established a crash test laboratory and an emission test laboratory to enhance its

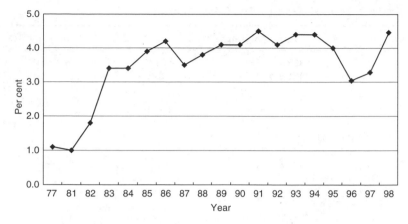

Figure 6.4   Ratio of R&D expenditures to sales in HMC, 1977–98
Source: Until the 1980s, HMC (1992); for the 1990s, HMC, *Annual Report*, yearly.

own capability to meet European and American safety and emission requirements.

In addition, HMC introduced the CAD/CAM system to computerize car designing. It was used for designing body parts first and then increasingly for designing body structure. Through simulations executed by the CAD/CAM, HMC's engineers were able to reduce the number of prototype cars, particularly those for crash testing. Consequently, HMC reduced expenditure on new products by 20 per cent (Chung M.-K. 1998).

The primary goal of the investment in vehicle testing functions and CAD/CAM was replacing imported and licensed technologies with in-house capabilities. The Sonata, developed during 1985–8, was the first case in which HMC tried to apply its own capabilities in various ways. The CAD/CAM system was used for designing body structure for the first time. In the case of the development of the Stellar, a compact car developed during 1981–3 (see the Table 6.2), prototype cars were built and tested but without simulation and analysis by the CAD/CAM system. This was one reason why the launch of the Stellar in the Canadian market in 1983 was followed by a chorus of consumer complaints arising from mechanical problems in the car structure. Learning from the failure, HMC emphasized the simulation of prototype cars using the CAD/CAM system before crash testing, and upgraded the mechanical performance of the body-chassis structure for the Sonata.

The Sonata was also the first car whose styling design was carried out by the company's own design studio. Of course, HMC also contracted

Table 6.3   Increasing capabilities of HMC in new car development, 1973–90

Car	Pony	Stellar	Excel	Sonata	Excel II	Scoup	Lantra
Launch year	1976	1983	1985	1988	1989	1990	1990
Segment (litres)	1.2–1.5	1.4–2.0	1.3–1.5	1.8–2.4	1.3–1.5	1.5	1.5–1.8
Styling design	0	0	0	2	2	2	2
Body design	0	2	1	2	2	2	2
Chassis design	0	1	1	1	1	1	1
Power train design	0	0	0	0	0	0	0

0 = developed mainly by foreign sources.
1 = developed partly by HMC and partly by foreign sources.
2 = developed mainly by HMC.
Source: Kim G. (1994: p. 218).

the car's styling design to ItalDesign, but this was only in order to secure various choices. In the final styling of the Sonata, HMC chose the in-house design. In the 1990s, HMC continued to contract style design to various foreign design houses. However, the purpose of the foreign outsourcing was, in contrast to the previous period, mainly to acquire and refer to information on new trends and concepts in car style in the world markets (Kim G. 1994: p. 219). Table 6.3 shows that, beginning with the Sonata, HMC did its own major body design and styling.

Throughout the 1970s and 1980s, however, HMC continued to license designs of power train and chassis layout from Mitsubishi. To overcome this dependence, HMC in 1984 founded the Mabukri Research Institute for power train development and launched long-run projects.

In 1984, the first engine development project started: it was called the Alpha project, and its aim was to develop a 1.5-litre engine for a sub-compact car. Because HMC had no knowledge of engine design, the company contracted it to Ricardo, a British engine design house. Ricardo was contracted to produce blueprints and a prototype engine, but it was also contracted to train six HMC engineers in basic engine design. As part of their training, they were allowed to participate in Ricardo's work for HMC.

In September 1985, Ricardo completed the engine design and presented a prototype engine and the blueprints, but the prototype engine was too big and heavy for a subcompact car and too expensive to manufacture. It was now up to HMC's engineers to modify the engine design. By 1989, the Alpha engine had undergone three full changes of basic design and 288 minor changes in detailed design. HMC's engineers successfully completed this task by themselves.

Without Ricardo's initial designing, training and instruction, HMC could not have developed the Alpha engine. However, it was HMC's engineers who completed the project (see also Chapter 8).

Mastering conventional car technology: the 1990s

In the 1990s, HMC expanded engine development projects and gradually replaced Mitsubishi-designed engines and platforms with its own (see Table 6.4). The Alpha engine was first installed in the Scoup, a small coupe car launched in 1990, for smaller scale mass production. But the Scoup still used the Mitsubishi-designed chassis structure developed for the Pony Excel because Hyundai had not yet developed a platform matching the Alpha engine. The Accent, a subcompact car launched in 1994, was the first Hyundai car that replaced the Mitsubishi-designed engine and platform.

The technological know-how acquired during the Alpha project was transferred to the second and third engine project, the Beta (1.6–2.0 litres) and the Gamma (2.0–2.4 litres). For the Beta project, HMC changed from Ricardo to AVL, an Austrian engine design house, in order to avoid becoming dependent on a single source of technology. This time, AVL was contracted only for the basic design. HMC's engineers completed detailed designing. AVL supervised the final stages of designing and testing prototype engines. The Beta engine was installed in the Avante,

Table 6.4 Capabilities of HMC in product development, 1991–8

Car	Scoup	Grandeur	Sonata II	Accent	Avante	Atoz	EF Sonata
Launch year	1990	1992	1993	1994	1995	1997	1998
Segment (litres)	1.5	2.0–3.0	1.8–2.4	1.3–1.5	1.5–1.8	0.8–1.0	1.8–2.5
Styling design	2	2	2	2	2	2	2
Body design	2	2	2	2	2	2	2
Power train design	2	0	1	2	2	2	2
Chassis design	1	0	1	2	2	2	2

0 = designed by Mitsubishi.
1 = designed by Mitsubishi and modified by Hyundai.
2 = designed by Hyundai.
Source: Kim G. (1994) for 1991–94 and various company data for 1995–98.

launched in 1995. The Gamma engine project ended in failure in 1994. The basic design by AVL caused too many problems with regard to manufacturability.

In the latter half of the 1990s, HMC developed the 0.8-litre Epsilon engine and installed it in the Atoz, a mini car launched in late 1997. The Delta engine (2.0–2.4 litres) was completed and installed in the EF Sonata, a compact car launched in 1998. In the meantime, HMC also developed the V6 Sigma engine (2.5, 3.0 and 3.5 litres) and the Alpha Lean-Burn engine independently of foreign design houses. By 1999, the company was fully capable of developing petrol-powered car engines. In late 2000, Hyundai succeeded in developing its first passenger car diesel engine. The Avante XD (called Lantra in European markets), fitted with a 2.0 litre diesel engine, was launched by 2001.

The EF Sonata marked a turning point in the technological capability building of HMC. Not only is it fitted with Hyundai's in-house designed platform, including the Delta engine, but it is also noteworthy for the technical data used for its development. HMC had previously used technical data acquired from Mitsubishi and other foreign sources. Technical data included not only officially licensed blueprints; data acquired through reverse engineering of foreign rival cars were also important. In CAD/CAM simulations and car crash testing, for instance, data and parameters acquired from such foreign sources played an important role. This meant that HMC continued to imitate technical specifications and engineering ideas. But during the two decades of indigenous car development efforts, HMC had accumulated its own empirical data and parameters acquired through repeated cycles of design, test, analysis and redesign. For the development of the EF Sonata, HMC applied those data and parameters for the first time.[14] That meant that HMC had become capable of developing cars without significant technology transfer from foreign sources. Now, the cycle of design, simulation, real testing, analysis of test results and redesign could be carried out within HMC.

6.4   HMC during and after the 1997 crisis

Slump and recovery

HMC's vehicle production increased steadily in the 1990s. It doubled from 650,000 vehicles to 1.28 million between 1990 and 1996. But the company also faced a sales slump due to the recession and the financial crisis during 1997–8. As a result, the capacity utilization rate, which had

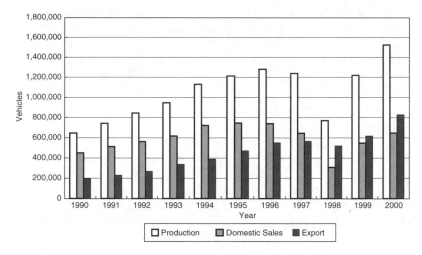

Figure 6.5 HMC's vehicle production, 1990–2000[a]
[a] For passenger cars and commercial vehicles.
Source: KARI, *Korean Automotive Industry*, 2000.

stayed around 90 per cent for the three years of 1994–6, dropped to 71 per cent in 1997 and 46 per cent in 1998.

However, its production recovered as early as 1999 and then soared to over 1.5 million vehicles by 2000. Exports led the production increase. In particular, cars fitted with Hyundai's in-house designed engines and platforms contributed to the second export boom. This was primarily because the engines and platforms developed by Hyundai significantly improved the quality of Hyundai cars. In the past, when Hyundai had used the blueprints of Mitsubishi-designed engines and other power train parts, it was not able to solve lots of technical quality problems occurring in these areas.

This is because tacit knowledge is difficult to transfer (Reber 1996; Sternberg and Horvath 1998): that is, Hyundai's engineers were, on the one hand, not able to understand the know-how, even less the know-why, of every design point, and on the other hand, Mitsubishi was not able to assist Hyundai because many of the problems were due to Hyundai cars' specific structures and components. In contrast, for Hyundai's in-house designed engines and platforms, Hyundai's engineers possessed the know-why of all relevant design points and could solve power train problems quickly.

Hyundai's car export to the US market has been growing rapidly from 1998. It nearly tripled between 1998 and 2000, from 90,000 vehicles to 244,000.

It increased again to 320,000 in 2001. The company's US market share increased from 1 per cent to 3 per cent between 1998 and 2001. Hyundai believes that the most important reason for the rapid increase is the 100,000 miles power train system warranty for first owners of Hyundai cars. Toyota is known to provide a 50,000 mile warranty for power train. Without the long-run capabilities building in power train development, Hyundai could not have set up such a risky and aggressive marketing strategy.

In the North American market, the company made efforts to dispel its low-end image by introducing medium and large-sized cars and recreational vehicles (RVs). They also recorded sales increases during 1998–2001. In spite of this, Hyundai cars' product quality values still belong to the median group in the US market. For instance, Hyundai cars' CSI (Consumer Satisfaction Index) in the US market ranked them twenty-ninth out of 37 automakers. This is similar to those of Nissan (twenty-seventh), Volkswagen (thirty-first) and Mitsubishi (thirty-third) and lower than that of Toyota (nineteenth: see *Korea Economic Daily*, 6 September 2001). And Hyundai cars' score of IQS (Initial Quality Study, conducted by J.D. Power) was 257 in 1998 and 224 in 1999. In the latter half of 2000, the score fell to 189, indicating a major improvement in the quality of Hyundai cars. Nevertheless, the score is still above the world industrial average of 157 (KARI 2001: p. 100). Hence, the company is making further efforts to enhance product quality.

Financial restructuring of HMC after the crisis

Figure 6.6 shows that Hyundai's sales increased steadily between 1989 and 2000, except for the period of stagnation in 1997 and downturn in 1998. The operating profit followed the same tendency, but the company's net profit shows a noticeable trend over the period. From 1989 to 1995, it followed the same tendency as the operating profit. But during 1996–7 it dropped, although the company's sales and operating profit increased. While the negative net profit in 1998 can be regarded as a natural consequence of the financial crisis, the sudden striking increase in the company's net profit in the following years, breaking records, demands an explanation.

The noticeable fluctuation of net profits can be understood as a result of changing financial expenditures. Historically, HMC's debt/equity ratio had remained between 300 and 500 per cent between 1985 and 1995. This ratio was usual for Korean firms. However, Figure 6.7 shows that HMC's debts grew fast during 1995–7, faster than the increase in assets.

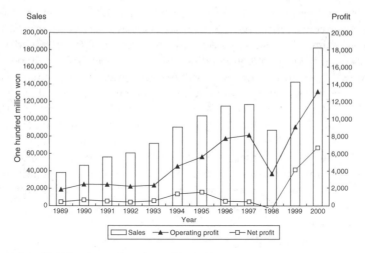

Figure 6.6   HMC's sales and profit, 1989–2000
Note: Operating profit refers to operating income and net profit refers to net income.
Source: HMC, *Annual Report*, yearly.

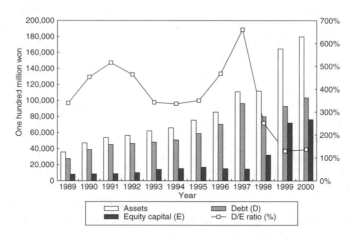

Figure 6.7   Financial structure of HMC, 1989–2000[a]
[a] The abrupt increase in assets in 1999 was due to the merger of Hyundai Precision Company's RVs unit and Hyundai Auto Service Company with HMC. As mentioned previously, Hyundai Precision Company (renamed Hyundai Mobis in 2000) is now the quasi-holding company of HMC. Chung Mong-Gu, the eldest son of the founder Chung Ju-Young, inherited HMC, and merged Hyundai Precision Company's RV unit and Hyundai Service Company, both belonging to him, with HMC.
Source: HMC, *Annual Report*, yearly.

We mentioned in Chapter 3 that deregulation and the opening of Korea's financial sector during 1993–7 resulted in excessive credit expansion. At the same time, the company's equity capital decreased for 1996 and 1997. Consequently, the debt/equity ratio grew steeply, from 350 to 660 per cent between 1995 and 1997, and fast growing interest payments pressed HMC towards low and negative net profits between 1996 and 1998.[15]

Faced with the financial crisis from late 1997 and throughout 1998, HMC radically restructured its financial structure by reducing debts and raising equity capital. As a result, the debt/equity ratio fell to 251 per cent by late 1998 and then to around 129 per cent by 1999. Since then it has remained at around 130 per cent. Lower financial expenditure, in spite of rising operational profits, contributed to the rapid growth in net profits since 1999.

6.5   Conclusion

HMC's remarkable accomplishments in technological learning and car exports have made the company an excellent example of Korea's achievement in catching up industrially. The competitive advantages of HMC today are the result of its firm-specific strategies and capabilities developed over the past few decades. HMC's success owes much to its insistence on maintaining national corporate control. Hyundai rejected any cooperation with transnational carmakers which might have limited its ability to export. By retaining full corporate control and unlimited access to the world market, HMC set out on a path of technological learning and this strategic choice eventually paid off. This in turn shows that the concentrated ownership and control structure of the *chaebol* has been crucial, in spite of what the advocates of shareholder value theory say about the distortions of shareholder values and firms' incentive structure.

Also, the strategic determination of top management, supported by the government's industrial policy, resulted in active technological learning. In contrast with Kia and Daewoo, HMC searched for various foreign sources of technology to avoid dependence on particular foreign providers of technology.

Product market pressure from export markets pushed HMC to technological and organizational learning. In contrast with Kia and Daewoo, who were not interested in car exports, or were reliant on GM and Ford, Hyundai continually faced problems arising from diverse requirements of export target countries. This forced the company to search for technical and organizational solutions.

HMC did not significantly change its strategies in the 1990s, in spite of liberalization and globalization in the Korean economy. In the 1990s, HMC succeeded in developing and launching its own engines and platforms, gradually replacing Mitsubishi-designed technology. The company has mastered conventional car technologies, and is shifting its focus to cutting edge R&D areas.

In spite of a serious sales slump during the financial crisis, especially in 1998, it soon recovered. Since 1999, the company's car exports to the US market have been increasing. In particular, cars fitted with Hyundai's in-house designed engines and platforms contributed to the second export boom. On the basis of this sales success, HMC restructured itself financially by reducing debts and raising equity capital. Rising sales, combined with lower interest payments, have contributed to rapid growth in profitability since 1999. Now, together with Samsung Electronics and other well-performing *chaebol* companies, HMC is once again leading the Korean economy. Its pre-crisis achievements in technological learning and car export laid the foundation for post-crisis success.

7
Daewoo's Global Management

Founded in 1962 as Saenara Auto Company, Daewoo Motor Company (DMC) is Korea's oldest carmaker. In 1998 it was the second largest carmaker in Korea, with an annual production capacity of 2 million cars worldwide.

The first studies of DMC appeared in the late 1980s, when the company was still under GM's control. Ryu *et al.* (1989) reported that the company's ongoing crisis throughout the 1970s and 1980s was largely due to GM's transnational strategy. On the verge of bankruptcy in 1992, DMC separated from GM. At about this time, Daewoo Group commenced an ambitious period of global expansion, including the car business. Between 1995 and 1997, when Daewoo's global network of production, R&D, and sales and marketing was being set in place, business scholars carried out case studies of Daewoo (see Kim T.-K. 1997; Choe J.-Y. 1998; Park C.-H. 1998).

Unfortunately Daewoo Group and DMC collapsed in August 1999 under massive debts amounting to US$60 billion. This was one of the world's largest bankruptcies. The scale of Daewoo's collapse has caused it to be seen as the embodiment of 'inefficient East Asian firms'. Liberal scholars and policy-makers felt that industrial policy and cronyism, wrong corporate governance and low transparency, high debts and low profitability were the primary causes of the corporate failure.

DMC's failure in the 1970s–1980s and then Daewoo's bankruptcy in 1999 paint quite a different picture, however. First, DMC (GM-Korea in the 1970s) was exempt from industrial policy until 1992, because of the dominance of its 'partner'. Section 7.2 will show the ways in which this transnational dominance prevented the company from developing organizational capabilities. Second, Daewoo's global expansion in the 1990s, which ultimately led to the collapse, had been made possible by the opening of the capital account and abolition of industrial policy. Sections 7.3–7.6 will analyse Daewoo's strategies and capabilities in the 1990s, in association with the liberalization and globalization of the Korean economy in the period, and discuss the real reasons for the failure. Third, as we will see in section 7.1, DMC's corporate governance was very similar to that of HMC, and yet HMC performed very well. Daewoo's failure was rather due to its path dependency in organizational routines (its reliance on entrepreneurial core capabilities), which turned out to be core rigidities.

7.1 Daewoo Group and Daewoo Motor Company

History and business

DMC was one of the largest companies of Daewoo Group. Daewoo Group, the second largest *chaebol* (by assets) in 1997, included 33 domestic companies (see Figure 7.1) and 372 overseas affiliates in the diverse business areas of trade, finance, automotives, shipbuilding, machinery, electronics, telecommunication, construction, and so on. The group employed 320,000 people around the world, and accounted for 8 per cent

Trade, Finance and Services	Automobile and Services
Daewoo Corporation	Daewoo Motor Company
Daewoo Securities Company	Daewoo Motor Sales Company
Daewoo Financial Service Company	Daewoo Capital Management Company
Daewoo Venture Capital Company	4 other companies
Daewoo Hilton Hotel	**Shipbuilding and Machinery**
4 other companies	Daewoo Heavy Industry Ltd
Construction	**Electronics and Telecommunications**
Daewoo Corporation (construction division)	Daewoo Electronics Company
Kyengnam Enterprises Company	Daewoo Telecom Ltd
Daewoo Development Company	Orion Electronic Company
4 other companies	6 other companies

Figure 7.1 Daewoo Group and its 33 subsidiaries, 1997

of the Korean economy. It recorded sales of US$71.5 billion in 1997, and was ranked eighteenth in *Fortune* magazine's Global 500 list.

Daewoo Group's origins lie in a trading company. Kim Woo-Choong, the founding chairman of the group, established the Daewoo Industrial Company(DIC), a small apparel trading company, in 1967. It soon became the second largest apparel exporter in Korea. In the early 1970s, the company moved from apparel trading to textile manufacturing. In the early 1970s when the Korean government prompted *chaebol* groups towards heavy industrialization, the company diversified further into manufacturing industries such as shipbuilding, automobiles and consumer electronics. In 1978, DIC acquired a 50 per cent share of GM-Korea, the second largest car manufacturer at the time.

Whereas other *chaebol*, such as Hyundai and Samsung, have been known for their technological catch-up, Daewoo Group has been characterized by its strength in international trading know-how and outstanding financing skills. The founding chairman, Kim Woo-Choong, created Daewoo's special competence. From the beginnings of Daewoo in the late 1960s, he continually travelled worldwide to exploit new overseas markets and to establish global branches. He was a born international businessman.

In 1982, DIC was transformed into a general trading company and renamed Daewoo Corporation (DC). DC encapsulated the core capabilities of Daewoo, and played the role of quasi-holding company for most of the subsidiaries and overseas branches. Daewoo's globalization strategy in the 1990s can be regarded as a global expansion of DC's existing capabilities into emerging markets, making use of the new financial market liberalization.

Between 1993 and 1998, DC made major investments in Poland, Romania, the Czech Republic, Uzbekistan, Vietnam, China and India, primarily for global manufacturing and sale of motor vehicles. In contrast with the 1970s–1980s, when GM dominated DMC, the car business became one of the most important aspects of Daewoo's global operation. Manufacturing bases for home appliances and consumer electronics were also established in France, Vietnam, Mexico and Latin America. There were, moreover, many overseas investment projects in the fields of telecommunications services, local banks and financial institutions. As of December 1997, Daewoo was involved in over 380 overseas investment projects mobilizing US$20 billion.

Ownership and control

The ownership and control structure of Daewoo is typical of the Korean *chaebol* (see Figure 7.2). At the top of the pyramid hierarchy were the

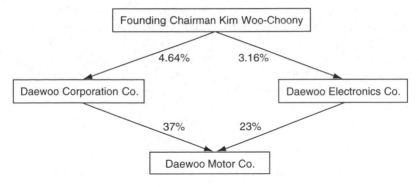

Figure 7.2 Ownership and control structure of DMC, 1997
Source: People's Solidarity for Participatory Democracy (1999: p. 119).

shareholdings owned directly by the founding chairman, Kim.[1] His shareholdings were concentrated in a small number of subsidiaries. He firmly controlled DC and Daewoo Electronics (DE), the two cash-cow companies of the group, by owning 4.64 per cent and 3.16 per cent of their shares respectively.[2] In the case of DMC, DC and DE were the primary shareholders, owning 37 per cent and 23 per cent respectively. Together with 8.5 per cent of shares owned by Daewoo Telecom, the intragroup shareholding of DMC amounted to 68.5 per cent.[3]

The pyramid structure of intersubsidiary shareholdings made it possible for the chairman to control DMC without owning any shares. Legally, he was neither a member of the directorial board nor a manager of DMC. Nonetheless, he used to nominate all company directors and managers and control strategic decision-making. In the following sections, we will see how he led the group with his vision and strategy.

7.2 Legacies of GM dependency: 1972–92

Birth of a KD assembler

Daewoo Motor Company (DMC) is the oldest automaker in Korea. It dates from 1962 when the military government of Park Chung-Hee passed the Auto Industry Law. The law prohibited imports of finished cars and instead promised favourable tariffs for components imported for assembly. As a result, Saenara Auto Company was established with the first modern assembly plant in Korea. It was a small plant with a capacity of 6,000 passenger cars a year, assembling imported semi-knocked down kits of the Nissan Bluebird. It was initially a profitable business but was forced to cease operation in 1963 because of a foreign currency shortage.

In 1966, Shinjin took over Saenara and started to assemble the Corona, a Toyota subcompact car, under a licensing arrangement. Shinjin's operation was profitable as the Auto Industry Law continued to guarantee Shinjin's monopolization of over 80 per cent of vehicle production in Korea. However, faced with criticism of Shinjin's monopolist profit, the government changed the law and allowed other companies to enter the car industry. By 1971, five automakers – Shinjin, Hyundai, Kia, Asia and Hadonghwan (later Ssangyong) – were engaged in KD production.

Establishment of GM-Korea in 1972

In spite of the other companies' entrance, Shinjin expected to maintain its leading position, but Toyota suddenly withdrew from Korea in 1970 when China announced 'Chou's Four Principles', which prohibited foreign companies from operating in China if they invested in South Korea or Taiwan. Consequently, Shinjin had to look for another foreign partner. Shinjin came to a 50:50 joint venture agreement with GM and established GM-Korea in 1972.[4] GM succeeded in acquiring management control of the company due to its technological, financial and strategic advantages.[5] GM-Korea built plants with a capacity of 35,000 cars and 50,000 engines a year.

GM-Korea's failures in the 1970s

GM-Korea's dependence on GM's transnational strategy seriously impeded its performance, however. First of all, the company failed to adapt to the rapidly changing Korean market. GM-Korea produced cars developed originally for the American market. It assembled CKD kits of the Chevrolet 1700 from September 1972, in the midst of the First Oil Shock. But this vehicle was too heavy and large and its fuel consumption was notorious among Korean drivers. The car was known to have failed in the American and Australian markets for the same reasons. Nonetheless, GM chose the wrong car for the Korean market, hoping to compensate for the failure. But GM sold merely 4,591 units in 1973, 1,099 in 1974, 675 in 1975, and 399 in 1976. The Chevrolet 1500, despite its smaller displacement of 1.5 litres, had an even worse fuel economy and only 907 units were sold during 1976–8.[6]

GM-Korea's market share in Korea dropped from over 60 per cent to 15 per cent between 1972 and 1976. Kia's Brisa, a small car licensed from Mazda, dominated the market. Then Hyundai's Pony, launched in 1976, introduced a fundamental change into the Korean car market. In spite of continuing failures, however, GM did not change its market strategy. Scale economies on a worldwide basis seemed to be more important for GM than adapting to a small market in a developing country. The losses of GM-Korea led Shinjin, the Korean partner, to bankruptcy in 1976. The Korea Industrial Bank, a government bank specializing in industrial promotion, took over the equity of Shinjin and then sold it to the Daewoo Group in 1978.[7]

Exemption from industry policy

As we mentioned in Chapter 5, the turning point in the development of the Korean automobile industry was 1973, when the government enacted its Long-term Promotion Plan for the Automobile Industry. The government selected three major carmakers – GM-Korea, Hyundai and Kia – for production of a 'People's Car'. The car was required to be small and affordable. In addition, in view of the export ban imposed by foreign carmakers based on intellectual property rights, the car was required to have a national proprietary design for the purpose of free export. The 1973 Plan also anticipated that content localization could be best achieved by localization of new car development and it required 100 per cent localization of parts and components manufacturing by 1981. In return, the government promised full financial and fiscal support to successful companies.

As already mentioned, HMC was the star pupil of the industrial policy. It successfully developed the Pony and immediately became a market leader. The car's rate of content localization reached 85 per cent in 1976 and 100 per cent in 1980. In addition, the Pony could be exported to countries in Latin America and the Middle East.

In contrast, Kia did not follow government industrial policy. Even though it steadily increased content localization, the company continued to produce cars licensed from Mazda, Fiat and Peugeot. The Brisa licensed from Mazda was a big hit due to its fuel efficiency. Kia was satisfied with its success and sceptical about the government's national car plan.

GM-Korea, as a subsidiary of the world's biggest multinational firm, was exempted from the 1973 Plan from the beginning.[8] While Hyundai and Kia shifted to full localization, GM-Korea maintained its KD production until 1979. Despite continuing failures, GM regarded a localized car for the small Korean market as unnecessary, and exporting cars from Korea to foreign markets was out of the question. The American management of GM-Korea, responding to the government plan and Hyundai's Pony project, asserted in 1974 that, in view of the low technological capabilities of Hyundai and the country, Hyundai could never develop a national car. It announced at the same time that GM-Korea would not follow the Korean government's reckless plan.

GM-Korea's content localization had reached only 35 per cent by 1975. Most primary components (body panels, transaxles, transmissions, etc.) were imported as KD kits. Only secondary components (tyres, pipes, lamps, seats, etc.) were localized. It was not until 1979 that GM-Korea localized body panel production.

Restructuring in the early 1980s

As mentioned in Chapters 5 and 6, GM-Korea and Hyundai came into conflict in 1980 when the new military government, concerned about excessive capacity in the car industry, ordered Hyundai and GM-Korea to merge their car operations and establish a monopolized carmaker. But the plan failed when GM refused to turn management control over to Hyundai.

In the meantime, the viability of GM-Korea (renamed Saehan in 1976) steadily deteriorated. In 1980–2, the capacity utilization rate fell below 30 per cent. In fact, the company hardly made a profit in its first 10 years of operation. Daewoo Group, the Korean partner of GM-Korea since 1978, had not been very interested in GM-Korea's operation. But in 1982, Daewoo and GM agreed that Daewoo would take charge of daily operations. The name of the company was changed from Saehan to Daewoo Motor Company, and the Daewoo Group strengthened marketing, services, and financing for the company. In spite of this, however, GM continued to dominate DMC. Although Daewoo was in charge of personnel, labour relations, production and domestic sales, GM held veto rights on strategic investment plans. Besides, it was GM that held the key to the foreign technology.

In 1983, DMC launched the Maepsy, an updated subcompact car. As the domestic car market recovered from the Second Oil Crisis, the Maepsy helped DMC increase domestic car sales. In 1983, the company earned record profits.

1987–92: the LeMan project for OEM export

In 1984, GM and Daewoo announced that they would produce small cars for sale in Korea and America. According to the project, DMC would produce the LeMan, a minor variation of the Opel-designed Kadett, and export it to the US market with the GM-Pontiac brand.[9] In June 1984,

GM and Daewoo signed an agreement on the LeMan project. Daewoo's chairman Kim explained his strategy by saying that 'we needed a car urgently and did not have time to do it ourselves. Besides, it's better not to gamble too much. Everyone knows the GM and Pontiac name' (Badaracco 1988).

The LeMan project was a quantum leap in the company's business history. First, DMC's production capacity increased ten fold from 40,000 to 400,000 units. The first LeMan plant was completed in 1986 with a capacity of 167,000 cars and a second plant, with the same capacity, was completed in late 1988. For the new operation, Fordist and Taylorist principles were introduced for the first time. Before the LeMan, manual hoists and plates were used, allowing a production of five or six cars an hour. But the new assembly plant's conveyor machines finished 28–29 cars an hour, and this soon increased to 38 cars.[10] Daewoo's managers also introduced the concept of TQC (total quality circle) learned from Isuzu and Nissan.

The second major development was that the LeMan was the first car exported by DMC, even though export was limited to the US market and marketing and sales were organized not by DMC but by GM's Pontiac division.

In spite of great expectations, however, DMC was once again left with big losses. Originally, GM promised that it would import 100,000 LeMans to America yearly. This was a part of GM's plan to supply one million subcompact cars produced overseas to the US market. In reality, however, the total number of LeMan exported to America between 1987 and 1992 was only 321,500 units (see Figure 7.3). Moreover, domestic sales did not increase, either. Hyundai's Pony Excel and Kia's Pride (Ford Festiva) defeated the LeMan in the Korean market. The capacity utilization rate of the LeMan plants averaged only 35 per cent.

The failure of the LeMan project was partly due to Daewoo's expansion strategy. The establishment of the second LeMan plant proved to be a major error. It was Daewoo that had insisted on the establishment of the second LeMan plant even though GM opposed the plan. The chairman, Kim, expected that DMC would eventually export the LeMan not only to the US market but also elsewhere. Later when the failure of the LeMan project became apparent, GM blamed Daewoo for reckless investment in the second plant.

However, the failure can be regarded as a result of DMC's full dependence on GM. First, GM only allowed DMC to export the LeMan to America. Indeed, Daewoo wanted to export the car to other countries due to stagnating sales in America. However, this was unthinkable for

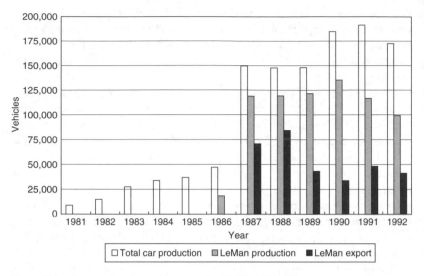

Figure 7.3   Car production and export by DMC, 1981–92
Source: KAMA (Korea Automobile Manufacturers Association), *Automotive Statistics*, yearly.

GM because Opel, the German subsidiary of GM and the proprietor of the car design, was exporting the Kadett worldwide except America.

Second, GM was not very interested in sales of the LeMan in the US market. In the late 1980s, DMC was merely one of the various OEM car suppliers to GM. The Nummi plant in America had been in operation since 1984 and Isuzu of Japan also supplied subcompact cars to GM. Besides, the product quality of cars manufactured by Nummi and Isuzu was higher than that of DMC. This was partly because DMC was suffering from chronic labour disputes at this time and partly because of the low technological capability of Korea's component suppliers. In view of continuing labour disputes and increasing labour costs, GM lost confidence in DMC. Falling oil prices also made GM inclined to sell bigger and more lucrative cars.

Third, the production costs and sales price of the LeMan were higher than those of the Hyundai Excel and Kia Pride.[11] This was partly due to the total dependence of DMC on GM technology. All the blueprints of the car and components had been bought from Opel. DMC paid a licensing royalty of US$120 for each sale. Besides, several key components for, say, engine and transmission, were imported directly from German suppliers of Opel or from Japanese suppliers of Isuzu, regardless of unfavourable foreign exchange rates.

Limited capability building under GM dominance

The limited authority of DMC in technology caused many problems. DMC was experiencing technical problems with both the car and the manufacturing process, but was not allowed to make anything other than cosmetic changes to the design.

For instance, engine noise was a serious problem for DMC in the local market.[12] The engine had been developed for German driving conditions but, because of the speed limit on Korean highways, Korean drivers did not need high-speed performance and were unhappy with the car's engine noise.[13] DMC demanded that Opel redesign the engine to lower the noise, but Opel and GM refused. That is, Opel and GM-Pontiac wanted a certain level of engine noise for German and American customers but, as DMC had only one engine plant, it was impossible for the company to manufacture engines for both the Korean and the American markets. Moreover, around 50,000 DMC-manufactured engines were supplied to Opel for the Kadett. This was yet another reason for Opel to resist any modification of the engine designs.

Problems also occurred with respect to the manufacturability of Opel-designed parts and components.[14] DMC's engineers often found it either too complicated or too expensive to manufacture parts exactly according to Opel's blueprints. This was partly because of the different technological and industrial conditions found in Korea and partly because the technological capabilities of DMC and its suppliers were lower than those of their German counterparts. DMC then sent letters to Opel demanding design changes but Opel either did not respond for months or answered with comments that were irrelevant to the Korean situation and therefore useless.

Clark and Fujimoto (1991: p. 121) point out, however, that engineering changes (changes to product and manufacturing process) are the rule rather than the exception in car production, and that good management of the content, timing and method of changes is critical.

Strong and active communication and feedback between DMC and Opel on technological matters were rare. Of course, Opel did train DMC engineers in accordance with the OEM licensing agreement. During preparations for production of the LeMan, DMC sent hundreds of engineers and technicians to Germany for six months, mainly to learn manufacturing technology. Later, in the pilot production stage, dozens of Opel's technical personnel were relocated to Korea and assisted DMC in setting up.[15]

Once commercial production began, however, Opel was responsible only for product quality. The task of finding solutions for technical problems in product and manufacturing was DMC's alone. DMC acquired additional manufacturing technology from machinery and equipment suppliers. They not only trained DMC's technical personnel, but also helped DMC to find solutions for problems arising from Korea- and DMC-specific industrial and technological conditions.[16] This was a typical case of incremental innovation based on user-producer interaction, as described by Lundvall (1992: p. 45). Of course, such interactive learning between user and producer was also seen in Hyundai and Kia.

Chronic losses with the LeMan production

Low production and sales figures for the LeMan meant deteriorating financial performance for DMC. The company recorded net losses for every year of LeMan production (1987–92), except 1990 (see Table 7.1). The cumulative losses, in 1991 and 1992 in particular, reduced equity capital from 247.8 billion won in 1990 to 3.5 billion won in 1992. At the same time, the debts grew rapidly, from 976.5 billion won in 1987 to 2,963.3 billion won in 1992. By 1992, the company was on the verge of collapse.

Separation from GM

In the 1980s the 50:50 ownership and control shared by GM and Daewoo did not change. The directorial board consisted of four GM members and four Daewoo members, and hence important investment decisions could only be made through negotiations and compromises. This governance structure limited the company's strategic choices and capability building, as we have seen. A DMC executive explained Daewoo's growing need for a more independent strategy as follows: 'GM considered DMC as just one more factory in its worldwide network serving the

Table 7.1   Financial statements of DMC, 1987–92 (hundred million won)

	1987	1988	1989	1990	1991	1992
Sales	9,618	10,491	11,413	15,430	15,956	17,067
Operating income	340	297	401	992	0.7	864
Net income	−53	−97	−163	102	−1,467	−956
Assets	12,400	12,295	15,366	19,977	24,569	29,668
Debts (D)	9,765	9,760	12,991	17,499	23,568	29,633
Equity capital (E)	2,635	2,535	2,375	2,478	1,000	35
D/E ratio (%)	371	385	547	706	2,357	84,666

Source: *Maeil Economic Daily, Annual Corporation Reports.*

Korean domestic market and providing low cost vehicles for the U.S. market. However, DMC wanted to pursue a larger market opportunity' (Park C.-H. 1998: p. 4).

Once the pilot production of the LeMan was completed, Daewoo wanted to develop a proprietary car like the Hyundai Pony. However, GM's directors opposed the idea. For the four years during which the LeMan was produced and exported, GM had no plan to launch new cars for the Korean subsidiary. As a matter of fact, GM itself was facing strategic difficulties in America at the time and was not concerned about DMC.[17]

In the early 1990s, while Hyundai and Kia were benefiting from the motorization of Korean society, DMC's domestic market share dropped to 17 per cent and capacity utilization rate fell below 50 per cent in 1992. Daewoo Group wanted to rescue DMC by raising funds. Because of the 50:50 capital participation agreement, however, Daewoo alone could not increase capital investment if GM did not want the same investment. Daewoo proposed that GM and Daewoo each invest US$100 million in DMC and establish a new car R&D organization, but GM rejected this proposal.

In 1990, DMC launched the Espero, its first proprietary car. It was developed during 1987–9 without assistance from GM. Because its platform was only a slight variation of the LeMan, GM-Opel limited sales to the Korean market. But the car proved to be a total market failure, even in the Korean market, because of poor quality. This in turn was because GM did not provide technical assistance and DMC itself had lower technological capabilities than either Hyundai or Kia.

In 1992, Daewoo finally concluded that only separation from GM could save DMC from ongoing crisis. GM also wanted to withdraw. In December 1992, Daewoo acquired GM's 50 per cent equity and management control.

7.3   Daewoo Group's 'global management' strategy in the 1990s

After the break-up with GM, Daewoo made important strategic changes. This coincided with the new Korean government's push for free market economic reforms, the abolition of industrial policy and deregulation of the financial sector, including the opening of the capital account. It was Daewoo that most welcomed the new policies. In March 1993, the group chairman, Kim, announced 'global management' as Daewoo's new strategy. During 1993–7, when Korean *chaebol* were overflowing with foreign capital, Daewoo made efforts to globalize its financial network as well as its production. It particularly sought out emerging markets in Eastern Europe, Central Asia and Southeast Asia.

As the auto sector was only one, even though it was the most important, of the diverse business lines of the Daewoo Group, and because DMC was not an independent company but merely a subsidiary of the group, we will first look at the strategy of the group overall.

Underdeveloped technological capabilities

In the late 1980s and early 1990s, the competitiveness of Daewoo's major manufacturing sectors was deteriorating. Hyundai took the lead in automobile and shipbuilding and Samsung and LG in electronics and information technology (IT) industries, based on long-run technological learning. In contrast, Daewoo's competitive advantage was in finance and trade.

The reason for the relative backwardness of Daewoo in manufacturing products was more strategic than structural. Even though Daewoo had an ownership and control structure similar to that of the other *chaebol* groups, the group had followed a strategy that neglected the importance of technological capability building. While Samsung and LG were shifting their core competence in electronics from house appliances to semiconductor and IT products, and Hyundai was developing its in-house designed engines and launching higher-priced cars and ships, Daewoo remained satisfied with the position of cost leader in lower-priced product markets.

Daewoo's new strategy of 'global management' did not involve any significant change in its attitude to technology; rather, Daewoo extended it globally. In projecting the strategy, Daewoo's top management described itself in the following terms:

> The technological capability of Daewoo in automobile and electronics is not sufficient to compete with rivals in high-tech product markets. We will not reach such a level of capabilities until 2010. Thus, world-class products are not our rational choice of strategy for the time being. But we are still competitive in manufacturing technologies. Technical and managerial skill and know-how of factory engineers and other technical personnel are comparable to those of our rivals ... The low-priced products market is our niche. Small cars of 1.5–2.0-litres, TVs, refrigerators, washing machines, and microwaves are such products. These price-sensitive markets are the targets of the 'global strategy'. (Choe J.-Y. 1998: p. 293)

Hence, Daewoo did not want to concentrate on markets in industrialized countries, where first-class firms dominate. In the Korean market Daewoo also found that the price-sensitive product markets narrowed as national incomes grew. Thus, Daewoo decided to focus on emerging market regions. 'In North America and Western Europe, it is unavoidable to compete with rivals with first class technology and global brands. But in developing countries and emerging markets, Daewoo's products of mid-quality and relatively low prices would be competitive enough' (Song I. 1998: p. 37).

Using financial market globalization

Even though Daewoo's manufacturing companies were weaker than their counterparts, Daewoo's financial and trade companies, especially the Daewoo Corporation (international trade and finance) and Daewoo Securities (securities brokerage), were leaders in their areas. Daewoo's founding chairman, Kim Woo-Choong, created these characteristics. Led by Kim directly, DC explored and exploited new markets, organized regional and global trading and financing, took over local companies and established joint ventures, and solved problems in Daewoo-specific ways.

The financial market opening and deregulation urged by the WTO and IMF provided Daewoo with a great opportunity. As mentioned in Chapter 3, financial liberalization made it possible for *chaebol* groups to acquire foreign credits and capital directly, without the mediation of Korean financial institutions and government bodies. To fund its global projects, Daewoo relied directly on the international loan and bond markets.

As seen in Table 7.2, the total overseas investments of Daewoo amounted to US$20 billion in January 1996. Daewoo needed to raise only US$3.5 billion to pay for its equity shares in these 168 projects. Local partners raised around US$2.4 billion, and US$12 billion (60 per cent of the total investments), was financed directly from international financial markets in London and elsewhere.[18] International lenders included the largest banks such as Chase Manhattan, Citibank, HSBC, Tokyo-Mitsubishi and UBS.

Use of financial market globalization meant that, at the end of 1997, only 15 per cent of the total debt was owed to Korean financial institutions. Some 85 per cent (US$16 billion) had been borrowed directly from the international financial market. For intragroup control of Daewoo's global financial transactions, Daewoo had established the BFC (British Financial Centre) in London as a department of DC.

Table 7.2 Daewoo's overseas investments, as of January 1996 (US$ million)

	Recently announced			Still under negotiation		
	Projects[a]	Total costs	Daewoo's contribution	Projects	Total costs	Daewoo's contribution[b]
Asia	41	6,903	1,529	52	4,425	676
Africa/Middle East	7	277	68	7	355	136
CIS/Europe	14	3,452	587	26	3,753	392
America	11	396	83	10	71	9
Total	73	11,028	2,267	95	8,604	1,213

[a] Projects include joint ventures, and exclude completed and operating.
[b] Daewoo's contribution is the amount of paid-in capital.
Source: *The Economist*, 27 January 1996.

In order to reduce the risks inherent in the huge international investment, Daewoo preferred establishing joint ventures to creating local subsidiaries. In the case of the Polish firm, Fabryka Samachodow Osowych (FSO), Daewoo needed US$1.2 billion during 1995–8. Some 60 per cent of the funds were provided by international financial institutions, for which the Polish government guaranteed repayment. For the 50:50 joint venture, the Polish government and Daewoo each provided capital of US$240 million. In this way, the Polish government shared the risk.

Besides, Daewoo made every effort to minimize its own contribution. In the case of FSO, Daewoo did not pay all of the US$240 million of paid-in capital from its own coffers; 80 per cent of the money was borrowed from the Trade Bank of Korea. Consequently, Daewoo needed only US$48 million cash for FSO.

Daewoo was further able to reduce its own cash contribution to total overseas projects by around 15 per cent by contributing in kind: for example, by contributing machines manufactured by or dismantled from Daewoo's subsidiaries in Korea (Choe J.-Y. 1998: p. 289).

Despite all its efforts to lessen risk, the huge international debts and, at the same time, the small amount of cash contributed by Daewoo made Daewoo's global business extremely vulnerable to global financial market turbulence, as events were to show.

Diversification as capability and strategy

The top management of HMC, particularly Chung Se-Young, wanted to transform the company into a specialized carmaker, independent of the

Hyundai Group. Since its entrance into the North American markets in the mid-1980s and throughout the 1990s, HMC had extended its autonomy in finance, personnel and technology. By contrast, DMC, under the direct leadership of the chairman, was always, despite its importance, only a business unit of the conglomerate. DC, Daewoo's leading company, profoundly influenced DMC's business. DMC was dependent on DC in recruiting top managers, raising funds, launching strategy and setting organizational routines.

The chairman, Kim, regarded Daewoo group's diversification into various product lines as one of its core capabilities. In advanced economies, firms specializing in specific products with excellent product technology predominate in each sector: Sony in electronics, Ford, GM and Toyota in cars, ABB in machinery, and so on. According to Kim, however, Daewoo's conglomerate form of corporate organization could turn into a strength in emerging market countries, where industries were underdeveloped and governments wanted to learn from the success of Korea's industrialization strategy from the 1960s to the 1980s, when the mixed business lines of the *chaebol* worked well.

Thus when DMC entered the Polish market, Daewoo Electronics, Daewoo Construction, Daewoo Telecom, and so on, moved simultaneously. DC coordinated the complicated investment projects. This strategy proved to be successful when, in 1995, Daewoo took over FSO, the largest Polish carmaker. General Motors was defeated by Daewoo even though it had endeavoured for years to acquire the Polish state enterprise. General Motors' approach to the Polish auto market had been careful because, as a specialized automaker, it could not run the risks of a transitional economy. By contrast, Daewoo's proposal to invest in important industries simultaneously was very attractive to the Polish government which was seeking foreign investors after the introduction of market economy.

Daewoo's investment project in Uzbekistan was yet another typical case of Daewoo's diversification strategy. After gaining independence from the Soviet Union, President Kharimov's ambition was to turn Uzbekistan into a strong economic power in Central Asia through industrial development and export promotion. This required foreign investment. However, companies from the industrialized countries were cautious because of political uncertainty, the large current account deficit, the growing external debt burden, regulatory controls on banking transactions and so on and so on. Siemens, Lufthansa and Cargill, amongst others, had business interests in Uzbekistan, but none of them had been willing to make a substantial investment. Japanese firms, which had invested in developing countries in the 1960s–1970s, were also reluctant. Daewoo was the first foreign firm that committed itself to a large-scale manufacturing plant in Uzbekistan. The Uz-Daewoo auto plant became a leading symbol of Uzbekistan's industrial development (Park C.-H. 1998).

Kharimov was impressed by Korea's history of government-led high-growth economic development in the 1960s and 1970s, and hoped that Uzbekistan might be able to replicate the experience. Daewoo's diversified lines of business and its sheer size also helped the government's plan. Daewoo increased its role in other key industries such as cotton, electronics and telecommunications. A Western businessman watched:

> Size helped in Uzbekistan. Small [foreign] companies are often frustrated by the regulations and bureaucracy. Given the limited currency convertibility and the various development needs, Daewoo's multiple lines of business helped a lot. For example, it seems that Daewoo can buy cotton with local currency earnings and export it, which is impossible for me to do. While other firms are still hesitant to invest, Daewoo has a myriad of business opportunities to offer to Uzbekistan, because the company operates in so many fields. (cited in Park C.-H. 1998: p. 10).

Daewoo was able to solve the hard currency problem, the most serious risk in investing in an emerging market, through its diversified business. The business of Uz-Daewoo Auto was designed so as to generate hard currency through car exports to the CIS countries, as the Uzbekistan government gave the company a higher priority in hard currency allocation. Despite this, currency convertibility was an ongoing challenge and constrained further investment in the auto plant. Kim Woo-Choong wanted to solve the problem through the cotton business: that is, DC could export cotton from Uzbekistan worldwide to earn US dollars, which would then solve the hard currency problem. To earn more hard currency, DC expanded the cotton business and established a range of value-added operations from cotton spinning to apparel manufacturing. Consequently, Daewoo helped the Uzbekistan government not only to solve the hard currency problem but also to establish new export industries.

Uz-Daewoo Electronics was established in 1994 and Aloca-Daewoo, a joint venture between Daewoo-Telecom and the Uzbekistan government, in 1995. Aloca-Daewoo was the only manufacturer of digital switching board telephone systems in the CIS region outside Russia. But both companies faced a hard currency problem because electronic components were all imported from Korea on the dollar base. DC tried to solve the problem by organizing a regional trading and manufacturing network of copper and cable between Uzbekistan and Kazakhstan (Song I. 1998: p. 58).

Daewoo moved even in sectors in which it had no previous experience. Cotton plantations in Uzbekistan, cable manufacturing in Kazakhstan, rubber plantation and timber processing in Myanmar, broadcasting in Central Asia, cement production and express bus transportation in China, tyre production in Philippines, rice production in Vietnam, and oil-refining in Belgium, for example, were organized by DC as package investments.

Obtaining preferential treatment in target countries

Kim regarded emerging markets as attractive because competition was limited. Daewoo consciously used the local governments' restriction on free market competition to eliminate rivals. Korean *chaebol* groups had received advantageous treatment from the Korean government during the 1960s, 1970s and 1980s. The benefits included preferential disposal of government-vested properties, preferential allocation of foreign exchange, preferential treatment in obtaining loans, taxation and financing. Daewoo transferred the Korean experience to emerging market countries.

The chairman usually kept in close contact with the state presidents of Poland, Uzbekistan, Kazakhstan and Bulgaria, and talked to them personally about Daewoo's investments and troubles and, at the same time, acted as an adviser on industrialization. The home governments wanted to learn from him on matters of rapid industrialization. In return for Daewoo's cooperation and advice, the governments issued new regulations that would provide benefits for Daewoo's investment projects.

In the case of the Uz-Daewoo Auto project, the company enjoyed all kinds of government support. For the 50:50 joint venture between Daewoo and the Uzbekistan government, the National Bank of Uzbekistan provided credits and the Uzbekistan government guaranteed repayment of Daewoo's US$222 million loan. In addition, by issuing a 'Cabinet Decree on Uz-Daewoo Auto', the government not only injected investment money directly but also provided bank credits and exemption from taxes. The government established a special bank for Uz-Daewoo that supported car sales and exports (Park C.-H. 1998). Uz-Daewoo Auto advertised daily on Uzbekistan's national television network, and on one occasion President Kharimov personally appeared on television to promote the company's cars. Daewoo's involvement in Uzbekistan's industrialization policies was so deep that Daewoo's collapse resulted in significant changes in the country's economic policy.

In the case of Romania, Daewoo occupied a 90 per cent share of the imported vehicle market in 1995. In return for taking over a shipbuilding yard and an automaker, Daewoo was allowed to import KD kits without paying any customs duty for seven years. Daewoo was also allowed to import finished cars from Korea without paying customs for two years (Kim T.-W. 1996).

The Myanmar operation was another case of preferential treatment. Myanmar was cut off from foreign investment funds because of sanctions imposed after the military coup. Daewoo treated this situation as a favourable business opportunity: there was practically no competition. Daewoo built an electronics plant inside a state defence industry complex, and enjoyed a market monopoly due to import sanctions. Daewoo enjoyed similar benefits for its automotive operation.

7.4　Daewoo's global expansion of automotive business

In its 'global management' strategy, Daewoo concentrated its resources on the auto business. In late 1992, after separation from GM, the group chairman, Kim, personally took over management of DMC. Then in March 1993, he announced 'global management' as the group's primary strategy and mobilized all possible resources to rescue DMC from impending collapse. Daewoo launched a group-wide campaign for car sales to its employees and suppliers and their relatives and friends. In addition, Kim urged Daewoo's financial companies to raise funds for DMC. As a result, the equity capital of DMC recovered to 568 billion won as of 1993, from 3.5 billion in 1992.

After the rescue of DMC, Kim made every effort to expand Daewoo's automotive business. We will now look at specific features of the 'global management' for the auto sector.

New car development by using a global R&D network

The product technology of DMC during the joint venture with GM had been limited to minor changes of car designs licensed from Adam-Opel. Hence, when Daewoo broke off from GM, the most serious problem it faced was the lack of proprietary cars and of the technological capability for product development. Even so, Daewoo reached the conclusion that the success of 'global management' in the auto business depended on

Table 7.3   Daewoo's new car development, 1992–2000

1992	Separation from GM
1993	Development of proprietary cars began
1994	Worthing Technical Centre, England, acquired in January
1995	German Technical Centre (GTC) set up in March
1996	Lanos (1.3–1.5 litres) and Nubira (1.5–1.8 litres) launched in September and November
1997	Leganza (1.8–2.0 litres) launched in January
1998	Matiz (0.8 litres) launched in February
1999	Magnus (2.0–2.4 litres) launched in December
2000	Rezzo (2.0 litres), an RV car, launched in February

Source: DMC company reports.

the development of proprietary cars, which could be sold worldwide (Kim T.-K. 1997: p. 11).[19]

In 1993, Daewoo decided to develop four proprietary cars as quickly as possible. For this purpose, DMC expanded investment in R&D. The number of engineers and technicians in Bupyong Technical Research Centre, the centre of DMC's product development, increased rapidly, from 900 in 1992 to 2,027 in 1995. At the same time, Daewoo built a global R&D network by acquiring or establishing foreign technical institutes. In January 1994, DMC took over the Worthing Technical Centre from the IAD Group in England. IAD (International Automotive Design) was an excellent engineering firm that had designed many of the world's famous cars. Through acquisition of the Worthing centre, DMC gained hundreds of car designers. In addition, Daewoo established Daewoo Motor Engineering GmbH in Munich, Germany, in 1995. This small office organized the development of Daewoo's proprietary engines by European engine design houses.

Subsequently, Daewoo launched four proprietary cars successively (see Table 7.3). The Lanos (1.3–1.5 litres), the Nubira (1.5–1.8) and the Leganza (1.8–2.0) were launched between late 1996 and mid-1997 in the Korean and world markets, and the Matiz (0.8 litres) in early 1998. They replaced all existing cars designed by Adam-Opel.

Focus on scale economies and capacity expansion

In the context of the underdeveloped technological capabilities of Daewoo, the group chairman, Kim, said: '70 per cent of world demands are for low-mid quality products. With its mid-technology, Daewoo is able to occupy the Eastern European markets that demand mid-quality, low-price products rather than high-quality, high-price ones' (cited in

Kim T.-W. 1996: p. 20). To this end, Daewoo's top management believed achieving scale economies was the best way to maintain low prices. The chairman summarized his strategy of scale economies as follows: 'To have competitiveness in the international automotive industry, DMC must produce 2 million units per year from now on. Only then can it absorb the US$1 billion needed per year for the development of new products and R&D investment, and maintain R&D costs per car below US$500' (cited in Kim T.-K. 1997: p. 6).

Hence Daewoo's marketing strategy focused on dominating emerging markets as quickly as possible, so as to attain a world market share large enough to achieve the scale economies it needed. During 1993–8, Daewoo expanded its auto production capacity worldwide to reach the goal of 2 million vehicles a year. A senior manager said: 'by 2000, DMC will have established a production and sales system of 1 million units domestically and 1.5 million units abroad, and it will occupy 4.5 per cent of the world market share and will strive to become one of the world's top 10 automobile companies in terms of quantity and quality' (cited in Kim T.-K. 1997).

It was argued that such capacity expansion, given the overcapacity of the global automobile industry and the sluggish increase in demand in the emerging markets, would be dangerous. However, Kim was confident that Daewoo's global strategy to achieve scale economies would work:

> For the last twenty years, there have always been concerns about overcapacity in the global automobile industry. Daewoo is creating new demand in the emerging markets of Eastern Europe, the former CIS countries, and Asia. With the rapid industrial development and the growth of consumer buying power, Daewoo can benefit from being the first mover in these markets. There, we will define unique market niches and adopt differentiated marketing strategies. Our U.S. market launch in 1998 will show the way.
>
> To remain competitive in the international market, we have to commit to an annual product development investment of $1 billion across five platforms. We need 300,000 to 400,000 units production for each platform (including the variants such as convertibles and wagons), totaling 2 million units of annual production. At this level of production, per unit R&D cost can be kept under $500. This is why leading automobile makers are maintaining production output of over 2 million vehicles per year. To maintain consumer interest, Daewoo is planning to introduce two or three new models every year. (cited in Park C.-H. 1998: p. 6)

Acquisition of existing companies in emerging markets

A unique characteristic of Daewoo is that it grew by acquiring existing companies. Almost all of the Daewoo companies (except for DC, the founding company) fell into this category. This is in sharp contrast with other Korean *chaebol* groups, and especially with Hyundai, which preferred establishing new companies. In addition, when taking over insolvent existing companies, Daewoo usually acquired various advantages from the Korean government and banks: debts were written off and new credit obtained.

Daewoo applied the same strategy to 'global management' in order to reduce production costs. Daewoo preferred establishing overseas plants by acquiring insolvent automakers in emerging market countries. Daewoo's senior managers were proud of having established an overseas production capacity of one million cars a year with only 1 trillion won for the four years 1994–7, while Samsung Motors was building a car plant of 240,000 units a year by investing 5 trillion won (Song I. 1998).

Automakers from Western countries did not want to take over existing production facilities in Eastern Europe which were not compatible with their automated facilities and higher-level technology. General Motors, for instance, in its negotiations with the Polish government about privatizing FSO, refused to take over the old plants for these reasons. As this would have meant a mass lay-off of workers from the existing plants, the Polish government would not accept. In contrast, Daewoo promised to take over the existing plants and workers and, in return, received various advantages, including a lower price for FSO.

In similar ways, Daewoo took over existing auto plants in Eastern Europe by offering only 20–30 per cent of the real asset price (Lee Y.-W. 1998: p. 233). According to a calculation by Daewoo, it needed only $200 or $300 million to establish a car production plant with 200,000 units a year, whereas building a new plant of the same capacity would have cost $750 million (Choe J.-Y. 1998: p. 294). This helped Daewoo reduce unit production costs.

With its mid-technology, Daewoo was able to solve the problem of technical incompatibility. By renovating plants one by one, it could not only reduce production costs but also the time necessary to occupy the emerging markets. Kim stated:

> To seize the opportunity in emerging markets, Daewoo is acquiring plants in those countries. We cannot rely on direct exports of finished vehicles in those countries because they will inevitably come up

against trade barriers. Acquisitions save time and money for both sides. The capital-intensive nature of the automobile industry is such that it takes around $1,000 fixed cost per unit of annual production to build a new plant. With careful renovation of existing plants, a large part of this cost can be saved. Daewoo's expanded market base will be the basis for achieving the necessary scale economies. (cited in Park C.-H. 1998: p. 6)

Expansion of auto production into emerging market countries

In order to reach the target of 2 million units a year, Daewoo increased overseas production rapidly. By extending the competitive strength of Daewoo in global financing and trading, the chairman exploited the markets of Eastern Europe, Central Asia and Southeast Asia. While automakers of the industrialized countries still hesitated to enter these markets because of high risks, his strategy was to be the first into those markets.

Kim signed a 50:50 joint venture agreement with the Uzbekistan government in August 1992 to build a car plant with an annual capacity of 200,000 vehicles. With construction completed in July 1996, it became the first modern auto producer in Central Asia. In 1994, Daewoo acquired RODAE, the biggest automobile (commercial vehicles) plant in Romania. In 1995, Daewoo took over FSO, Poland's biggest carmaker. Daewoo also agreed to establish DMP, a joint venture with FSL, Poland's state-run commercial vehicle manufacturer. In the Czech Republic it acquired AVIA, a state-run truck manufacturer. In addition, Daewoo established KD assembly plants in Vietnam, China, the Philippines, Iran, Indonesia and India during 1993–5 (see Table 7.4).[20]

By the end of 1996, Daewoo had established 11 car assembly plants and many parts plants in 10 countries. Annual production capacity of the overseas plants amounted to 589,000 vehicles. The plants started operations, beginning with the Cielo, a modified version of the LeMan, in the Indian plant in July 1995. In that year, the overseas plants produced 15,989 cars through KD assembly. In 1996, with the main overseas plants in full-scale operation, overseas production amounted to 217,000 units, including 115,383 units of KD assembly. Daewoo sold 636,000 vehicles worldwide in 1995 and 857,000 in 1996.

Around half of the sales outside Korea were made in emerging markets and the other half in developed markets. Daewoo became the eighteenth largest automaker in 1996 with US$12 billion car sales and 27,000 Korean employees.

Table 7.4   Expansion of Daewoo's overseas vehicle production sites, 1993–96[a]

Start of operation	Country	Name	Staff number (1996)	Capacity (1996)	Capacity (2000)[b]
March 1993	Uzbekistan	Uz-Daewoo	3,116	200,000	200,000
March 1994	Vietnam	VIDAMCO	274	22,000	22,000
Aug. 1994	China	Guiling Bus	1,069	3,000	5,000
Oct. 1994	Philippines	TAMC	70	1,000	10,000
Oct. 1994	India	DDML	2,813	70,000	240,000
Nov. 1994	Romania	RODAE	5,032	100,000	200,000
Feb. 1994	Iran	KMC	19	0	50,000
June 1995	Czech	AVIA	2,428	25,000	25,000
July 1995	Indonesia	PT-SD	192	3,000	50,000
Nov. 1995	Poland	DMP	6,894	40,000	170,000
March 1996	Poland	Daewoo-FSO	19,850	125,000	400,000

[a] Production capacity refers to the capacity announced by Daewoo itself, and is not recalculated on the basis of uniform work hours.
[b] Planned number.
Source: Kim T. K. (1997).

Daewoo planned to build three regional networks of auto business in the emerging markets (see Table 7.5). The engine/transmission plants in Romania, India and China were established to operate as regional suppliers to production networks in Eastern Europe, South Asia and East Asia respectively. In the case of Eastern Europe, for instance, Daewoo established a regional network of parts supply by producing engines, transmission, transaxle and brake systems in Romania, bearings and air filters in Hungary, and suspension system and shock absorbers in Poland.

In contrast to Daewoo, Hyundai was more cautious in developing a global manufacturing strategy. Since the failure of the plant in Canada in the late 1980s Hyundai had expanded mainly through low-risk CKD ventures, rather than take risks in emerging markets (Bursa *et al.* 1998). Hyundai's overseas plants had a production capacity of 390,000 units a year in 1998; but, except for the Indian plant, all of these were CKD operations (see Table 7.6).

As mentioned above, one of Daewoo's most important strategic goals was to establish a production system of 2 million units capacity: 1 million in Korea and 1 million abroad. With the opening of a new car plant in Kunsan, Korea, with an annual capacity of 300,000 units, in early 1997, domestic capacity reached 1 million. Overseas production capacity reached 900,000 units in 1999. As a result, Daewoo's total capacity amounted to around 2 million units, a fivefold increase between 1991 and 1998 (see Table 7.7).

Table 7.5 Regional networks of Daewoo's overseas vehicle production, 1999

	Country	Passenger car	Commercial vehicle	Engine	Transmission
Eastern	Poland (FSO + DME)	240,000	64,000	55,000	
Europe	Romania	100,000		300,000	200,000
	Czech		20,000		
	Ukraine	136,000			
	Uzbekistan	160,000			
India	India	60,000		300,000	300,000
China	China		5,000	300,000	300,000
	Iran	24,000			
	Egypt	24,000			
KD	Libya	20,000			
assembly	Vietnam	20,000	2,000		
	Indonesia	3,000			
	Philippines	10,000	600		
Total		797,000	91,600	955,000	800,000

Source: DMC company reports.

Table 7.6 Hyundai's overseas car plants, 1993–98

	Start of operation	Country	Capacity
	May 1993	Botswana	40,000
	Aug. 1994	Egypt	10,000
	Feb. 1995	Thailand	10,000
	May 1995	Philippines	10,000
KD assembly	Feb. 1996	Venezuela	20,000
	May 1997	Brazil	30,000
	July 1997	Taiwan	20,000
	Sept. 1997	Turkey	100,000
	July 1998	Pakistan	10,000
	Aug. 1998	Malaysia	20,000
Car manufacture	Oct. 1998	India	120,000
Total			390,000

Source: O'Brien (1998: p. 122) and HMC company reports.

Table 7.7 Increase in Daewoo's vehicle production capacity, 1990–99[a] (thousand vehicles)

Year	Domestic	Overseas	Total	Factor of increase
1990	373	0	373	
1991	423	0	423	New mini car plant in Changwon, Korea completed[b]
1992	581	0	581	The mini car plant expanded
1993	760	0	760	Production lines in Bupyong, Korea speeded up[c]
1994	760	0	760	
1995	760	50	810	Overseas KD assembly plants in operation
1996	760	590	1,350	Overseas plants in operation
1997	1,060	n.a.	1,650	New car plant in Kunsan, Korea, in operation
1998	1,060	900	1,960	New plants in Ukraine and elsewhere
1999	1,060	900	1,960	

[a] Production capacity refers to the capacity announced by Daewoo itself, and is not recalculated on the basis of uniform work hours.

[b] The mini car plant in Changwon, Korea, officially belonged to Daewoo Heavy Industries (DHI), a shipbuilder. The car plant was completed in 1991 when DMC was still a joint venture with GM. Daewoo, in order to bypass GM's objection to expansion of auto production, chose DHI to produce the mini car. The plant was officially merged with DMC in 1998.

[c] The increase in the production capacity in Bupyong plant from 37,300 in 1992 to 520,000 in 1993, without any additional production facilities, was due to a speeding up of production lines, including conveyor belt speed, which accompanied a significant strengthening of management control over labour. See Lee E.-S. (1996).

Source: Compiled from company data of DMC and Daewoo Heavy Industry (DHI).

7.5 Domestic and overseas operations compared

Increasing production and export by domestic plants

In the first stage of 'global management' (1993–5), Daewoo's automotive business achieved remarkable growth. In two years, domestic production increased by 94 per cent. Car export led the growth. Daewoo's domestic market share grew only slightly from 15.6 per cent to 16.5 per cent in the same period, but its share in Korea's car exports doubled, from 12.8 per cent to 26.9 per cent in 1995. In car exports, Daewoo surpassed Kia for the first time. Daewoo exported a total of 260,000 units in 1995, an increase of 450 per cent from 58,000 units in 1992. Successful entry into Eastern European markets in 1995 resulted in a sharp increase in car exports (143 per cent growth over the previous year).

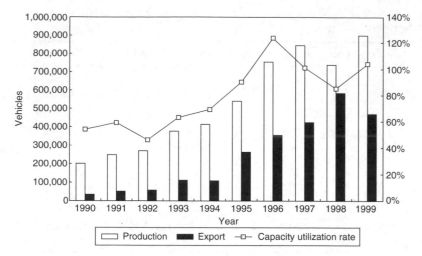

Figure 7.4   Car production and export by Daewoo's domestic plants, 1990–9
Note: Capacity utilization rate is based on the uniform work hours.
Source: KAMA, *Automotive Statistics*, yearly

In the second stage, with the commencement of operations at overseas car plants in 1996, car exports continued to grow. In the four years from 1996 to 1999, domestic car production increased by 45 per cent. During the same period, however, car export by domestic plants grew by 221 per cent. Therefore, the share of exports in domestic car production grew rapidly. It remained below 30 per cent in the first stage, but soared to over 50 per cent in the second stage. In 1998 when the Korean economy faced a financial crisis, 81 per cent of Daewoo cars produced domestically were destined for export markets (see Figure 7.4).

Daewoo celebrated the export increase while Hyundai and Kia were suffering from falling domestic sales and exports due to the financial crisis. Daewoo's 'global management' strategy appeared to be at the peak of its success. In the domestic market Daewoo emerged as number two, surpassing Kia in 1997.

As a result of increasing production and sales, the capacity utilization of Daewoo's domestic car plants stayed at over 80 per cent during 1995–9, and even surpassed 100 per cent during 1996–99, except for 1998.[21] Not including Daewoo Heavy Industries (DHI), which manufactured the mini car, Matiz, DMC's sales jumped from 1.7 trillion won to 5.8 trillion won between 1992 and 1997, an increase of 340 per cent over 5 years (see Table 7.8). DMC suffered net losses for the 4 years following

Table 7.8 Financial statements of DMC, 1992–97 (hundred million won)

	1992	1993	1994	1995	1996	1997
Sales	17,067	21,594	27,859	34,700	43,543	57,977
Operating income	864	1,366	3,075	3,357	4,148	6,368
Net income	−956	−847	−91	105	229	2,512
Assets	29,668	38,913	40,765	49,000	52,724	85,134
Debts (D)	29,633	33,231	35,180	43,290	45,027	74,741
Equity capital (E)	35	5,682	5,581	5,815	7,698	10,394
D/E ratio (%)	84,666	585	630	745	585	719

Source: *Maeil Economic Daily, Annual Corporation Reports.*

its separation from GM. In 1995, however, it reported positive net profits for the first time in the 1990s.[22] The turnaround was attributable to booming exports.[23]

Poor operation of overseas plants

Most of the overseas plants, the core of the 'global management', however, failed to increase production and sales in proportion to their growing production capacity. Even when total overseas capacity jumped from 50,000 in 1995 to 590,000 in 1996 and 900,000 in 1998, actual production grew moderately, from 217,000 in 1996 to 364,864 in 1999. Contrary to Daewoo's expectation, the economies of the emerging market countries were not growing quickly. Moreover, the East Asian and Russian financial crises of 1997–8 impacted on them immediately. Consequently, the capacity utilization rates of the overseas plants remained below 45 per cent, except in 1997 (see Table 7.9).

Furthermore, half of the performance of the overseas plants was achieved by FSO-Daewoo in Poland. The share of FSO-Daewoo in

Table 7.9 Daewoo's actual overseas vehicle production, 1994–99

	1994	1995	1996	1997	1998	1999
Total capacity (C)	0	50,000	590,000	590,000	900,000	900,000
Total production (P)	0	15,986	217,000	281,150	299,897	364,864
KD assembly	0	15,986	115,383	94,184	95,975	140,610
Capacity utilization: P/C (%)		32	37	48	33	41

Note: Production capacity refers to the capacity announced by Daewoo itself, and is not recalculated on the basis of uniform work hours.
Source: Own calculation from DMC company reports.

Daewoo's total overseas production increased from 43 per cent to 58 per cent between 1997 and 1999 (see Table 7.10).

Only FSO-Daewoo achieved over 80 per cent capacity utilization rates (see Table 7.11). In contrast, most of Daewoo's overseas plants recorded an average capacity utilization rate of below 25 per cent.

From the quite low capacity utilization rate, we can assume that most of the overseas production plants did not bring returns but made big losses. However, financial data on the operation of the overseas plants are not available to the public. First, all the overseas plants belonged to DC, not DMC, but these data were never released. Second, because DC organized complicated global and regional financing and trading, coupled with package investments in multiple product lines, the data, where they existed, were neither clear nor comprehensive.

In addition, because of Daewoo's well-known one-man leadership, the data were not known even within the company. To facilitate financial transactions for its overseas investments, Daewoo established a financial unit inside DC called the British Finance Centre (BFC), which was located in London. The BFC was under the direct control of the chairman, Kim. The public did not know of its existence until 2000 when the Financial Supervisory Commission of Korea (FSC) was investigating Daewoo's massive fraudulent manipulation of financial statements.[24]

Table 7.10   Share of FSO-Daewoo in Daewoo's overseas vehicle production

	1997	1998	1999
Total overseas production (T)	281,150	299,897	364,864
Production by FSO-Daewoo (F)	119,513	161,105	211,656
F/T (%)	43	54	58

Source: Own calculation from DMC company reports.

Table 7.11   Production by FSO-Daewoo, 1997–99

	1997	1998	1999
Capacity (C)	125,000	n.a.	240,000
Production (P)	104,907	142,380	197,226
P/C (%)	84	n.a.	82

n.a. = not available
Note: Production capacity refers to the capacity announced by Daewoo itself.
Source: Compiled and calculated from DMC data.

Daewoo itself did not expect that the overseas plants would bring returns immediately (Choe J.-Y. 1998: p. 300). Assuming that the globalized financial markets would remain stable and provide further funds, Daewoo projected a long-term financial strategy and continued to invest in emerging market countries without making profits for years. Transnational firms usually ensure healthy cash flows by transferring annual returns in the form of dividends, royalties or commissions to their headquarters. Daewoo had, by contrast, quite a different plan for yielding returns: listing the overseas joint venture companies on regional or global stock markets and selling founders' stocks on the markets. Senior managers believed that the plan to list on the stock markets would be fulfilled in 7 to 10 years (i.e., by 2000–2003).[25]

7.6 The financial crisis and Daewoo's collapse

Continuing business expansion in 1997–8

Even after the outbreak of the Asian financial crisis, Daewoo continued to expand its business to complete the 'global management' project. As seen in Table 7.12, the number of Daewoo's overseas subsidiaries increased in the period between April 1997 and April 1999. Furthermore, in December 1997, just as Korea was signing the IMF bailout package, Daewoo announced that it would take over Ssangyong Motor Company.[26] Kim also announced plans to take over Hanwha Energy, a troubled Korean oil company, and Ansaldo, a large Italian heavy industry company. In a press interview, furthermore, he revealed that Daewoo, together with its foreign associates, would establish a large international investment bank with capital funds of US$4 billion, in the hope of taking full advantage of financial globalization.

Table 7.12 Number of Daewoo's subsidiaries, 1995–99

	1995	1996	1997	1998	1999
Domestic subsidiaries	21	25	31	36	36
Overseas subsidiaries	117	147	219	239	253
Total	138	172	250	275	289

Note: Figures given are for April of each year.
Source: Financial Supervisory Commission, *Process of Corporate and Financial Restructuring and Policies for the Future*, Press Release, 24 August 1999.

Repayment of foreign credits and increasing domestic credit

According to the *Korea Economic Daily* (25 September 2001), Daewoo Group's cash flow began to worsen as early as 1995, when it continued to expand investments without making profits. But the true amount of its losses is still not known because Daewoo manipulated its financial statements. In any case, from late 1997, when the Asian financial crisis was significantly affecting Korea and emerging market countries, Daewoo faced not only falling sales and production in domestic and overseas markets, but also suffered from the financial turbulence per se, as its foreign creditors – the international banks – rejected a rollover of existing loans to Daewoo.

Daewoo, as we have seen, had endeavoured to reduce its own contribution to the overseas investments by relying on direct borrowings from international financial institutions. But Daewoo's core competence turned into a 'core incompetence' when, in the midst of the Asian and Russian financial crises of 1998, the international lenders demanded immediate repayment of matured loans.

Under pressure from foreign creditors, Daewoo managed to repay US$9.3 billion of foreign loans between December 1997 and March 1999, reducing its total foreign debt from US$16 billion to US$6.7 billion. But the company raised this money mainly from the Korean financial market because it did not have overseas subsidiaries bringing in cash.

The costs of repaying foreign debts in the midst of a financial crisis were enormous. First, a doubled foreign exchange rate brought Daewoo enormous exchange losses.[27] Second, as the Korean financial market itself was hit by the financial crises, Daewoo was able to raise funds only by issuing corporate bonds and commercial papers at exorbitant interest rates (well over 20 per cent in the first half of 1998).[28] Consequently, Daewoo's financial expenses increased rapidly in 1998, as shown in Table 7.13. Net losses, according to Daewoo's financial statements, ballooned to a record 554 billion won.

As the financial statements of Daewoo were falsified, however, particularly for the year of 1998, we can regard even this figure as significantly understated. According to a secret KDI report compiled in early 1999 and published in the *Korea Economic Daily* on 22 August 2001, Daewoo recorded net losses of 4 trillion won in 1998.[29] Daewoo's biggest problem then became short-term domestic liabilities that caused a continuing heavy drain of interest repayments.

Table 7.14 shows that Daewoo's domestic debts increased by 15.5 trillion won between December 1997 and March 1999. The increase in

Table 7.13   Profitability of Daewoo Group, 1996–98 (billion won)

	1996	1997	1998
Operating income	2,397	3,091	3,192
Financial expenses	2,210	2,996	5,924
Net income	–110	135	–554

Note: The data are based on the financial statements published before investigation into account manipulation.
Source: Financial Supervisory Commission, *Daewoo Group's Workout and Policies*, Press Release, 4 November 1999.

Table 7.14   Increase in Daewoo's domestic debts (December 1997–March 1999, trillion won)

	Dec. 1997 (A)	March 1999 (B)	Increase (B – A)
Commercial bank loans	8.6	8.4	–0.2
Other bank loans	8.1	4.0	–4.1
Corporate bonds	8.4	19.7	11.3
Commercial papers	3.6	12.1	8.5
Total	28.7	44.2	15.5

Source: Financial Supervisory Commission, *Daewoo Group's Workout and Policies*, Press Release, 4 November 1999.

short-term credits, in the form of corporate bonds and commercial papers, amounted to 20 trillion won while, at the same time, bank loans declined by 4.3 trillion won.

The increase in Daewoo's domestic short-term debts, which amounted to 20 trillion won (US$16 billion), between December 1997 and March 1999, was caused primarily by the withdrawal of foreign creditors (US$9.3 billion) and partly by the rejected rollover of domestic bank loans (US$3.5 billion). The rest of the debt increase, US$3.2 billion (4 trillion won), was used to cover the net losses in the period.

Moral hazard, Daewoo's bankruptcy, and accounting fraud

It was in this period from December 1997 to 1998 that Daewoo benefited from the logic of 'too-big-to-fail'. Domestic financial institutions – mostly investment trust companies – continued to buy Daewoo's bonds and papers in this period because they believed that the government would not allow Daewoo to fail, due to its sheer size. The high return on Daewoo's bonds and papers and high market interest rates, plus a

Daewoo risk premium of 2–4 per cent extra, made them run the excessive risk. It was these financial institutions – the deregulated investment trust sector – that fostered the 'moral hazard', rather than the strictly regulated commercial banking sector (see also Chapter 3).[30]

Faced with intensifying financial troubles, Daewoo announced plans in late 1998 to combine 36 domestic companies into 10 companies, divided into four business areas of auto, heavy industry, trading and construction, and finance and services. According to this plan, Daewoo would give up electronics and communication. In early 1999, Daewoo negotiated with Samsung about a possible swap of Daewoo Electronics with Samsung Motors. The chairman, Kim, expected that the deal would bring 4 trillion won to Daewoo. At the same time, he approached GM with a joint venture proposal, but GM was not interested unless it got full management control of the company. At the end of June 1999, Samsung also announced its decision not to accept the swap.

With the failure of all its contingency plans, Daewoo was on the verge of bankruptcy in July 1999. It could no longer repay the enormous amount of maturing short-term credits (more than 1 trillion won every day). On 19 July, Daewoo Group announced its inability to service its debts. The chairman announced that he had offered private and Daewoo assets valued at 10 trillion won as collateral for a further 4 trillion won in loans from domestic banks. At the same time, he said, he would step down when operations at Daewoo's auto business became normalized.

However, the 4 trillion won provided by banks was far from enough to rescue the sinking Titanic. On 26 August 1999 the Korea Development Bank, a state-run bank and the representative of Daewoo's domestic creditors, announced that the domestic creditor banks had decided to put all Daewoo's companies into a workout programme: that is, bank-controlled restructuring. The chairman lost his position and property as well, as the creditors disposed of the collateral.

Under the workout programme, repayment of debts and interest was frozen and commercial papers and corporate bonds ceased to circulate. More funds were injected into the group and the ownership and control of Daewoo's domestic and overseas companies were transferred to the creditor banks. Korea Development Bank announced plans for restructuring the companies, including the sale of DMC in an international auction. (DMC was sold to General Motors in late 2001.)

The FSC investigated the Group's accounts and revealed a large-scale manipulation of financial statements. According to an FSC press release of 4 November 1999, Daewoo had inflated the group's assets by 30.7

trillion won to hide its troubled finances and persuade financial institutions to supply new credits. Total debts were revalued to 86.8 trillion won, an increase of 9 trillion won, and the net assets (capital) were estimated at minus 25.6 trillion won (US$20 billion), a decrease of 39.7 trillion won (see Table 7.15). Daewoo's three main companies, DC, DMC and Daewoo Electronics, were responsible for 90 per cent (23 trillion won) of the negative net assets amounting to 25.6 trillion won. DC had the largest negative net assets: −14.5 trillion won. This was partly because of the enormous losses made by its overseas subsidiaries.

An investigation of DMC's financial statements also showed account fraud (see Table 7.16). The company's assets were revalued to 12.9 trillion won, down from 20.6 trillion, and the liabilities were revalued to 18.6 trillion won, up from 15.6 trillion. The capital value was revalued to −5.7 trillion won, a drastic fall from 5.1 trillion.

Daewoo collapsed under debts of US$60 billion. The dream of 'global management' turned into the world's biggest corporate bankruptcy.[31] The group founder and chairman, Kim, once one of Korea's most respected businessmen, went into hiding in late 1999 as Korean prosecutors began to investigate Daewoo executives on suspicion of one of the world's biggest accounting frauds.

Table 7.15   Results of Daewoo Group audit, 1999 (trillion won)

	June 1999 (A)	August 1999 (B)	Increase (B − A)
Assets	91.9	61.2	−30.7
Liabilities	77.8	86.8	9.0
Capital	14.1	−25.6	−39.7

Source: Financial Supervisory Commission, *Daewoo Group's Workout and Policies*, Press Release, 4 November 1999.

Table 7.16   Result of audit on DMC's account, 1999 (billion won)

	1997	1998	June 1999	August 1999
Assets	8,513	15,864	20,646	12,936
Liabilities	7,474	11,791	15,560	18,638
Capital	1,039	4,073	5,086	−5,702

Source: For 1997 and 1998, *Maeil Economic Daily, Annual Corporation Reports*; for 1999, Financial Supervisory Commission, *Daewoo Group's Workout and Policies*, Press Release on 4 November 1999.

The collapse of Daewoo, the second largest *chaebol* group by asset value in 1998, caused heavy damage to domestic and foreign financial institutions. In negotiations with Korean banks about Daewoo's debts, the international lenders, including the largest banks such as Chase-Manhattan, Citibank, HSBC, Tokyo-Mitsubishi and UBS, were pressed to agree to write off 60 per cent of the US$6.7 billion debt. Originally, they had required a guarantee from the Korean government for Daewoo's total foreign debt, but this was criticized as a 'moral hazard'. The Korean financial institutions involved in Daewoo also wrote off more than 60 per cent of their 60 trillion won credits. The Korean government in 1999 was forced to put more than 30 trillion won of public funds into the troubled financial institutions (primarily the four largest investment trust companies) to protect the financial system from a possible second crisis.

7.7   Conclusion

DMC provides in all aspects the counterexample to HMC, and Daewoo's collapse in 1999 provides evidence to contradict the neoclassical argument that saw it as an example of 'failed crony Asian capitalism'. The company was under transnational control during the 1970s and 1980s. There is no doubt that transnational control had had a negative impact on the company, providing a strong illustration of dependency theory. GM put a curb on product development, exports and learning of technology. GM-Daewoo's continuing failures led Daewoo to dissolve its partnership with GM in 1992. Daewoo's global car business in the 1990s, however, began with the negative legacy of the period of GM dominance.

Daewoo's global expansion projects in the 1990s were launched on the institutional basis of liberalization and globalization. Abolition of industrial policy made it possible for Daewoo to establish many overseas production plants. The opening of the capital account made it possible for Daewoo to raise investment funds of US$20 billion for overseas projects. Daewoo's BFC in London, which handled all offshore financial transactions, was the symbol of Daewoo's financial globalization. Among Korean *chaebol* groups, it was Daewoo that most welcomed the liberalization and globalization because of its existing organizational capabilities in international trade and finance, which it sought to magnify to new proportions by global expansion.

In the 1990s, Daewoo did not make great efforts to overcome its relative backwardness in technological capabilities. Rather, its expansion into emerging markets was based on existing strengths in lower-priced products. Besides its expertise in international financing and trade, Daewoo's existing capabilities (such as quick decision-making by the founding chairman, gaining preferential treatment from target countries' governments, and package investments in diverse product lines of the conglomerate business) also made rapid expansion into emerging market countries possible.

To expand in lower-priced car markets, Daewoo focused on scale economies and capacity expansion. Daewoo rapidly increased overseas production in emerging markets. Daewoo's strategy was to be the first mover into those markets, but most of its overseas plants failed to increase production and sales. The economies of the emerging market countries did not grow as fast as both Daewoo and international financial institutions expected. When the financial crises in East Asia and Russia in 1997–8 hit, Daewoo was the most exposed as panicked international banks required immediate repayment of matured loans. Daewoo collapsed in mid-1999 amid rapidly rising debts and interest payments. The IMF policy of raising market interest rates over 20 per cent also contributed to the bankruptcy.

In Daewoo's case, moral hazard problems appeared in 1998, when Korea's deregulated investment fund sector, confident that the government would not permit Daewoo to go bankrupt, kept purchasing Daewoo's short-term bonds and company papers, even when commercial banks had ceased to lend to Daewoo. Daewoo consciously took advantage of this situation. International banks also showed moral hazard when, in late 1999, they claimed a government guarantee for their remaining credits to Daewoo. Moral hazard problems appear therefore to be more related to financial deregulation and globalization than to government intervention and to the *chaebol*'s distorted corporate governance.

In conclusion, both the rise and the collapse of Daewoo in the 1990s were essentially associated with the liberalization and globalization that occurred in that period. They appear to be closely related to the boom and crash of 'emerging markets' in the 1990s.

Daewoo presents a clear case of a firm that is 'locked in' to its existing capabilities, rather than building dynamic capabilities. Daewoo's concentration on such capabilities as finance, trade, and political relationships led it to neglect long-term building of organizational capability. In the next chapter, we will look in more detail at this issue by comparing the respective approaches of Daewoo and Hyundai to R&D.

8

Comparison of Hyundai and Daewoo in Research and Development

As Gerschenkron (1962) indicated, backwardness in technology is one of the common characteristics of all late industrializing countries.[1] Germany and the United States, the latecomers in the nineteenth century, overcame this problem with their own technological and industrial innovations which constituted a second industrial revolution. By contrast, economies that began industrialization in the twentieth century tended to develop on the basis of learning from borrowed technology, rather than invention or innovation (Amsden 1989). The Northeast Asian economies – Japan, Korea, and Taiwan – followed this pattern during their fast growth periods.[2]

In capitalist economies, firms are the main unit of technological activities. Leading Korean companies have actively invested in learning from foreign technologies in order eventually to challenge the firms in the industrialized countries. Many studies on Hyundai Motors, Samsung Electronics, and several other Korean companies report such cases in car, electronics, D-RAM, computer, telecommunications, and other sectors (see, e.g., Kim G. 1994; Choi 1996; Kim L.-S. 1997, 1999; Kim S.-R. 1997; Lee K. 1997; Hwang 1998). Assisted by the government's industrial policy, they made every effort to achieve technological parity, instead of relying on rent-seeking activities. As a result of these efforts, Korea's main industries gradually changed from a shop floor oriented system into a more R&D oriented one from the mid-1980s onwards (Kim L.-S. 1997, 1999). Moreover, industries such as semiconductors, electronics and biotechnology have been stretching their in-house R&D activities to transform themselves from learners into innovators.

Technological learning is not a passive process. To be successful, it requires strategic determination and investment in the capability to improve and adapt. This is because learning is a complex process including uncertain, subjective and tacit elements. Many *chaebol* companies successfully acquired relevant technologies by vigorously investing in capabilities building, but many others have instead concentrated on non-R&D activities, such as capacity expansion and unrelated diversification. Eventually, they were defeated by the technologically competent companies in market competition in Korea.

The massive collapses of *chaebol* groups and companies which began in 1997 were partly due to failures in catching up with Korea's industrial dynamics. We have already discussed some of the differences in general strategies. On the basis of different general orientations, HMC and DMC had quite different approaches to product technology. In this chapter, we will investigate the different strategies adopted by these two companies in the area of capabilities building in product technology. Much of this chapter will rely on interviews with engineers from both companies.

Section 8.1 will give an overview of both companies' product development. Organizational systems, investments, and product development performance of R&D institutes will be compared. Section 8.2 will analyse both companies' new car development processes, including a comparison of Hyundai's self-reliant process and Daewoo's global R&D network. In the case of Daewoo, we will focus on its Bupyong Institute, the centre of its global network, and investigate its achievements and weaknesses in technological learning. Section 8.3 will look at the different paths taken by the two companies in engine development. We will compare Hyundai's self-reliance and long-run projects with Daewoo's foreign outsourcing and short-termism.

Section 8.4 will compare their organizational systems for new car development. Daewoo's project-oriented system and Hyundai's lightweight product manager system will be analysed with respect to the reduction of product development time and the accumulation and sharing of technological knowledge. Section 8.5 will compare the different styles of achieving company-wide coordination for new car development. We will show how Daewoo's one-man leadership and HMC's formalized procedures were reflected in organizational routines.

8.1   Different approaches to car development

Hyundai's strategy of self-reliance

The success of Hyundai's in-house developed cars led Kia and Daewoo to choose the same strategy in the early 1990s. Nonetheless, only HMC had a self-sufficient product development system. Hyundai's strategy, following Hyun (1999), can be called 'self-reliant'.

In 1979, HMC had only a small product development organization with four departments; but by 1992, it had evolved into an organization with three R&D institutes consisting of 38 departments and six teams. In the early 1990s, the company built a second testing track in Namyang that is four times bigger than the testing track built in Ulsan in 1984. In 1996, it opened the Namyang Institute, the company's fourth R&D organization. This institute is responsible for passenger car development and is also the organizing centre of all HMC's in-house R&D activities. Today the Ulsan Institute is responsible for smaller passenger cars and light commercial vehicles, while the Mabukri Institute specializes in power train development and advanced technology research, and the Chonju Institute undertakes heavy commercial vehicle development. Including institutes for manufacturing and machining technologies, HMC had eight institutes in Korea in 1998 (see Table 8.1).

As seen in Chapter 6, there were three stages in the history of HMC's product technology (see Table 6.2, 6.3, 6.4). In the first stage (1973–85), for the Pony and Pony Excel, HMC relied largely on foreign technological sources. In the second stage (1986–93), beginning with the development of the Sonata, HMC developed the capacity to design styling and body in-house. This capacity extended partly to chassis design. At the same time, the company invested in learning the technologies it needed for developing its own engines, transmissions, and other chassis parts. Subsequently, in the third stage from 1994, the company launched new cars with completely new platforms installed with its own engines (see Table 8.2). In the period of the Pony, HMC had only some hundreds

Table 8.1   HMC's organization of product development, 1998

Organization	Staff number	R&D area
Ulsan Institute	983	Smaller passenger car and light commercial vehicle
Namyang Institute	863	Passenger car
Mabukri Institute	1,266	Power train and advanced research
Chonju Institute	637	Heavy commercial vehicle
Design Institute	150	Styling design
Overseas	25	Window on foreign trends and information
Administration	204	Planning, patent, coordination, finance, etc.
Total	4,128	

Source: HMC, *Annual Report*, 1998.

Table 8.2   Evolution of HMC's product development technology

Launched	Car	Grade (litre)	Styling design	Body design	Chassis design	Engine design
1975	Pony	1.2–1.5	0	0	0	0
1983	Stellar	1.4–2.0	0	2	1	0
1985	Excel	1.3–1.5	0	1	1	0
1988	Sonata	1.8–2.4	2	2	1	0
1989	Excel II	1.3–1.5	2	2	1	0
1990	Scoup	1.5	2	2	1	0
1990	Lantra	1.5–1.8	2	2	1	0
1991	Scoup II	1.5	2	2	1	1
1992	Grandeur	2.0–3.0	2	2	0	0
1993	Sonata II	1.8–2.4	2	2	1	0
1994	Accent	1.3–1.5	2	2	2	2
1995	Avante	1.5–1.8	2	2	2	2
1997	Atoz	0.8–1.0	2	2	2	2
1998	EF Sonata	1.8–2.4	2	2	2	2

0 = licensed from foreign sources.
1 = improved by HMC based on borrowed technology.
2 = developed by HMC.
Source: For 1976–94, Kim G. (1994: p. 205).

of technical personnel; this number increased rapidly in the early 1980s, from 700 to over 2,000 by 1985. In 1989, it jumped to 3,500, and again to 4,000 in 1994. In 1998, the company had more than 4,000 personnel in new product development.

Daewoo's global approach

When Daewoo launched its 'global management' project in 1993, it planned not only to expand its annual car production capacity to 2 million units, but also to launch four proprietary cars by 1997. However, because of the long period of dependence on GM, DMC had poor capabilities in product technology. Its only experience had been the development of the Espero. The number of R&D personnel and their know-how were far from sufficient for the task of developing four cars within four years.

Daewoo expanded technical personnel and facilities at the Bupyong Institute, its central R&D organization near Seoul. Its complement of engineers and technicians jumped from 900 to 2,030 between 1993 and 1995, and had increased to 2,805 by 1999 (see Table 8.3). Nevertheless, as the Bupyong personnel lacked skills and experience, Daewoo still needed foreign sources of technology transfer.

Table 8.3   DMC's organization of product development, 1996 and 1998

Institute (location)	Personnel number		Main areas
	1996	1998	
Bupyong (Korea)	2,260	2,805	Car body and chassis development
Worthing (UK)	850	863	Car body and chassis development
Munich (Germany)	100	44	Administration of engine development
Design Forum (Korea)	130	145	Styling design
Kunsan (Korea)	200	212	Heavy CVs development
Total	3,540	4,069	

Source: For 1996, Hyun (1997: p. 17) and for 1998, company reports of DMC.

The chairman's solution for this problem was to establish a global R&D network. Acquisition of the Worthing Institute from IAD in January 1994 brought DMC more than 700 experts in vehicle design, test and analysis.[3] Daewoo also contracted ItalDesign of Italy for the development of the Lanos, and established Daewoo Motor Engineering GmbH in Munich in 1995. This office administered engine development projects that were carried out by Porsche (Germany), Lotus and Ricardo (UK). The overseas institutes worked in collaboration with the Bupyong centre.

As of 1998, DMC had five institutes for product development in Korea and abroad (see Table 8.3). The Bupyong Institute and the Worthing Institute were responsible for passenger car development, including design, test and analysis. The institute in Munich was an office for the administration of outsourced engine development projects. There was also the Daewoo Design Forum, a car styling design organization, but its role in the development of Daewoo's cars was limited, as we will see later.

The global R&D network made it possible for Daewoo, despite its inexperience, to develop four new cars within just 3½ years (see Table 8.4). The Lanos (1.3–1.5 litres), Nubira (1.5–1.8 litres), Leganza (1.8–2.0 litres), and Matiz (0.8 litres) were launched between October 1996 and March 1998, and replaced all existing cars designed by Adam-Opel. After completion of the first series of car development projects, DMC commenced a second series immediately, in 1998. The Magnus (2.0–2.5 litres) was launched in late 1999 and the Rezzo, an RV based on the Nubira platform, in February 2000.

Table 8.4 History of DMC's car development, 1972–99

1972	CKD production of Chevrolet 1700
1972–86	SKD production of cars licensed from Adam-Opel
1987–92	Licensed production of the LeMan (Opel Kadett)
1987–90	Development of the Espero, based on the Kadett platform
1992	Separation from GM, in December
1993	Begins development of four proprietary cars
1994	Acquisition of the Worthing Institute, in January
1995	Establishment of the Munich Institute, in March
1996	Lanos (1.3–1.5 litres) launched in October
1996	Nubira (1.5–1.8 litres) launched in December
1997	Leganza (1.8–2.0 litres) launched in February
1998	Matiz (0.8 litres) launched in March
1999	Magnus (2.0–2.4 litres) launched in December

Comparison of input and output for car development

During the period of GM dependence, DMC's investment in product development was insignificant. But between 1992 and 1995, it soared tenfold, from 37 to 370 billion won, and remained around 350 billion won until 1998. This figure approached that of HMC (see Figure 8.1).

Similarly, DMC's number of R&D personnel approached that of HMC in the latter half of 1990s (see Figure 8.2). Until 1992, DMC had fewer

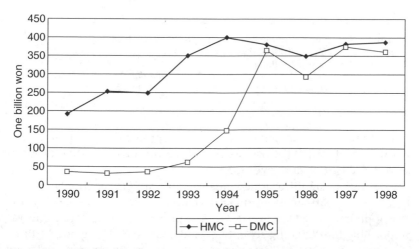

Figure 8.1 R&D expenditures in HMC and DMC, 1990–8
Source: For HMC, *Annual Reports*; for DMC, *Maeil Economic Daily, Annual Corporation Reports*.

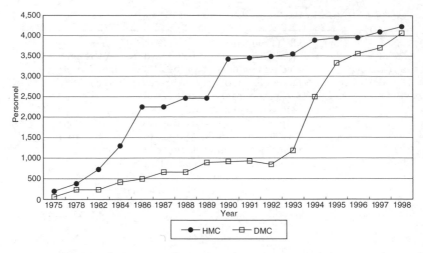

Figure 8.2   Number of R&D personnel in HMC and DMC, 1975–98
Note: The number of DMC staff includes that of the Worthing and Munich Institutes.
Sources: HMC and DMC, *Annual Reports*, and other company reports.

Table 8.5   Evolution of Daewoo's car development technology, 1993–8

Launched	Car	Grade (litres)	Styling	Body	Chassis	Engine
Oct. '96	Lanos	1.3–1.5	0*	1*	1*	1
Dec. '96	Nubira	1.5–1.8	0***	1**	0**	1
Feb. '97	Leganza	1.8–2.2	0*	2	2	0
Mar. '98	Matiz	0.8	0*	1**	1**	1

0 = developed by foreign technologies, including the Worthing Institute.
1 = improved by Bupyong Institute, based on foreign technologies.
2 = developed by Bupyong Institute.
* for ItalDesign of Italy; ** for Worthing of UK; *** for IDEA of Italy.
Sources: Hyun (1997) and company reports of DMC.

than 1,000 technical personnel for new product development, but expansion of R&D facilities brought these numbers up sharply: there were 3,300 in 1995 and over 4,000 in 1998.

In spite of significant dependence on foreign technology, DMC increased its participation in car development (see Table 8.5).[4] In the development of the Lanos, DMC's first proprietary car, ItalDesign was responsible for designing style, body and chassis; the Bupyong Institute then worked on detailed improvements of the ItalDesign-designed body and chassis. In the case of the Nubira too, Bupyong's role was limited

Table 8.6   Engineering lead time in DMC and HMC for car development, 1998

Company	Car	Styling freeze	Start of commercial production	Engineering lead time (months)
Daewoo	Lanos	1 July '94	1 Oct. '96	27
	Nubira	1 Feb. '94	1 Dec. '96	34
	Leganza	1 July '94	1 Feb. '97	31
	Matiz	1 Sept. '95	1 March '98	30
Hyundai				34

Source: Company reports of DMC and HMC.

as Worthing was primarily responsible for designing body and chassis.[5] However, in the case of the Leganza, Daewoo's engineers at Bupyong, using knowledge and experience gained from the Lanos and Nubira projects, were able to design the body and chassis independently.

Between 1994 and 1998, Hyundai launched four fully changed models with new platforms, besides making minor changes to existing models. Daewoo also launched four completely new cars in the period 1996–8. In view of DMC's weak technological capability in product development, its performance in development lead time was remarkable.[6] The average lead time for product engineering, from styling freeze to start of commercial production, achieved by Daewoo was 30.5 months, less than Hyundai's 34 months (see Table 8.6). DMC's increased R&D investments enabled the company to reduce engineering lead time. Consequently, Daewoo was able to launch four proprietary cars in the Korean and overseas markets faster than HMC.

However Daewoo's successful focus on 'time-to-market' was achieved by the sacrifice of long-run consideration of capabilities. This will be the focus of our next sections.

8.2   Comparison of car development capabilities

Carmakers organize product engineering in a series of 'design–build–test' cycles, the elements of which are almost uniform throughout the industry. Basic and detailed blueprints are drawn for a vehicle system, its subsystems and components. Prototype components and a prototype vehicle are built, based on the preliminary drawings. Then, the prototypes are tested against established targets. The test results are evaluated and designs are modified as necessary. The cycle is repeated and repeated until an acceptable level of performance is achieved (Clark and Fujimoto 1991: p. 116).

HMC built an integrated car development system, in Korea, to carry out the 'design–build–test' cycles with as little foreign assistance as possible. The self-reliant organizational system was a part of the company's long-run efforts to build its own technological capabilities. In contrast, DMC depended on a global network of product development, in which the Worthing Institute and other design houses (such as ItalDesign, IDEA and Lotus) played important roles.

Daewoo's improving capabilities: the Bupyong Institute

In spite of its dependence on foreign institutes, however, Daewoo's Bupyong Institute can be regarded as the heart of its product development activities. The Bupyong Institute's technological capabilities improved rapidly from 1993. Daewoo's Korean engineers and technicians learned much from their counterparts at the Worthing Institute. Worthing was in full charge of developing body and chassis for the Nubira (1993–6). It was also responsible for the initial development of the Matiz (1995–7), but 100 Korean engineers had been relocated to the Worthing Institute to work with the British engineers. In this joint work, the Koreans learned the fundamentals of car body and chassis design.[7]

Another important source of technological learning for the Bupyong engineers was their direct participation in the car development process itself. Faced with many failures, they had to search for solutions by themselves: that is, they learned from repeated cycles of design, testing, analysis of failures, and redesign.

After the completion of the first series of product development projects (1993–7), the engineers were ready to design both the car body and the chassis with little foreign assistance. Now it was the Worthing Institute which took a secondary role. It was responsible only for minor design changes to cars intended for European markets. The Bupyong Institute was responsible for the development of the Magnus, launched in December 1999, and the Rezzo, launched in February 2000.

Bupyong's weaknesses in comparison with HMC

While Bupyong had improved its capabilities in body and chassis design, and also in prototype building, it had yet to develop its own vehicle testing and analysis capability. Of course, the institute had some facilities and personnel for this purpose (for example, it had had a crash test department since 1995), but major testing capabilities were lacking. For instance, Bupyong did not have sufficient facilities and personnel for testing and analysis of the mechanical structure of body and chassis. Thus, Bupyong continued to depend on Worthing and other foreign institutes for major testing of both body and chassis. Even worse, it had no test track. Important driving tests and analysis were contracted to MIRA or Millbrook, both British car engineering firms. The Bupyong Institute carried out only secondary driving tests on paved and unpaved roads nearby.

Due to this weakness, DMC spent as much as 21 per cent of the total cost of the first series of car development projects on outsourced testing and analysis. Dependence on foreign contractors, including the Worthing Institute, amounted to 82 per cent for the Nubira project, and 70 per cent for the Leganza. Bupyong carried out only 18–30 per cent of total testing and analysis. By the end of 1999, in the midst of the second series of car development, the company still had no plan to reduce its dependence on outsourced testing and analysis.[8]

This situation appears to have resulted from strategic decisions made by top management rather than from structural constraints. For example, there was no inevitability about Daewoo's lack of a test track: 20 years of GM dependence had left the company without one of its own. And yet, when the company built a new plant for the Nubira in Kunsan, Korea, no test track was included, even though the site was large enough and Daewoo had sufficient funds at the time. Many of Daewoo's senior managers advised the chairman that the company needed a proving ground; but he had a different vision, and chose to invest in acquisition of overseas plants rather than strengthening Daewoo's technological capabilities. In contrast with DMC, HMC invested heavily in its test facilities and now has one of the best testing and analysis organizations in the world.

Daewoo's dependence on outsourced testing and analysis created other problems. Prototype cars built by Bupyong were sent overseas by air for testing and analysis, and then returned. This was a serous disadvantage, considering the importance of reducing development lead time. However, the most significant problem lay in difficulties in communication and cooperation. Many misunderstandings and conflicts arose between Bupyong and the foreign institutes because of different languages and cultures on the one hand, and different technical and industrial backgrounds on the other.

To be effective, 'design–build–test' cycles require frequent and intensive communication between functional organizations (Clark and Fujimoto 1991). It is often necessary for working level engineers – say, designers and testers – to have formal and informal communication through direct meetings and talking with each other. As is well known, transfer and sharing of tacit knowledge is possible primarily through personal and direct communication. Hyundai's integrated R&D system facilitated such communication but, in the global system of Daewoo, it was not so easy. Although Daewoo's engineers travelled frequently to the Worthing and the other foreign institutes, and had access to the global network of telecommunications and Intranet, organizing intensive communication proved problematic.

For instance, during the Matiz development, material for the body panel caused serious problems during pilot production. In designing the panel, Worthing engineers specified steel sheet according to DIN (Deutsche Industrie-Norm, or the German Industry Standard). However, Bupyong's engineers were not able to find a Korean steel supplier who could produce the steel sheet, and so they replaced it with a sheet according to Korean Standards. Unforturnately, this sheet proved to be not strong enough when pressed to Worthing's specifications.

This problem could be solved in various ways. Worthing could redesign the body with the Korean Standard steel sheet, but this could mean redesigning all body components and body structure because of different mechanical specifications, such as weight, crash-testing features, and so on. Alternatively the press department in Bupyong could search for technical solutions, including introduction of new press machines, or the steel supplier could improve the product and production of the steel sheet. All of these solutions were theoretically feasible.

It was essential for the engineers concerned to resolve the problem quickly and with the greatest cost-benefit combination. However, differences in language and culture, and the sheer distance between Korea and Britain, made this process very difficult. The first difficulty for Bupyong's engineers was to make Worthing's engineers understand a situation which they had never experienced before and, as much tacit knowledge was involved, (because of different industrial, technical, and economic backgrounds), both institutes had to overcome many misunderstandings.

8.3   Differences in engine development

For the Pony, launched in 1976, Hyundai licensed engine and chassis technology from MMC. This practice continued in the development of Pony Excel, launched in 1986. However, as the scale of production grew – from 70,000 a year to 300,000 for the Pony Excel – royalty payments to MMC also increased rapidly. This was the primary reason for Hyundai's decision to develop proprietary engines. As Hyundai expected its car production to increase to over 1 million units a year by 1990, it also thought that the minimum scale economies for developing proprietary engines would be achieved. In the mid-1980s, engine development became one of the company's most important R&D investments.

There were two ways for Hyundai to acquire proprietary engines. First of all, there were specialized engine design houses, particularly in Europe. The client retained the intellectual property rights pertaining to these engines. This was the quicker and lower risk option. Daewoo chose this way in the 1990s.

The second choice was to develop proprietary engines by building one's own technological capabilities. This path required more time, and was accompanied by higher risk. With success, however, this path would reduce dependence on foreign technology.

HMC's in-house engine development by learning from foreign technology

Hyundai's top management supported the second strategy. The founder, Chung, was firmly determined to build HMC's own engine development capability. Many senior managers opposed the strategy in view of the high risk.[9] Mitsubishi also warned about the risks involved and advised Hyundai to continue licensing its engine technology.[10] But the top management was convinced that, without in-house designed engines, a carmaker could not survive in the long run. Chung insisted that engine technologies were not too difficult for Korean engineers to master. A Korean engineering adviser, who had studied in the USA and worked in GM's engine department, also supported the founder's vision. They believed that the young engineers of the Mabukri institute would overcome initial failures and eventually master engine design.

In fact, it took seven years for Hyundai to complete development of its first proprietary engine. If it had been contracted fully to foreign engine design houses, it would have taken only three or four years.[11]

The year 1984 saw the commencement of the first long-term project of engine development: the Alpha project, which aimed to develop a 1.5-litre engine. The project leader was a Korean who had studied in the USA and worked as an automotive engineer in Detroit. Other members were all newly recruited from Korean universities.

At first, Hyundai had no idea about basic engine design. Ricardo, a British engine design house, was contracted to create a prototype engine and hand the blueprints to Hyundai. But Ricardo was also in charge of training six Hyundai engineers in basic engine design. As part of on-the-job training, they were allowed to participate in Ricardo's work for Hyundai. Most importantly, they carried out detailed design work under the guidance of Ricardo engineers.[12]

In 14 months, Ricardo completed all designs and built a prototype engine (HMC 1992: p. 765). But the prototype engine was too big and heavy for a subcompact car, and too expensive to manufacture. Ricardo was merely an engine design house, and was not responsible for matching the engine with engine room, transmission and transaxle, and neither was it responsible for questions related to mass production. Ultimately, Hyundai's engineers had to go beyond modification of the Ricardo-designed engine.[13]

When HMC contracted to Ricardo for the Alpha project, it was not with the intention of completely redesigning the engine and learning from the process. However, by the time the pilot production of the Alpha engine began in 1989, the prototype engine had gone through three full design changes and 288 detailed design changes (HMC 1992: p. 895). Over four years, Hyundai's engineers successfully completed this complex task by themselves.

The Alpha engine was first installed in the Scoup II, a subcompact coupe car intended for a small niche market in Korea. The engine was commercially produced from 1990 on a small scale. This was partly because Hyundai was not yet sure of the engine's performance, but also because it had not yet developed transmission and other power train components that were compatible with the Alpha engine. The Scoup II used the Pony Excel's chassis licensed from Mitsubishi.

In 1994, HMC completed the development of a new power train system and chassis for the Alpha engine. This was installed in the Accent, a subcompact car launched in that year. Thus, the Alpha engine project was successfully accomplished after 10 years.

The Alpha engine had not been completed by Hyundai's engineers alone, but the project was their 'initiation' into engine design. The know-how and skills acquired during the Alpha project were transferred to the second and third engine projects, the Beta and Gamma. For the Beta project (1.6–2.0 litres), only basic designing was contracted to AVL, an Austrian engine design house. The Mabukri Institute was in charge of detailed designing, which then came under final examination by AVL. Hyundai began to produce the Beta engine commercially for the Avante and Tiburon in 1995. The Gamma project ended in failure. AVL's basic design proved to have too many problems in manufacturability. Since then, Hyundai has carried out almost all design work by itself.

Between 1996 and 1998 HMC launched four more engines: the Epsilon engine (0.8–1.0 litres) for the Atoz; the Delta engine (2.0–2.4 litres) for the EF Sonata; the V6 Sigma engine (2.5–3.5 litres) for the EF Sonata and New Grandeur; and the Alpha Lean Burn engine for the new Accent.[14]

After mastering conventional gasoline engine technology, the company turned to the new technology of common rail diesel engines. Throughout the 1990s, HMC's RV and commercial vehicles were still fitted with Mitsubishi-designed diesel engines. HMC began a diesel engine development for RV and light truck in the mid-1990s by contracting to and learning from European engine design houses. But this project – the Zeta project – failed because of the difficulties of manufacturability. The second diesel project for light trucks began in 1998.

In late 2000 Hyundai succeeded in developing its first passenger car diesel engine with common rail technology. The Avante XD (called the Lantra in European markets), fitted with the 2.0 litre diesel engine, was launched in 2002.

In the 1990s, HMC was the only Korean carmaker capable of developing its own engines. Kia and Daewoo also developed proprietary engines for passenger cars, but these were all designed by foreign engine specialists.[15]

Daewoo's dependence on foreign engine specialists

Daewoo had no proprietary engine until the late 1980s. The engine for the Espero launched in 1990 was the only case of a proprietary development. However, this engine had been designed not by DMC but by Lotus, a British engine design house, and DMC's engineers carried out only minor changes of detailed design for manufacturability.

After separation from GM, Daewoo planned for production worldwide to exceed one million units a year from late 1996, when three proprietary cars would be launched. As the economies of scale permitted the development of proprietary engines, Daewoo discussed possible strategies. Some senior managers maintained that Hyundai's strategy was right, but the chairman, Kim, who wanted speedy global expansion in emerging markets, rejected this option: that is, because of the time-to-market strategy of Daewoo, Daewoo did not have enough time to drive a long-term strategy of capability building. Daewoo needed proprietary engines as soon as possible, for proprietary cars that would be launched in 3–4 years.

Daewoo decided on outsourcing of proprietary engine development and established the Munich Institute in March 1995. In spite of Daewoo's claims, the Munich Institute was not an R&D institute but an office for administration of foreign outsourced development projects. It had only 40–100 staff and little test equipment. Its role was limited to mediation between the engine department in Bupyong, Korea, and the European engine design houses.

Daewoo developed a 1.5-litre engine, called the Family One engine, by outsourcing to Ricardo. Ricardo carried out basic and detailed design.

Bupyong made only minor design changes for manufacturability, as with the Espero engine project. The engine was installed in the Lanos (1.3–1.5 litres) and the Nubira (1.5 litres). Daewoo also developed a 0.8-litre engine for the Matiz in a similar process. Cosworth, a British engine design house, contracted the development. For minor design changes, Daewoo itself built prototype engines.[16]

The dependence on outsourcing proprietary engine development is understandable if we take into account the urgency of launching four cars by late 1996 under the global expansion strategy. However, even finishing the first series of car development projects, Daewoo continued dependency in engine technology. Daewoo developed a 1.8–2.4 litres engine and a 2.5–3.5 litres engine during 1998–2002. Both engines were again contracted to European design houses. DMC made only minor design changes for manufacturability. Consequently, even today, Daewoo's engine development organization has little technological capability to carry out design of engine system and engine parts.

As we have seen, Hyundai made an official agreement with Ricardo about training of the company's engineers.[17] As a result, HMC acquired know-how in engine design. In contrast, DMC made no training agreement with Lotus, Ricardo or Cosworth. The company sent some engineers to the Munich Institute and to the foreign contractors, but their role was limited to merely administrative mediation between Bupyong and the foreign developers.[18] The foreign contractors transferred the completed prototype engine and its design blueprints to Daewoo, and their job finished at that point; they were not responsible for answering design questions. Consequently, even after 13 years in which Daewoo developed five proprietary engines, the company still has little know-how as regards engine design.[19]

8.4   Different approaches to organizational structure

Diverse R&D organizations for car development

In their famous book, *Product Development Performance – Strategy, Organization, and Management in the World Auto Industry*, Clark and Fujimoto depict four types of new car development systems by capturing essential features of many different kinds of organizations they surveyed (1991: pp. 253–6).

In the *functional* structure, development is organized by functional discipline, and engineers are relatively specialized. Senior functional managers (e.g., the head of body engineering) are responsible for allocating resources as well as the performance of the department. No individual has overall responsibility for total product quality. Coordination or integration among functional disciplines occurs through rules and procedures, detailed specifications, shared traditions among engineers, occasional direct contacts, and meetings.

In the *lightweight product manager system*, the basic organization remains functional, and the level of specialization is comparable to that of the functional structure. What makes it different is the existence of a product manager, who coordinates development activities through liaison representatives from each function. Product managers in this organization are lightweights in several respects. They have no direct access to working-level engineers and, compared to functional managers, have less status or power. In addition, their responsibility is limited to 'internal' integration within the R&D organization. They have no power for 'external' integration (i.e., company-wide coordination with marketing, sales, production, finance, etc.). Hence, they have no direct contact with the market or consumers.

In the *heavyweight product manager structure*, there is now a product manager with broader responsibility although the organization is still largely functional. Heavyweight product managers are usually senior in the organization, often having the same rank as the heads of the functional organizations, and sometimes higher. Some of their work occurs through liaison representatives, but the liaison personnel themselves are more important than in the lightweight system; they serve as local project leaders within their functional groups. The product managers, when necessary, have direct access to the working level functional engineers in charge of their project. They exercise strong direct and indirect influence on all functions of the product project. However, the product managers have no formal authority over engineers. Engineers still work within functional areas and may work on more than one project at a time, but they have stronger project orientation than engineers in the purely functional or lightweight systems. The heavyweight product managers are responsible not only for internal integration but also for external integration (e.g., for product concept development together with marketing organization).

The *project execution team structure* takes the product orientation further. A product manager works with a team of people who devote all their time only to the product project. This is not the same thing as a team of liaison people. People on the execution team leave their functional organization and report directly to the product manager.

According to the depiction of Clark and Fujimoto, Hyundai's organization is close to the lightweight product manager system and Daewoo's organization of Bupyong Institute is similar to the project execution team system.

Hyundai's lightweight product manager system

According to Hyun's survey (1999) on the product development organization, Hyundai had a lightweight product manager system with component-focus.[20] A product manager at Hyundai was only responsible for internal integration inside the R&D institutes. He was not in charge of external coordination with the marketing organization; even less was he responsible for consideration of customer needs. The product manager's job begins after product concept planning has been completed, usually by the corporate planning office and the marketing department (see Kim G. 2000: p. 202).

He is a chief engineer who is responsible for coordinating the activities of functional organizations for body, chassis, trim and electric parts within the R&D institute. Supported by an assistant engineer, he works through liaison engineers belonging to each function, but he has no direct access to the working level engineers. Power to decide about, say, chassis components belongs to the functional manager of the chassis department. A functional department works on several product development projects at a time. Hence, the status and power of a product manager is lower than that of functional managers (Kim G. 2000). The main role of a product project manager is to gather information on the status of work carried out by functional units, to help them solve conflicts, and to facilitate achievement of overall project targets. Besides, a product manager is in charge of one major project as well as of a few minor projects at a time. Consequently, his power is additionally dispersed among diverse projects.

Daewoo's project execution team system

In the development of the Espero during 1987–90, DMC's R&D organization followed the traditional functional form (Hyun 1997). But the group chairman's decision in mid-1993 to develop three cars simultaneously within three years forced the company to reorganize.[21] In November 1993, Kim initiated the transformation of the Bupyong Institute into a sort of project execution team system. The primary goal of the organizational renovation was the reduction of engineering lead time.

The reorganized Bupyong Institute consisted of three car project teams in charge of the Lanos, the Nubira and the Leganza, respectively. The functional organizations for body and chassis engineering, electric systems, and trim were divided into three projects, each of which came under the exclusive command of one project manager.[22] Consequently, car project managers acquired the power to drive the functional units to accomplish project-focused targets such as lead time reduction.[23]

They were not in charge of external coordination, however, as we will see in section 8.5. Thus, as regards company-wide coordination, the power of a product project manager at Daewoo was much weaker than that of Toyota's heavyweight product managers. But within the Bupyong Institute, they had much stronger authority than those working for Toyota, to say nothing of Hyundai's light product managers. As Hyun (1997) points out, 'through this organization, the project managers have relatively strong power to try to meet their initial target date for the start of production, which was one of Daewoo's most important objectives'.

The dynamic capabilities approach to firms and R&D organizations

In comparing firms' organizations, a historical-dynamic approach is important because firms and their organizations are in certain historical contexts and evolutionary stages of capability building (Chandler, Hagström and Sölvell 1998).

In their book, *Product Development Performance* (1991), Clark and Fujimoto compare three parameters of product development performance – lead time, engineering productivity, and product quality – for American, European, and Japanese carmakers, and show that some Japanese companies were much better in all aspects. They believe that their outstanding performance was mainly due to superior organizational systems. Their evidence suggests that organizational integration of development processes is the underlying source of reduced lead time, improved engineering productivity, and higher total product integrity. The best firms have not only achieved internal integration within their R&D organizations, but also external integration (i.e., the integration of customer needs into the design and development process). Clark and Fujimoto point out that a strong product manager system is essential for strong internal and external integration. Thus, their main concern is not technological but organizational capability.

The book has the same limitation as all research that uses international comparative surveys: namely, it does not focus on how and under which historical conditions the Japanese, European and American systems evolved, but simply assumes that the technological capabilities of the Japanese, European and American companies being studied are already on the same level. Therefore, the book is not interested in how the Japanese companies, the latecomers, made efforts to learn technologies from Europe and America not only before the war, but also after. The historical dynamism of the interactive influence between technological capability and organizational structure rarely comes into question.

In his recent book, *Evolution of a Manufacturing System at Toyota* (1999), Fujimoto shifted his focus on to the ways that firms with lasting superior performance built their competitive capability. As regards Japanese automakers, he suggests the following model of historical stages:

1960s–'70s: Pursuit of better functions and technology at the individual component level. Organizational capability built around element technologies. Element-focused strategy for product development. Functional organization best fits this stage.

Late 1970s to early 1980s: The element-focused strategy reaches its limit. Firms find they cannot differentiate their products by superiority in component technologies alone. The companies with superior component technology tend to fail in the market at this stage.

1980s: Companies start focusing on product integrity as a key differentiator at the system level. System-focused strategy for individual product development is chosen. Tight project teams and heavyweight project managers are better structure for this stage.

Early 1990s: Companies pursuing customer satisfaction through total product quality face over-quality and increasing costs as side effects of their efforts toward higher product integrity and variety... Heavyweight product manager system and strong cross-functional teams, designed for higher product integrity, often lead to a lack of cross-project coordination.

Mid-1990s: Companies start to cut product costs dramatically by applying lean product design. Shifting focus from individual products to company-wide product line may be a key for this stage...Reorganization for multiple projects management often becomes the issue. Strong multi-product planners...often become essential people. (Fujimoto 1999: pp. 213–14)

Fujimoto adds that the shift from component focus and functional organization to system integrity and heavyweight product manager organization is likely to be accompanied by an improvement in the customer's ability to discern subtle differences in the total product quality.

However, it is not only the improving *customer's ability* but also the improving *producer's ability* which is the factor that enables the shift. In other words, the shift was feasible for the Japanese automakers only after they had mastered the technologies of car components (engine, chassis, body, and so on) by learning from America and Europe in the 1950s–1970s. Without learning the component technologies through the functional or lightweight product manager system, they could not have shifted the focus to total product integrity and heavyweight product manager organization in the 1980s.

The historical experience of the Japanese carmakers is a good reference standard for evaluating the organizational systems of Korean automakers, also latecomers.[24]

Technological expertise and knowledge sharing

The negative effects of a project-oriented organization, which were rarely referred to by Clark and Fujimoto in *Product Development Performance* (1991), are described well by Fujimoto in *Evolution of a Manufacturing System at Toyota* (1999). A project-oriented organization, as shown in the case of Daewoo's Bupyong Institute, is not appropriate for long-run capabilities building because it hinders knowledge sharing and knowledge accumulation.

Working space of project teams and knowledge sharing

Fujimoto notes that, even in the Japanese firms with a heavyweight product manager system, each of the product project teams was not brought together into one large room, except in the case of a few especially urgent projects. Engineers' desks were normally located in the rooms for functional units. For instance, they were located in the space allocated to the body design department or the chassis design department, although these units themselves were usually located fairly close to each other (Fujimoto 1999: p. 193). This kind of spatial organization enables functional engineers, say, chassis engineers who are working for different project managers, to communicate directly with each other and to share their chassis-specialized knowledge.

In the case of Daewoo, however, each of the three product teams occupied an entire floor of the central building at the Bupyong Institute: the Lanos project team was located on the second floor, the Nubira team on the third floor and the Leganza team on the fourth floor. Engineers for body and chassis engineering were divided between floors, over which the relevant product manager had exclusive authority. This hindered chassis engineers, say, sharing chassis-specific knowledge.

In contrast, the working spaces of Hyundai's engineers were located in the rooms of functional units. Product managers had small office rooms where they held meetings with the liaison representatives. They usually visited the functional unit rooms for coordination purposes. Hence, the functional engineers, say, for chassis design, could share their knowledge easily with each other.

In the heavyweight product manager system at Toyota functional engineers were usually assigned to more than one project, rather than dedicating themselves to one project at a time (Fujimoto 1999). In this way, knowledge transfer and sharing among various projects was facilitated. In the lightweight product manager system of Hyundai, too, functional engineers were engaged in more than one project. But at Daewoo, functional engineers dedicated themselves to one project only, so that knowledge sharing among the projects was difficult.

Authority on personnel issues and promotion of functional experts

In Toyota's heavyweight product manager system, functional managers had formal authority even in personnel issues. Product project managers could only informally influence appraisal and promotion of engineers and hence the functional units held strong formal power to facilitate an engineer's professional development. Because of the advantage of facilitating professional expertise, even the project execution team systems surveyed by Clark and Fujimoto allowed functional managers to retain responsibility for personnel issues (1991: p. 256).

In the case of Daewoo, however, it was the project managers who determined personnel issues. Engineers were appraised and promoted not according to their contributions to functional expertise building, but according to those regarding a product project. This helped Daewoo develop cars quickly, but at the same time hindered expertise building.

In contrast, HMC's product managers had no power in personnel issues; functional managers retained authority. Hence, individual engineers had a strong motive to enhance their know-how and skill within the functional specialization. Functional specialists were promoted, although development engineering lead time might take longer.

Technical expertise and component-focused strategy

In the 1990s, HMC kept its component-focused strategy with lightweight product managers (see also Kim G. 2000). To the question of why HMC did not adopt the heavyweight manager system, a manager of the company's development organization answered as follows:

> I think, without an overall development of component technologies, introduction of a heavyweight manager system would be absurd. In

Hyundai, some component technologies, for example, body designing and gasoline engine development, are now OK. But our technological ability with regard to diesel engine, automatic transmission, high-tech suspension and brake system, safety technique, etc., is far from enough to compete with automakers in industrialized countries. In these areas, we are still in a stage of learning existing technologies from foreign sources. Hence, we cannot yet concentrate our resources on more advanced technologies like fuel cell engines so long as we can outsource them.

Many functional departments still lack technological expertise. For example, we still lack a specialist of piston technology who has worked at least 10 years in the area. We have just reached a stage of such expertise that we now have a piston specialist who has several years' experience. Insofar as we do not reach the level of capabilities in major component technologies close to that of the Japanese or American carmakers, it is unavoidable for us to adopt the component-focused strategy with lightweight product managers.

By contrast, Daewoo achieved a reduction of engineering lead time with its project-focused strategy with stronger product managers, but this was at the cost of long-run formation of technical expertise in functional organizations.

Clark and Fujimoto (1991: p. 284) report that, like Daewoo, Chrysler also adopted so-called 'dedicated-co-located product development teams' for each of the base models (e.g., for the Neon car). Some Japanese makers have also used this type of organization in the past; but Clark and Fujimoto point out that even these automakers hesitated to go as far as the 'project execution teams' structure. Their main concern was loss of expertise by dispersing engineers to different projects on a full-time basis. Therefore, they generally preferred more regular product manager systems in which one working engineer is allowed to work on more than one project. Japanese practitioners argue also that, although the product-oriented approach would shorten lead time, 'using this approach regularly results in a duplication of engineering resources, insufficient accumulation of component technologies, and lack of inter-project knowledge transfer' (Fujimoto 1999: p. 203).

Using common parts and knowledge sharing

Clark and Fujimoto (1991: p. 260) point out that even heavyweight product managers have no formal authority with regard to design specifications of components. Functional managers retain the authority and a product manager can only influence design indirectly, through cross-functional coordination. Such practices facilitate adoption of common parts because functional managers prefer it. Fewer common parts – say, a unique brake system for each new car – would certainly improve product integrity, and would strengthen the product variety, which would be desirable to product managers. But this could also result in cost increases (Fujimoto 1999: p. 208).

In Daewoo, product managers acquired the power to decide on parts, too. With functional organizations completely divided into three project units, functional managers had no formal authority on design specifications of parts. Consequently, product managers tended to strongly avoid adopting common parts. In Hyundai, the functional managers had the authority to decide on design specifications of parts and components.

Competition among product managers

Fujimoto speaks of the side effects of a project-oriented organizational strategy (1999: p. 217). When each product project manager is powerful, cross-project coordination may become difficult. This is because individual managers tend to behave too autonomously. In particular, when product project managers are competing for internal promotion, knowledge transfer and sharing among the projects become difficult.

O'Brien (1998: p. 92) points out that Korean automakers did not utilize a 'multi-project management policy' that emphasizes interproject platform sharing, knowledge sharing and design transfer.[25] But above all, Korean carmakers did not have enough of their own models to allow them to adopt a multi-project management policy. Throughout the 1990s, HMC replaced cars with the old Mitsubishi-designed platforms with new ones; DMC also concentrated on launching completely new cars with new platforms.

Despite this, the competition among project managers at Daewoo was surely much stronger than at Hyundai, so that they tended to avoid sharing knowledge of possible common subsystems and parts. The group chairman, Kim, intentionally promoted competition among product project managers in order to drive them to reach targets as quickly as possible.

8.5   Differences in company-wide coordination for car development

Product development requires more than an R&D organization; it needs a coordinated effort from planning, purchasing, marketing, engineering, finance and production organizations. Hence, achieving company-wide coordination is an important factor in the product development process. This entails a conscious organizational effort to enhance the integrity of the development process by matching the philosophy and details of product design to the expectations of target customers.

In the case of a heavyweight product manager system, product managers are in charge of external coordination. They are responsible for coordination in wide areas (including manufacturing, marketing and sales) for the entire project period. They also have leadership in conceptual development through direct access to customers.

In the 1990s, however, all Korean carmakers were in an early stage of developing new cars. They had only a few proprietary cars, so that the success or failure of a new car project significantly impacted on overall corporate performance. Therefore, as Hyun (1999) points out, top management usually paid great attention to the new car development process, and used directly to intervene in the decision-making on new car projects. Consequently, the power of product project managers was limited in R&D areas. This was the case not only in Hyundai and Kia, which used a light product manager system, but also in Daewoo, which had a strongly product-oriented system.

In spite of this common feature, however, Hyundai and Daewoo showed clear differences in their methods of achieving company-wide coordination. These differences in turn reflect differences in organizational routines with regard to the product development process.

Product commission in Hyundai

In HMC, a committee organization, whose name in English means something like 'the Product Commission', took charge of company-wide coordination of new product development.[26] The commission consisted of all chief managers from marketing, R&D, manufacturing, finance, export and so on, who were directly involved in a new product development. It was not an organ of execution, but a planning and decision-making organ. It held monthly meetings. Often, the CEO and other top managers also attended the meeting. The commission made important decisions about matters such as product concept, target market and customer, cost and price, model variations, and so on. For instance, the commission had the power to decide on styling freeze and prototype freeze.

A product planning department, which belonged to the marketing function, organized the commission by preparing agendas and reports. It gathered information and organized small meetings among middle-level managers from R&D, marketing, sales, manufacturing, finance, and so on. In the monthly meeting, the chief functional managers had discussions and made decisions only about important matters and resolved conflicts.

Entrepreneurial leadership in Daewoo

In Daewoo, the chairman himself took the role of company-wide coordinator. Daewoo was famous for its one-man leadership. For instance, The *Economist* called the globalized Daewoo a 'one man empire' (27 January 1996). As one of Daewoo's senior managers said proudly:

> Chairman Kim always initiates our business deals and takes charge not only of *strategic decisions* but also of *operational details*. Experienced aides in the corporate office and operating divisions provide analysis reports to aid him in his decision-making. However, it is usually Chairman Kim who senses the opportunities and judges the business prospects. He really thinks that every street is paved with gold. After a project has progressed to a certain stage, he focuses on key strategic issues and delegates operational issues to the corporate staff and local subsidiary managers. As the project matures further, the local subsidiary takes more of the initiative. *Whenever necessary, Chairman Kim intervenes and deals with a problem*, but the process is quite simple. *With only a couple of phone call or faxes, he cuts to the heart of the problem and identifies a solution.* He also benefits from the wisdom of experienced executive assistants and front-line managers, but the process mainly involves very brief informal discussions. I've never seen him sit through a lengthy internal presentation. This business style is reflected in the simple internal reporting process of Daewoo. The direct experience of front-line managers is appreciated more than an ornate analysis written from behind a desk...*Bureaucratic haggling and sticking to routine procedures are the biggest enemies of progress in Daewoo. Having started as a trading company, Daewoo still values flexibility and deal making rather than building and running routinized operating systems.* (cited in Park C.-H. 1998; italics are my own)

Thus, instead of relying on organizational capabilities building, Daewoo's managers believed in the chairman's entrepreneurship as an excellent dealer and trader, and ignored the formalization of organizational processes. They usually considered formal market studies prepared by marketing and planning offices to be 'ornamental'. This is one of the most important reasons why Daewoo expanded so fast and recklessly in the emerging market countries. Daewoo's senior managers did not seem to have been warned by any corporate organization about the potential risks.

In DMC, the chairman not only made strategic decisions but also looked after operational details. In order to reach the target of launching proprietary cars as quickly as possible, the chairman personally took charge of new car development, too. Hyun (1997) points out that Kim undertook the role of chief technology officer (CTO) in DMC, while he was also the CEO and Chief Finance Officer. A product manager appreciated Kim's role as CTO, saying: 'the most important success factor in the new product development effort was global R&D. But it was the strong driving force of the chairman Kim Woo-Choong, who, as the overall project manager, devoted himself to coordinating the inter-project cooperation, that made for success' (cited in Hyun 1997). Indeed, without the chairman's direct intervention in product development, Daewoo would not have succeeded in launching four cars during 1996–8.

DMC had no body to compare with HMC's Product Commission. The chairman, playing the role of an extremely powerful heavyweight product manager, undertook the company-wide coordination by himself. Without relying on routinized organizational procedures, he decided on product concept, product planning, target market, styling freeze, prototype car freeze, and so on.[27]

For instance, in developing the Lanos, a product-planning unit proposed a concept that targeted young customers. But, after scant discussion with relevant functional managers, the chairman chose a car style design himself, according to his own taste. (Foreign car design houses such as ItalDesign or IDEA proposed four or five style samples, and Kim made his choice.) Similarly, the chairman directly intervened in the prototype freeze. For instance, he several times demanded changes in seat designs of prototype cars. Each change of seat design caused an additional cost of around US$1 million for additional prototype building and crash testing.

It is noteworthy that the top management of HMC, by contrast, rarely intervened in the procedures of the Product Commission. They respected proposals by the marketing and design department and delegated authority to the commission.[28] For the styling freeze, for instance, special meetings about car style evaluation were organized by the commission. Relevant functional managers attended to see and evaluate clay models and prototypes from their own viewpoints. They discussed openly with each other and sometimes with the top management, including the CEO, Chung Se-Young. The Product Commission made the final decision.

8.6   Conclusion

In this chapter, we have examined the divergent strategies, capabilities and organizations of HMC and DMC for product development. We saw that Hyundai and Daewoo had very different approaches to R&D, and that these were conditioned by differences in 'vision'. This determined the different ways of building and organizing product development capabilities and procedures.

HMC was the only Korean carmaker that was capable of developing new cars without significant dependence on foreign technologies. HMC stressed long-term accumulation of technological capabilities and wanted to become innovative enough to compete with top-class carmakers in the world market. This self-reliant R&D was in sharp contrast with Daewoo's global R&D outsourcing. Daewoo sought to expand into emerging markets, where its existing technological capabilities were more or less adequate. Daewoo, to overcome its underdeveloped technological capabilities, simply outsourced necessary technologies. This strategy enabled Daewoo to launch cars quickly between 1996 and 1998, more quickly than HMC.

At the same time, however, Daewoo's focus on global outsourcing and 'time-to-market' was accompanied by the sacrifice of long-term capabilities building. Daewoo outsourced car testing and analysis and new engine development to foreign specialists, while HMC pursued and attained full independence in this area. Daewoo's use of foreign automotive institutes also meant problems in the acquisition of tacit knowledge, due to differences in language, culture and technical-industrial background. These problems entailed immediate and long-term inefficiencies.

We also noted that Daewoo's project-oriented R&D organization, introduced to reduce car development time, was not conducive to long-term accumulation of technological expertise in a company with underdeveloped technological capabilities. By contrast, HMC's more function-oriented R&D organization encouraged engineers to develop professional expertise.

And finally, Daewoo's firm-specific organizational style (organizational routine), built around the entrepreneurial leadership of the founding chairman, meant that organizational competencies were not developed. The entrepreneur directly intervened in decision-making on car development. HMC adopted a different approach: decision-making procedures were formalized and professional managers played an important role.

In conclusion, Daewoo's global approach and short-termism in technology, together with the entrepreneurial leadership, failed to compensate for its underdeveloped capabilities in product technology.

In this regard, the 1997 crisis revealed – and at the same time, accelerated – two aspects of the *chaebol*'s evolution in business. The first was their evolution from entrepreneurial organizations to managerialist ones; the second was the evolution from focusing on expansion to technology-related growth. The former aspect, organizational capability, was closely linked with the latter, technological capability. Those firms that did not follow these tendencies failed and eventually collapsed.

In the next chapter, we will further illuminate those tendencies, this time in relation to the question of diversification.

9
The *Chaebol*'s Diversification: Ssangyong and Samsung

Diversification was one of the principal pathways taken by the *chaebol* to expand business. As seen in Chapter 3, the abolition of industrial policy, which had previously limited industrial entry, allowed *chaebol* groups to diversify into new business lines. And in fact, starting in the early 1990s, there followed a wave of unrelated diversification across almost all major industries and, as a result, the number of companies in the electronics and semiconductors, automotive, iron and steel, petrochemical and oil industries, merchant banking, insurance and other sectors doubled and tripled.

In the automotive industry, for instance, Ssangyong (cement and construction), which had taken over Donga Motors (commercial vehicles) in 1986, began to produce luxury passenger cars and RVs in 1991. Hyundai Precision Company (railway systems and cargo containers) also entered RV manufacturing in 1990.[1] Samsung (electronics and chemicals) began producing commercial vehicles in 1992 and passenger cars in 1994. Halla (construction and shipbuilding) also attempted to enter commercial vehicle production in the mid-1990s.

Most *chaebol* groups wanted to diversify into any sector which seemed promising. In particular, small and middle-sized *chaebol* groups (the sixth to fiftieth largest) diversified into sectors in which the five largest *chaebol* groups – Hyundai, Samsung, Daewoo, LG and SK – had long been predominant. For instance, Jinro, a *chaebol* group (ranked nineteenth in 1997) whose core business had been alcoholic drinks, diversified into electronics and the transportation business; Haitai (ranked twenty-fourth in 1997), one of the two leading producers of food and drinks, diversified into electronics and construction. Deregulated financial markets supplied the investment funds.

However, these diversifications failed sooner or later. Corporate collapses among small and middle-sized *chaebol* groups continued between 1997 and 1999. In the automotive industry, Ssangyong and Samsung abandoned their loss-making carmakers in 1997 and 1998, respectively.[2]

Agency theory criticizes unrelated diversification for causing interest conflicts between managers and shareholders. Amihud and Lev (1981 and 1999), for instance, argue that managers, unless closely monitored by shareholders, will attempt to reduce their employment risk through unrelated mergers and diversification. This managerial misbehaviour (moral hazard) may not be in the shareholders' interest.[3]

Following this line of argument, some critics of the *chaebol* blame unrelated diversification for having caused the 1997 crisis in Korea (Choe J.-P. 1999; Kim K.-W. 1999; Jang 2001). They regard the unrelated diversification (and hence the conglomerate form of business) of the *chaebol* as a rent-seeking activity (Kang, Choe and Chang 1991; Kang, C.-K. 1995). Indeed, the massive failures of the *chaebol* companies during the 1997 crisis seem to provide the best support for this argument.[4]

However, this fundamental criticism of unrelated diversification has a significant weakness. It ignores the historical fact that the leading *chaebol* companies came into being through unrelated diversification. For example, HMC was established as a spin-off from HECC (construction) and Samsung Electronics as a spin-off from Cheil Textile (textile).

Shareholder value theory's ahistorical criticism does not explain the historical dynamics of the *chaebol*'s diversification. Rather, we should ask: why did unrelated diversifications in Korea in the 1960s and 1970s succeed by and large, while those in the 1990s did not? As the question itself implies, the answer should include an historical perspective.

In section 9.1 of this chapter, we will make use of just such a historical view, one developed by the 'dynamic capabilities approach', to re-examine the *chaebol*'s diversification.[5] Chandlerian notions such as first mover advantages and challenger disadvantages will be presented to explain diversification. Sections 9.2 and 9.3 will examine two cases of unrelated diversification into the automotive industry in the 1990s: Ssangyong and Samsung. We will see that both carmakers from the outset faced significant problems in the areas of technological capabilities and minimum scale economies, whereas first mover companies – Hyundai, Kia and Daewoo – had all the advantages. The new entrants' high costs, high debts and low profits, followed by the untimely collapse of the Korean car market after the outbreak of the financial crisis, ensured the demise of the struggling challengers.

9.1   Diversification of the *chaebol*, past and present

Diversification and capabilities

Diversification is a firm's entry into a new business area to expand its production or market. There are a variety of reasons for diversification.[6] When a firm's current product line matures or even declines, the firm may have to search for new business opportunities. Alternatively, when the firm is very successful in an industry and has substantial surplus resources, it may need new businesses in which to invest; or the firm may diversify simply to expand its business domain and increase its economic power. Alfred Chandler (1962) found that successful firms in the USA grew by diversifying from single product lines into multi-product lines that were related to their core business. This is referred to as related diversification (see also Penrose 1959).

Between the early 1960s and late 1970s, however, America's big business firms tended to diversify into businesses that were not related to their technological and other core capabilities (Chandler 1990: p. 622). This is usually called unrelated diversification (UD), and an enterprise group with this business structure is called a conglomerate. The conglomerate movement in American business, however, soon declined and faded in the 1980s. Firms divested from unrelated fields and reorganized themselves according to their core competence (Prahalad and Hamel 1990).[7]

Diversification in late industrialization

The Korean *chaebol* have grown by diversification. Both unrelated and related diversifications have been useful strategies for business expansion,[8] but here we will discuss only unrelated diversification.

In Korea's developmental system the unrelated diversification strategy was prevalent among the *chaebol* groups (Jung 1991). They had, however, good reasons for choosing this strategy. First, as Amsden (1989, 1997a, 1997b) argues, learning is central to the process of late industrialization. Because firms in late-industrializing countries do not have the technical or marketing expertise that industrialized enterprises already possess, they cannot grow by developing new related product lines or by moving into higher-quality niches in their existing markets. The only other way to grow is to begin with learning from the bottom. In the case of Korea, nearly every firm was just a beginner in its business at the start of industrialization, and particularly at the time of the Big Push of the 1970s. In those days, Korea was a rapidly expanding economy, presenting the *chaebol* with new business opportunities.

Second, the Korean market was relatively small. A successful company would saturate a market with a relatively small scale of operation and soon need to find new business (Kang 1996: p. 116). Hence, with the support of the government, *chaebol* groups were encouraged to enter new sectors that were not related to their existing capabilities. Both the *chaebol* and the government wanted to establish world-class big businesses that could effectively compete in the international market. Without specialized knowledge-based assets, big business groups diversified widely into technologically unrelated industries. Therefore, Amsden (2001: p. 197) argues, initial absence of proprietary know-how and the conglomerate form of business go hand-in-hand in late industrializing economies. Large *chaebol* groups in Korea conformed to this pattern of diversification in the three decades following the 1960s (Jung K.-H. 1987).

First mover advantages and challenger disadvantages

Diversified *chaebol* firms soon became the leading companies in their industries. Because these industries had large minimum economies of scale in production and distribution, the first entrants into them were strategically positioned to capture 'first mover advantages'. Chandler (1990: p. 8) points out that first mover firms in modern business history made three-pronged investments in production, distribution and management:

> The first was an investment in production facilities large enough to exploit a technology's potential economies of scale or scope. The second was an investment in a national and international marketing and distributing network, so that the volume of sales might keep pace with the new volume of production. Finally, to benefit fully from these two kinds of investment the entrepreneurs also had to invest in management: they had to recruit and train managers not only to administer the enlarged facilities and increased personnel in both production and distribution, but also to monitor and coordinate those two basic functional activities and to plan and allocate resources for future production and distribution.

By exploiting the minimum scale economies and core organizational capabilities, the first enterprises acquired powerful competitive advantages. These industries quickly became oligopolistic: that is, dominated by a small number of first movers.

Likewise, the first movers in the Korea's industrialization acquired sooner or later distinctive advantages through their production scale, market share, and technological and managerial competencies. The Big Push in particular created capital-intensive industries that usually required high minimum efficient scale economies and hence had high capital entry costs. Furthermore, the first movers built their own proprietary knowledge assets. In the 1980s, government promotion of private business was contingent on investing heavily in R&D, and leading firms not only mastered manufacturing technology but also invested in new product development, as seen in the case of HMC.

The Korean government, we have seen, practised licensing control of industrial entry. New entry in key industries was strictly controlled, so that minimum production scales for the existing firms was guaranteed. However, insofar as the first movers benefited increasingly from scale economy and core capabilities, industrial entry by challengers became increasingly difficult. An entry barrier based on the technological and organizational competence replaced the legal entry barrier from the late 1980s. This meant that the traditional strategy of the *chaebol*, unrelated diversification, became either unfeasible or very costly and time-consuming.

Nonetheless, the investment boom in the 1990s tended to follow the lines of UD. The *chaebol*'s organizational inertia simply created continuing impulses towards that goal: that is, unrelated diversification was usually initiated and driven by the *chaebol* entrepreneur and his office, usually known as the 'general planning office'.[9] As professional managers increasingly took charge of strategic decision-making in individual subsidiary companies, the managerial position of the *chaebol* entrepreneur and his office tended to decline. The latter then sought to retain their managerial competence by continuing diversification into new areas where professional managers had not yet developed expertise. In other words, the *chaebol*'s specific organizational routine – now turned into an organizational rigidity – created the inertia towards UD (see also Amsden and Hikino 1994; Amsden 1997b).

The entry moves of the challengers in the automotive, petrochemical, iron and steel, and electronics industries induced the general overinvestment in the period: that is, as a countermove, the first movers expanded their production vigorously in order to ensure that latecomers found no market niche.[10] The fierce market competition that occurred during the 1990s between the challengers and first movers in Korea's major industries ended with the defeat of the former; their successive collapses and restructurings are one of the most important features of the economic crisis during 1997–9.

In the Korean automobile industry, Ssangyong and Samsung were such entrants. They entered in 1986 and 1994 respectively and the moves were typical cases of unrelated diversification. They collapsed in late 1997 and late 1998 respectively.

9.2   Case one: the Ssangyong Motor Company

Ssyangyong's entry into car manufacturing

The Ssangyong group was the sixth largest *chaebol* in the 1990s. Its major business areas were trading and finance, engineering and construction, cement and machinery, and its competitive edge was in Ssangyong Cement in particular.

Its history is characterized by UD. Having started out as a small soap factory in 1939, it entered textiles, insurance and trade in the 1940s and 1950s, cement, paper and shipping in the 1960s, oil refining, machinery, engineering and construction in the 1970s, and information and tele-communications, securities and automobiles in the 1980s. Automobile production came in 1986, with the acquisition of Donga Motors, a small manufacturer of jeeps and large commercial vehicles. Donga Motors already had competitive advantages in these segments. However, Kim Suk-Won, the chairman of the Ssangyong group, had an ambitious vision to make it a large volume carmaker, challenging Toyota. In accordance with his vision, the Ssangyong Motor Company began to expand its product lines. As the first step towards entry into the passenger car business, it chose the luxury passenger car and RV segments.

As Chandler (1990) points out, challengers are disadvantaged by their lack of minimum scale economies and by poor organizational capabilities for solving technological and managerial problems. SMC faced exactly these difficulties. In order to learn the technical know-how to produce luxury cars and RV engines through technology-transfer, it came to a technical licence agreement with Daimler-Benz. Mercedes agreed to help Ssangyong build an engine plant and develop the chassis for a luxury passenger car model. As part of the deal, Daimler-Benz acquired a 5 per cent stake in SMC in November 1992.

Ssangyong established an R&D centre in 1992 and developed a chassis for the Musso, an RV model, and the Istana, a mini-bus. The vehicles were installed with Mercedes-designed engines manufactured by Ssangyong, and their commercial production began in 1993 and

1995 respectively. In 1995, the company also developed the Chairman, a luxury sedan, based upon Mercedes-Benz's E-Class. Ssangyong designed only the body and mounted it on a Benz-designed platform. Core technologies for the platforms of all the models were licensed from Daimler-Benz.

The company built new production lines and expanded production capacity rapidly. As shown in Table 9.1, its annual production capacity multiplied four times from 39,000 units to 154,000 units between 1993 and 1997. But even this increase was modest compared to the chairman's vision which, in 1995, anticipated an increase in capacity to 300,000 units by 1997 and to 650,000 by 2000.

Lack of scale economies and technological capabilities

In spite of launching new products and multiplying production capacity, actual production volume did not increase accordingly. Table 9.1 shows that the capacity utilization rate usually remained at under 60 per cent throughout the 1990s. This shows that the company never reached the production volume it needed for minimum efficient scale economies. Moreover, the rate peaked in 1994 and then went downwards even though its new models, the Istana and the Chairman, were launched in 1995.

The company faced intense competition with the first mover carmakers. In the RV segment where Ssangyong, as the successor of Donga Motors, was a powerful first mover, Hyundai Precision Company entered successfully with a model licensed from Mitsubishi. Furthermore, the strongest first movers (HMC and Kia) had competitive advantages in the mini-bus segment, with their scale economies and organizational competences. Worse, the Korean market for large luxury passenger cars did not grow as fast as the chairman, Kim, expected. And worst of all, Ssangyong was not allowed to export its products insofar as they included parts that were manufactured with licensed technology.

Chronic losses and financial vulnerability

The vision of Kim Suk-Won perished as the Ssangyong Motor Company never turned a profit after 1991, even after the launch of new products in 1993 and 1995. As shown in Table 9.2, the company suffered chronic huge losses in the 1990s.

The investment in production facilities and R&D and the low level of capacity utilization rate were the main causes of the losses. Moreover, the rate of material costs to total production costs was calculated to be 16 per cent higher than that of other automakers (Kim W.-P. 1999).

Table 9.1 Car production by Ssangyong Motors, 1990–8

	1990	1991	1992	1993	1994	1995	1996	1997	1998
Capacity (A)	39,000	39,000	39,000	39,000	59,000	112,000	120,000	154,000	154,000
Production (B)	22,148	24,668	21,439	22,075	46,375	54,758	77,538	80,813	44,562
B/A rate (%)	57	63	55	57	79	49	65	52	29

Note: Capacity utilization rate is based on the uniform work hours.
Source: KAMA, *Automotive Statistics*, yearly.

Table 9.2 Profitability of Ssangyong Motor Company, 1990–8 (hundred million won)

	1990	1991	1992	1993	1994	1995	1996	1997	1998
Sales	3,669	4,018	3,408	3,821	8,059	9,867	13,694	14,416	7,942
Operating profit	99	108	–74	–340	–45	22	168	247	369
Ordinary profit	n.a.	104	–85	–617	772	–1,278	–2,200	–3,112	–2,457
Net profit	58	94	–88	–621	–793	–1,262	–2,285	–3,133	–4,998

n.a. = not available
Source: Ssangyong Motors, *Annual Report*, yearly.

This high cost structure partly resulted from the use of expensive technology. As long as it licensed Mercedes-Benz technology for both engine and chassis, there was no choice but to use expensive material and components. The company's attempts at technological learning were constricted by the choice of Mercedes-Benz's advanced technology which was too expensive and too advanced to learn. This meant that there was little room for the company to upgrade its own technological capabilities for the purpose of cost reduction.

A further problem was that the company, in spite of higher manufacturing costs, could not set sales prices higher than those of rival automakers. Hence, even the increase in turnover from 1994 could not help it escape from the increasing losses. Table 9.3 shows that due to the repeated net losses, SMC's equity capital fell rapidly after 1993, finally reaching below zero in 1997.

The more the company recorded net losses, the more it borrowed from various financial institutions; and yet the company was able to survive for six years. How was this possible? It was possible only because some commercial banks and Ssangyong-controlled non-banking financial companies – Ssangyong Securities, Ssangyong Fire & Marine Insurance, and Ssangyong Capital – pumped funds into it.

We have seen that such intersubsidiary support was a feature of the group system of the *chaebol*. In the developmental system, the government restricted this practice through its industrial policy and credit control. However, after the financial market opening and deregulation, there was no regulatory institution that was capable of, and responsible for, monitoring and controlling intragroup financial support. The costs of lax deregulation were heavy. The practical default of the company at the end of 1997 left the Ssangyong-related financial institutions with huge non-performing loans.

Table 9.3   Financial statements of Ssangyong Motor Company, 1990–98[a] (hundred million won)

	1990	1991	1992	1993	1994	1995	1996	1997	1998
Assets	5,951	8,364	11,095	14,636	22,225	29,185	37,672	39,863	37,930
Debts (D)	4,394	5,870	8,054	11,951	20,133	26,590	37,316	41,372	27,468
Equity capital (E)	1,557	2,494	3,041	2,685	2,092	2,595	356	–1,509	10,462
D/E ratio (%)	282	235	265	445	962	1,025	10,482	-	263

[a] The company was taken over by Daewoo in December 1997.
Source: Ssangyong Motor Company, *Annual Report*, yearly.

Ssangyong Group's crisis and restructuring

In 1996, Kim decided to give up Ssangyong Motor Company. Because, like other *chaebol*, the group's companies were interconnected through intersubsidiary debt guarantee and shareholding, all of them risked financial default. At the end of 1996, he entered into negotiations with Samsung and Mercedes-Benz about the sale of Ssangyong Motors, recognizing that the group's survival was at stake, but without success. In the meantime, however, Ssangyong's capital and cash-flow crunch became much more serious. In the face of an ever-worsening crisis, he selected Daewoo as the buyer for Ssangyong Motors. Finally in December 1997, in the midst of the financial turmoil, the acquisition of Ssangyong Motor Company by Daewoo was announced.

In spite of this, 17 subsidiaries of the Ssangyong group made losses in 1998 that totalled 3.1 trillion won. Ssangyong, still the sixth largest *chaebol* in 1999, was not formally bankrupt, but it went into a workout programme with creditor banks. Of its 27 subsidiaries, only six retained their normal corporate status at the end of 1999. Two were in the bank bailout programme, seven had been sold or were to be sold, two were liquidated and ten merged with other subsidiaries. Responsibility for half of Ssangyong Motors' debts was still one of the main factors that forced Ssangyong Group to sell off assets and spin-off companies ahead of the most pressing creditors.

9.3   Case two: the Samsung Motor Company

Samsung Group's business and diversification

Samsung was one of the largest *chaebol* and some companies in the *chaebol* group, notably Samsung Electronics, symbolized all of the positive aspects of Korea's industrialization. Samsung group, with its 58 subsidiaries in 1998 (see Table 9.4), encompassed diverse business activities in the electronics, chemicals, machinery, automotive, and trade and finance sectors. Within the group, Samsung Corporation, Samsung Electronics and Samsung Life Insurance were the three leading companies in terms of assets, turnover and net profit, and they played the role of quasi-holding companies for the other subsidiaries.

Samsung was founded in 1938 as a small trading company. In 1948, the founder, Lee Byung-Chull, established Samsung Corporation and began international trade. In the late 1960s, when the military government of President Park Chung-Hee began to encourage the *chaebol* to invest in heavy industries, the founder established Samsung Electronics.

Table 9.4   Samsung Group and its 58 subsidiaries, 1998

Field	Company name
Electronics	Samsung Electronics Samsung Display Devices Samsung Eletro-Mechanics Samsung Data Systems Samsung Corning Samsung-GE Medical Systems* 6 other companies
Chemicals	Samsung General Chemicals Samsung Petrochemical Samsung Fine Chemicals 2 other companies
Machinery	Samsung Heavy Industries Samsung Aerospace Industries* Samsung Watch* Leechun Electric Manufacturing*
Automotive	Samsung Commercial Vehicle* Samsung Motor Co.*
Finance & Trade	Samsung Corporation Samsung Life Insurance Samsung Fire & Marine Insurance Samsung Card Samsung Finance Samsung Securities 2 other companies
Other businesses	Cheil Industries (design) Samsung Engineering (construction) Samsung Everland (entertainment) The Joong-Ang Ilbo (newspaper) Hotel Shilla (hotel business) 22 other companies

*Refers to the subsidiaries that Samsung abandoned in the restructuring of 1998–2001.

From then on, Samsung vigorously invested in electronics and became one of the first movers in the industry. The *chaebol* group also diversified into other electronics-related product lines and, in the 1980s, began semiconductor production. Samsung's electronics companies that diversified into interrelated technologies established internationally competitive core capabilities in the 1970s–1980s, enjoying first mover advantages in their industries. Even if relatively small, the group's chemical-related companies also became the national first movers in the industry.

Twice in its history Samsung diversified into unrelated industries: the first time was during the Big Push in the 1970s. The core capabilities of Samsung's manufacturing companies in electronics, the chemical industry and, to some extent, shipbuilding were founded in this period. The second drive occurred between the late 1980s and the early 1990s when the *chaebol* entered automobile production.

One of the most important reasons for the second drive was a change in chairmanship. Lee Byung-Chull died in 1987, and his son Lee Kun-Hee became the new chairman.[11] In 1988, he announced a 'second founding' of the group, presenting a vision for Samsung's growth towards world-class status. To this end, Samsung launched projects dealing with the reorganization of existing businesses and entry into new sectors.

Abolition of industrial policy and Samsung's entry into car production

Samsung entered automobile manufacturing in 1992 when the Samsung Heavy Industries Company reached a licensing agreement with Nissan. The company began manufacturing large commercial vehicles based on a Nissan-designed chassis in small quantities from 1994. But the new chairman's original intention was to establish a volume carmaker. Consequently, Samsung Motor Company was founded in 1995, and began commercial production in early 1998.

Samsung's efforts to enter the auto business date back to 1983 when it was preparing a joint venture agreement with Chrysler, but the government did not agree to Samsung's entry because of the industrial promotion laws which explicitly banned new entry into the automobile industry until 1989. From 1990, there was no explicit institutional barrier to new entry. In reality, however, the habitual practice of banned entry continued because the Ministry of Commerce and Industry still had the power to veto technical licensing agreements with foreign companies. Since the import of foreign technology was essential, because of the lack of technological capabilities, the government was able to block entry of the *chaebol* into unrelated sectors. In the event, the government did not permit the technology licensing agreement of Samsung with Nissan for passenger car production until 1993.

The existing carmakers – Hyundai, Daewoo and Kia – vehemently opposed Samsung's entry and this caused a big political and public debate. Moreover, a newspaper report that Samsung's financial companies were secretly buying Kia stocks in order to acquire it turned public opinion towards Samsung negative. The Samsung group used clever political manoeuvring to create sympathetic public opinion. It finally succeeded in changing the President's attitude by playing on traditional regionalist sentiments. It was later revealed that Samsung had secretly promised to place the production site in the President's home province.[12] At the end of 1994, President Kim Young-Sam announced that he would not oppose Samsung's entry because the government had already declared its commitment to a free market policy. Therefore, the government also abolished restrictions on the licensing of foreign technology.

Lack of technological capabilities and scale economies

Samsung Motor Company was established in 1995 and immediately began to build a passenger car production plant in Pusan. The plant had a capacity of 125,000 units a year and the management believed that the minimum efficient production volume would be 80,000 unit sales. It employed 6,300 personnel for production, sales and R&D. Because the existing component suppliers were not allowed by their incumbent customers (Hyundai, Daewoo and Kia) to supply Samsung, the new car-maker had to either make use of its subsidiaries (for instance, Samsung Electro-Mechanics Company for electric components) or help set up new suppliers financially and technologically. By the beginning of operations in early 1998, it had organized 2,323 suppliers.

Almost all of the technology was imported from Nissan. Production facilities were imported from Nissan directly. Engineers and technicians for production and R&D were sent to Nissan for training for at least three months and sometimes for one year. Many experienced middle and high level managers, engineers and technicians moved from the existing Korean automakers to Samsung to make the initial setting-up easier. In addition, 150 Nissan technical personnel were relocated to the Pusan plant for training and problem solving. Samsung also made an agreement with Nissan to have engineers and technicians from 90 Korean suppliers trained by Nissan's suppliers. An R&D centre with 1,000 personnel was established, and it developed Samsung's first passenger car, a compact car named the SM5. The body design was developed in-house, but chassis and platform designs were licensed from Nissan.[13]

Construction of the Pusan plant was completed in October 1996, and after having overcome various initial difficulties in test and pilot productions, the company began commercial production of the SM5 in February 1998. At the opening ceremony, the chairman, Lee, spoke of his dream to make SMC one of the 10 largest carmakers in the world within 10 years.

One of the biggest difficulties latecomer firms face is acquiring minimum scale economies and market share. According to Samsung's projections, the initial production capacity of the Pusan plant, 125,000 units per year, was not enough to ensure operational incomes. Production and sales of more than 200,000 units a year were necessary. Samsung planned therefore to build a second plant with the same capacity within five years, making the production capacity 250,000 units a year.

However, Samsung's market position with the SM5 was not promising. First, the three existing companies – Hyundai, Daewoo and Kia – had already launched new cars to compete with the SM5. Hyundai's EF Sonata in particular was a close rival of Samsung's compact car in price and technical performance.

Even though the sales price of the SM5 was similar to that of the EF Sonata, its production costs were much higher. First, the construction of the Pusan plant had cost four times more than the plants of Hyundai and Daewoo. Samsung's site lay on the seashore and needed special construction methods in order to make the ground solid. Samsung had known of this problem, but accepted the extra cost because of the political agreement with the President. Second, the production facilities imported from Nissan embodied the highest technology in the world and hence were very expensive. Samsung once again applied its business motto, 'Samsung makes only the best products with the best facilities' (Kang M.-H. 1998: p. 116ff). Even the buildings at the plant were of the highest quality. Third, components used for SM5 were also of a higher standard, and therefore more expensive, than those of rival cars. The chairman wanted to make the SM5 a kind of luxury passenger car (Kang M.-H. 1998). Finally, Samsung had to pay Nissan a technology licensing royalty of 1.6–1.9 per cent of car sales.

It was evident from the beginning that Samsung could not make a profit with the SM5. In fact, the more cars that were sold, the greater the losses would be. Of course, if sales of the car had reached the minimum efficient scale economies, losses would have been reduced significantly. Samsung's management calculated that 80,000 unit sales would be satisfactory in the first year of operation.

Samsung's entry timing could not have been worse, however. It began commercial production of the SM5 in late February 1998, in the midst of the panic shrinking of the consumer market in Korea. In March 1998 domestic sales of cars slumped and even the existing carmakers' capacity utilization rates fell below 50 per cent. From March to December

Table 9.5   Financial statements of Samsung Motor Company, 1995–8 (hundred million won)

	1995	1996	1997	1998
Sales	0	0	0	6,139
Operating profit	−32	−59	−161	−2,080
Financial expenses	0	0	2,200	2,621
Net profit	−7	−216	6	−6,771
Assets	7,573	21,566	33,936	41,458
Debts (D)	4,355	15,918	25,727	40,020
Equity capital (E)	3,218	5,647	8,209	1,438
D/E ratio (%)	135	282	313	2,783

Source: Samsung Motor Company, *Annual Report*, yearly.

only 44,719 SM5s were sold. Most of these sales were sales to Samsung group employees. The average capacity utilization rate reached only 35.8 per cent.

The enormous, yet unnecessary, investment in the site, buildings, production facilities and R&D facilities was the main factor in the cost blow-out. For the three years from 1995 to 1997, investment in facilities reached over 1 trillion won each year. Establishing a sales network cost an additional 900 billion won. A total of about 4 trillion won (US$5 billion) was invested, as shown in Table 9.5.

From 1995 to 1998, the company's liabilities increased from 435.5 billion won to 4 trillion won, an increase of 819 per cent. Therefore, the debt to equity ratio (a criterion of financial vulnerability) increased from 135 per cent to 2,738 per cent. With real production of 44,719 units, the company made a negative operating income of 208 billion won and a net loss of 677.1 billion won in the first year of operation.

Samsung's abandonment of Samsung Motor Company and restructuring

In December 1998, faced with soaring losses and debts, Lee decided to abandon Samsung Motors, a project in which he had been deeply involved. Operations at the production facility in Pusan were suspended. Kim Dae-Jung's new government imposed new regulations that were designed to avoid interrelated collapses of *chaebol* firms by restricting intersubsidiary credit guarantees and shareholdings. Cut off from financial assistance from Samsung group, Samsung Motor Company could not survive. It applied for court receivership in June 1999 and was finally sold to Renault-Nissan in 2000.

At the same time, Samsung profoundly restructured its business. Samsung consciously endeavoured to reorganize its subsidiaries according to the principle of core capabilities. As Table 9.4 shows, companies in electronics, chemicals, finance and trading were selected for future business but companies in the machinery and automobile industry, except for Samsung Heavy Industry (shipbuilding), were either liquidated or sold. Samsung reduced the number of its affiliates from 58 to 47. It sold ten business units to foreign companies. Samsung Heavy Industry's construction equipment business unit was sold to Volvo AB of Sweden and its forklift business unit to Clark of America. Samsung lowered 1997's 365 per cent debt/equity ratio to 183 per cent by late 1999 and reduced its labour force by almost 50,000.

9.4 Conclusion

Some critics of the *chaebol*, shareholder value advocates in particular, criticize UD and instead uphold specialization. They criticize the UD – and hence the conglomerate business style of the *chaebol* – for its alleged inefficiency and rent-seeking and attribute the 1997 crisis to it. Opposing this view, we emphasized the necessity of a historical-dynamic point of view.

UD was one of the major strategies used by the *chaebol* in the 1960s–1980s, and was undoubtedly a factor in Korea's rapid economic growth. Therefore, UD can be regarded as a legitimate method of growth for firms in a developing country with low initial capabilities in technology and organization. If unrelated diversification had not occurred in Korea in the 1960s–1970s, Korea would still be an economy with no heavy and high-technology industries.

It is true, however, that most of the unrelated diversifications of the 1990s ended in massive collapses. To explain this historical change, we applied the dynamic capabilities approach and used the concepts of 'first mover advantages' and 'challenger disadvantages', described by Chandler. Knowledge assets (organizational capabilities in technology and management) and scale economies built by first mover companies became the main entry barriers to new entrants in the 1990s, replacing the legal barrier expressed in the government's industrial licensing policy.

Nonetheless, many other *chaebol* firms attempted to enter the industries in the 1990s, when the legal entry barriers were abolished. It is

214 Crisis and Restructuring in East Asia

important to note that the *chaebol*'s entrepreneurial type of organizational capabilities created the organizational inertia (i.e., organizational rigidity) that tended towards unrelated diversification.

However, the challengers failed to jump the barrier set up by first movers. In other words, the challengers failed to overcome 'challenger disadvantages'. In the cases of Samsung and Ssangyong we identified the various disadvantages faced by the challengers, notably the difficulty of bridging the gap in technological capabilities and attaining effective scale economies. Then, hit by the economic contraction due to the financial crisis, they collapsed one after another.

In this regard, the 1997 crisis was a turning point in Korea's business dynamics. During and after the crisis, *chaebol* firms reorganized their business lines according to the principle of core competency. Korea's existing main industries, in their dynamic evolution, had reached a stage of sophistication in which diversification needed to be combined with specialization into technologically related areas. After the crisis, *chaebol* firms reorganized their business lines according to their core capabilities. This was, however, not because of any liberal reform policies, but simply because Korea's business dynamics and industrial development had removed the historical foothold of unrelated diversification.

10
Conclusion: Crisis, Restructuring, and the Future of Korea

10.1 Bubbles, crashes and *laissez-faire*

Liberal theories tend to axiomatically attribute economic crises to the absence of free market principles. Free market capitalism is supposed to be crisis-proof because there is, in principle, no moral hazard problem. And according to the theories, there are various sources of moral hazard in East Asia (primarily cronyism, state interventionism, and allegedly 'distorted' shareholder value). Yet, our analysis presents findings contrary to these liberal arguments.

The East Asian financial crisis was one of the financial burst-bubble syndromes that appeared in the global economy of the 1990s. The reason for this crisis, like the others, was that globalized financial capital tends to result in herd-like behaviour, thus creating 'self-reinforcing booms and bubbles', followed by 'self-reinforcing crashes'. The financial crises in Mexico and Argentina in 1994–5 were the first examples of the bursting of bubbles created by the 'emerging markets mania' of the first half of the 1990s. The Asian crisis in 1997 was the second example and the financial crises in Brazil and Russia in late 1998 were the third. Global capital subsequently flooded into the 'New Economy' sectors in 1998–9 which, in their turn, have crashed worldwide since the beginning of the new millennium.

Why were there so many financial crashes in the 1990s? What changed in that period? To answer this question, we directed our attention to the institutional aspects of the Asian crisis, and concluded that deregulation in East Asia during that period generated *laissez-faire* conditions, which allowed and encouraged financial and industrial bubbles. These bubbles burst in late 1997, when the economies of the five deregulated Asian countries – South Korea, Thailand, Indonesia, Malaysia and the

Philippines – crashed. Therefore, the global capital movement into and out of East Asia was the primary cause of the boom and crash in the 1990s in the region. This could not have occurred without the financial deregulation and globalization that provided the institutional framework of the border-crossing capital movement. In the case of Korea, the abolition of capital controls and industrial policies made it possible for global capital and Korea's deregulated financial sectors to supply excessive funds for *chaebol* groups, which then excessively invested in business expansion.

The Daewoo story typifies this process. Daewoo's ambitious expansion into emerging market countries was vigorously supported by 'emerging market mania' among global financial institutions. Korea's opening of the capital account brought direct access to funding from global financial markets. Also, the abolition of legal limits on investments abroad, which had been a part of industrial policies, opened the door for Daewoo to expand globally. However, the economies in emerging markets did not grow as rapidly as Daewoo and the global financial markets expected, while Daewoo's dependency on global financing made it extremely vulnerable to global financial instability. And when the Asian and Russian financial crises broke out in 1997 and 1998, Daewoo faced claims from panicked international banks for immediate repayment, finally filing for insolvency in August 1999.

10.2   Moral hazard, market competition, and late industrialization

In fact, moral hazard problems were more linked to free market principles, introduced in East Asia in the 1990s, than to East Asia's developmental institutions. In the Korean case, liberalization in the 1990s not only allowed and fostered the excessive flow of global capital into Korea's corporate sector, but they also created a situation of *laissez-faire* in corporate governance and financial supervision. The developmental system of the 1960s–1980s, which had effectively limited moral hazard, was dismantled through liberal reforms in the 1990s. The state-based model of corporate governance and financial supervision was abolished. But neither a bank-based nor a capital market-based model was introduced in its place, and this institutional vacuum created moral hazard problems among the *chaebol* and financial institutions.

In this regard we also criticized shareholder value theory's concentration on the *chaebol*'s firm-level governance, which was characterized by intragroup ownership and control. Instead, we stressed that the weakness of the *chaebol*'s corporate governance just prior to the crisis was at the national system level: Korea's state-based model of corporate governance had been abolished, but no alternative corporate governance mechanism was set in its place. This national institutional vacuum was the primary problem. The fact that many *chaebol* groups recovered from the crisis even though they strengthened the intragroup ownership and control suggests that intragroup governance problems were not a major cause of the crisis.

Furthermore, as the evolutionary theories of the firm suggest, even when corporate governance is absent or weak, '[product] market pressure' – from the world market in particular – can operate as an economic governance mechanism. This is also suggested by conventional neoclassical economics of trade. But, as dependency theory and the developmental state approach emphasize, a necessary condition for late industrializing economies entering the world market is national corporate control. As regards the *chaebol*'s corporate governance, concentration of ownership and control can be regarded as a means of maintaining national corporate control. Closed intragroup ownership as a way of keeping national control can also be seen in the Japanese pre-war *zaibatsu* and post-war *keiretsu*. Shareholder value theory, in its critique of the *chaebol*'s corporate governance, completely ignores this aspect.

'Market pressure' from the world's car markets provided the push that drove HMC's management towards rapid technological and managerial learning. In contrast with Daewoo or Kia, which did not export or relied on transnational automakers for car exports, Hyundai continually faced technical and marketing problems in export target countries, and had no choice but to rapidly find its own solutions. HMC succeeded not by rent seeking but by disciplined organizational learning.

National corporate control alone is not sufficient to explain HMC's success, however. Top management's vision and determination, closely linked with the state's nationalist goals of industrial promotion, played a vital role. Without paying attention to the cost, Hyundai gained its independence from transnational carmakers through the acquisition of skills and know-how. HMC was innovative in its approach to developing exports, and in the way it acquired technological learning. In this regard, HMC's *chaebol* entrepreneur can be regarded as a type of Schumpeterian entrepreneur in a developing country.

10.3   Business dynamics, industrial development, and organizational change

Besides financial and institutional aspects, however, the 1997 crisis in Korea included also industrial and business aspects. Korea was unique among the five crisis countries in that the bursting of financial bubbles was accompanied by large-scale collapses of big industrial firms. To explain this aspect of the crisis, we investigated *chaebol* firms' business. By analysing the strategies and capabilities of both successful and failed *chaebol* firms, using the dynamic capability approach to the firm, we identified innovative and expansive paths.

Korean industry began to develop R&D-related capabilities from the mid-1980s. While some *chaebol* firms led the change, choosing an innovative path, many others preferred a path of business expansion. The subsequent liberalization and globalization gave the latter a chance to recycle old strategies and capabilities. From 1993 to 1997 these firms enthusiastically made use of the new financial and business opportunities in order to expand into new markets and unrelated product lines. Most of them failed and eventually collapsed during the crisis. This is undoubtedly associated with a shift in the *chaebol*'s core organizational capabilities.

The shift in the *chaebol*'s core organizational capabilities is also manifested in the evolution of the *chaebol* firms' organization from an entrepreneur-centred system into a managerialist one. From the mid-1980s and throughout the 1990s, the groups' old strengths, such as rapid expansion, unrelated diversification and their founders' entrepreneurial leadership, gradually lost their importance. Instead, new capabilities (such as R&D-oriented growth and related diversification or specialization) became increasingly important. As knowledge in technology, marketing and finance gained importance, professional managers with expertise increasingly took charge of strategic decision-making.

Nonetheless, many *chaebol* firms, relying on the founder's or a successor's entrepreneurial abilities, followed the old routines. Daewoo's global expansion, like the unrelated diversification of Samsung and Ssangyong, was driven by the *chaebol* entrepreneur and his staff organization. Organizational routine and the entrepreneurial type of organizational capabilities apparently created a kind of inertia, an organizational rigidity, that tended towards expansionary strategies. These failures show that the *chaebol*'s old core capabilities had become core rigidities and that there is a specific path dependency in the *chaebol*'s organizational routine. After the crisis, some failed *chaebol* entrepreneurs increasingly delegated decision-making to professional managers, while retaining ownership and control. We observe this tendency in Samsung, for instance. A few other *chaebol* entrepreneurs resigned their position as their *chaebol* groups, including Daewoo and Kia, were completely dismantled. Non-family professional managers, under bank control, are now in charge of the former Daewoo companies.

We concluded on this basis that the real cause of massive corporate collapses between 1997 and 1999 in Korea is to be found in the expansive strategies and rigid organizational capabilities of many *chaebol* firms, rather than in the moral hazard problems which liberal critics claim to see.

10.4 Post-crisis reform towards the Anglo-American model

The Kim Dae-Jung government (1998–2002), under the supervision of the IMF, attempted to introduce Anglo-American standards in all areas of Korea's financial and corporate system. Establishing a full capital market-based system in corporate governance and financial systems was a prime goal of the liberalist reform. Shareholder value advocates supported this effort.

Despite this, the capital market-based system is not fully established. This is because the crisis revived a kind of state/bank-based system. Many of the largest commercial banks were nationalized during the crisis, due to the danger of a run on them. The banks, in turn, undertook control of failed *chaebol* firms through bailout loan programmes. Consequently, the government, by means of the banks, intervened extensively in financial and business matters, even though it claimed to be liberalist.

Not surprisingly, critics and advocates of the reform programme take very different positions on this partial revival of state/bank-based model of corporate governance. For the critics, it presents strong evidence for the assertion that the crisis was caused by massive 'market failures', rather than by 'government failures'. Furthermore, it confirms the validity of the notion of institutional path dependency and the need to have a strong state/bank-based system in the future.

For the advocates, however, the state/bank-based system is only provisional, an emergency prescription for failed banks and *chaebol* firms. Liberal policy-makers in the government and the IMF want to privatize all the banks and companies, preferably by selling to foreign transnational companies or foreign investment funds. In this way, a fully capital market-based model will replace the partial state/bank-based model.

10.5 Benefits and risks of the reform

Can the Anglo-American-style institutions solve the problems that caused the 1997 crisis? We can observe both positive and negative developments.

On the positive side, the introduction of a capital market-based model ended a period of institutional vacuum in corporate governance and financial supervision. Second, Korea successfully removed the immediate causes of the 1997 financial crisis: huge amounts of foreign short-term borrowings exceeding foreign exchange reserves. Short-term foreign borrowings have been transformed into long-term ones and various regulatory limitations imposed on new short-term foreign borrowings. Now, in 2003, short-term foreign borrowings account for only one-third of Korea's total foreign borrowings. At the same time, between 1998 and 2003, Korea built up US$145 billion of foreign exchange reserves to deal with the danger of sudden outflow of short-term international capital. This amounts to the fourth largest in the world, after Japan, China and Taiwan. Two factors are responsible for the growth in foreign reserves: (1) an increase in exports and current account surplus every year from 1998; (2) an increase in foreign capital inflow in the form of portfolio investment and direct investment (acquisition of Korean firms). The first factor is not the achievement of liberal reforms, but due to the strength of Korea's existing export industries. The second, however, represents an achievement of the reforms.

Nevertheless, we need to be aware of new dangers. First, in the Korean stock market foreign investors already own 40 per cent of total shares and thus hold more than half of freely floating shares (the highest level of foreign stock ownership in the world). Due to the unavoidable problem of informational asymmetry in global financial markets, global investors tend to exaggerate good and bad news. Consequently, with the liberal efforts to introduce a full capital market-based system, Korea's financial and corporate system – the core of its economic system – is increasingly exposed to the instability of globalized financial capitalism.

Even more serious is the fact that the future of Korea's large industrial and financial corporations is increasingly decided in the US stock market. A full capital market-based model will strengthen this dependency, which is a danger that dependency theory warns of. In the banking sector, global investment banks and funds such as Goldman Sachs, Carlyle Group, New Bridge Capital and Lone Star have already become controlling shareholders of Korea's largest commercial banks. If the privatization of commercial banks continues as the new Roh Mu-Hyun government (2003–7) plans, the transition to a fully capital market-based model will be essentially complete and most of Korea's financial institutions will be under transnational control or influence. This will make the danger of economic dependency more critical.

10.6 Changes in business dynamics and industrial development

We have already emphasized that a national model of corporate govern-ance and finance system should be understood not separately from, but in combination with, business dynamics and industrial development.

How have the Anglo-American-style reforms of financial and corporate institutions affected the *chaebol*'s business dynamics and Korea's indus-trial development? Some *chaebol* firms, which are leading the post-crisis recovery, seem to have successfully adapted themselves. These are the firms that now have strong competencies in organization, technology and finance. A good example is HMC. On the basis of increasing sales and exports after the crisis, HMC was able radically to reorganize its financial structure by reducing debts and raising equity capital. Because of its financial stability, the company can now acquire funds directly from capital markets at home and abroad. Furthermore, following its merger with Kia, the company established the Hyundai Motor Group, which is separate from the Hyundai Group and specializes in cars and car-related businesses.

Samsung, LG, and some other well-run *chaebol* firms have reorganized their business and financial structure along the same lines. These listed *chaebol* firms are now fully integrated in the capital market-based system, and claim to give priority to shareholder value. In the case of HMC and Samsung Electronics, 60–75 per cent of freely floating shares, 50–60 per cent of total shares, are now owned by New York and London-based investment funds, although the *chaebol* families have retained corporate control by means of pyramid shareholding.

Ironically, however, these successful *chaebol* firms are all the products of the developmental system in the 1970s-1980s. The fact is that Korea's rapid recovery from the 1997 crisis was made possible not by Anglo-American-style institutional reforms but by the existing strengths of Korea's export-orienting *chaebol* firms, all of which had been nurtured by state interventionism and bank (debt)-based finance.

This clearly illustrates the continuity or path dependency in Korea's business dynamics, in spite of the radical break in institutional settings, and underlines the need for a historical-dynamic perspective on the *chaebol*'s evolution.

A second group includes *chaebol* firms, such as the Daewoo companies, which collapsed during the crisis and were involved in bank bailout programmes and, hence, came under state/bank control. Many of them have been taken over by foreign transnational companies or global investment banks and funds. As liberal policy-makers have been interested only in selling all the failed firms as quickly as possible, the state–bank complex is far from operating as the developmental state did in the 1970s–1980s. To cite examples from the car industry only, Samsung Motor Company was sold to Renault-Nissan in early 2000 and Daewoo Motor Company to General Motors in late 2001. Ssangyong Motor Company is also waiting for a foreign buyer.

It is also true that the liberal reforms have weakened major, though failed, exporting firms. DMC is a prime example. Once the second largest car exporter, its exports dramatically decreased after 1998. Both creditor banks and the government were only interested in selling the company as quickly as possible and made no attempt to sustain car exports. Although DMC had enough export orders, creditor banks refused to provide minimum operational funds. Such behaviour on the part of the banks, and ultimately the liberal government, destroyed even the exiting capabilities (assets) of the company and enabled General Motors to acquire the company at a discount.

General Motors has promised that DMC will be allowed to develop small cars and export them, using 'existing' capabilities, but it is unlikely that it will help DMC develop larger segment cars and RVs by building its own technological capabilities. Consequently, there is no certainty that General Motors will help DMC build dynamic capabilities in the future. The same is true of other Korean firms that were acquired by trans-national companies or investment banks/funds.

From our analysis, one thing appears certain: the rapid growth of the *chaebol* and the Korean economy will not be repeated in the future as long as the efforts towards a capital market-based model continue. On the one hand, the first group of *chaebol* firms (say, HMC and Samsung Electronics) are now raising investment funds mainly from retained earnings. The Korean stock market, like its US counterparts, hardly plays an important role in supplying new funds for corporations. Banks also are not very interested in providing fresh loans to industrial firms. Consequently, cut off from external financing, even the well-performing Korean firms will not be able to grow as fast as in the past. On the other hand, the second group of *chaebol* firms will not grow fast because they do not get vigorous support from banks. *Chaebol* firms taken over by transnational capital are not expected to grow rapidly, either.

There is a growing fear that many Korean firms will lose business dynamism and be locked into 'existing' capabilities. 'Dynamic' capabilities are essential if a firm is to be effective in the long term. This is even more important to Korea's firms because the country – with an average per capita income of US$10,000 in 2003 – still needs dynamic and sustained growth. Therefore, South Korea needs rather to strengthen the state/bank-based model, instead of allowing the unilateral rule of capital market-based standards such as shareholder value. This will be the best way to help Korean firms build 'dynamic' capabilities.

10.7 Increasing private debts and property market bubbles

At present, the Korean financial market does not actively provide funds for industrial firms. This is mainly because many industrial firms in Korea are still not able to satisfy the so-called 'global investment standards' that New York and London-based investors – today's 'rule-makers' – require due to the lack of capabilities in technology, brand, marketing, and so on. Like most firms in developing and late industrializing countries, many Korean firms are considered too risky for global investors.

Shareholder value-oriented financial institutions are now more interested in private client and property market investment than industrial financing. This is shown by the fact that bank loans to the private sector have increased rapidly in the past few years. They amounted to 211 trillion won at the end of 1997, but had soared to 440 trillion won by the end of 2002, more than doubling over five years. The banking sector today provides more money to private clients than to corporate clients and, consequently, the ratio of private sector bank loans to corporate sector loans has been reversed. It was 10:90 in 1991 and 35:65 in 1997, but developed to 54:46 in 2002. This is the first reversal since the beginning of industrialization in the 1960s.

This historic change, however, has created a property market bubble. As more than half of the private loans are used for investment in the housing sector, real estate prices rose 60 per cent in the years between 1999 and 2002. At the same time, however, the real demand for housing decreased because the real income of the middle and lower classes declined. This suggests that most of the private investment in housing is speculative.

At the end of 2002, the danger of potential bad loans given to private clients became so explosive that the chairman of the Korean Financial Supervisory Commission officially warned of 'a possible second financial crisis due to the huge private debts'. The government is now making every effort to control private loans and housing prices. Despite this, there is no reason for optimism. Many credit card service companies, which went to the verge of insolvency in June 2003 due to rising bad loans to private clients and were rescued through bailout loans from banks, reported historic losses at the end of the year, losing all they had earned in the previous 10 years. Even more significantly, according to a research report publicized in October 2003, a 'self-reinforcing boom mechanism' is developing in the housing sector that will probably result in a financial crash.

10.8   Never-ending history

We have seen that the 1997 crisis was caused primarily by imprudent liberalization. Now, the IMF and the Korean government claim that they have achieved a 'prudent' liberalization and globalization, with the full introduction of Anglo-American norms. And yet the US stock market crashes accompanying large-scale accounting frauds in 2002 clearly showed that the Anglo-American model is far from preventing financial bubbles, cronyism and moral hazard problems. In the Korean stock market, too, the bursting of 'New Economy' bubbles after mid-2000 revealed innumerable cases of cronyism, accounting frauds, market manipulation, and so on. In this regard, financial historians are right when they say that moral hazard is an integral part of the financial bubble syndrome.

We should not forget that the Asian financial crisis of 1997 was a boom/bust phenomenon, and neither should we forget that the Anglo-American system of global financial capitalism tends to produce such bubble effects. The Enron and WorldCom scandals raise profound doubts about the aptness of the Anglo-American model.

The claim of 'victorious' liberalism that an 'End of History' (Francis Fukuyama) has been attained, or will be attained in the near future, is fading away. History has not ended, and there is no evidence of the ultimate triumph of a certain type of capitalism.

Notes

1 Introduction

1 For a comprehensive and comparative overview, see Corsetti, Pesenti and Roubini (1998a), Radelet and Sachs (1998), and Haggard (2000). A large number of contributions on the crisis are available online on Nouriel Roubini's Asian Crisis home page at http://www.stern.nyu.edu/globalmacro/

2 *The Economist* (15 April 1998) notes, 'American triumphalists and some academics, such as Paul Krugman, emphasize crony capitalism. Others, notably Jeffrey Sachs of Harvard University and Joseph Stiglitz, chief economist at the World Bank, believe panic was more important.'

3 We will use the concept of 'business dynamics' as described by Alfred D. Chandler.

4 *Chaebol* size is measured by the value of assets in 1997.

5 The 'dependent development' approach is summarized in Thomas Biersteker (1981), and Richard Newfarmer (1985).

6 To avoid confusion in references to Korean authors who have the same family names, we will follow the following rules. First, if we refer to only the family name of the author, this means that the literature is written in English or German language, and that in the reference list there is only one Korean who has the same family name. For example, Lim (1985) indicates that the literature is written in English or German, and that there is only one Lim. Second, if we refer to the family name and in addition the abbreviation of the given name of the author, this means one of two things: (1) the literature is written in the English or German language but there are several Korean authors in the reference list who have the same family name; or (2) it is written in Korean or Japanese, and can be found in the separate lists for Korean and Japanese language references.

7 On why they are called revisionists, Chalmers Johnson explains as follows:

> 'Revisionism' refers to my – as well as others' – observation that Japan has a political economy different from that of the Anglo-American countries in term of institutions, the role of the state, and the weight of economic nationalism. Most American academic economists maintain that the Anglo-American pattern is the orthodox norm that defines capitalism; hence Japan differs from this alleged norm, and those who point this out are said to be 'revisionists'. (1995: p. 12)

8 About the ideological character of the controversy over industrial policy, Leipziger and Petri (1993: p. 6) note, 'Just why an economy should utilize industrial policy is subject to much confusion. Some authors treat the question of industrial policy almost as a choice between religions – between the "old"

Anglo-Saxon economics of competitive markets, and the "new" political economy of government-directed capitalism.'

9 Leipziger (1997, p. 10) notes, 'Yet others like Wade (1990, 1993) and Haggard (1993) point out that mainstream economics places excessive emphasis on the export promotion story and provides inadequate attention to the governance story.'

10 Amsden (1989: p. 14) writes:

> in exchange for stunning performance in the areas of exports, R&D, or new product introduction, leading firms were rewarded with further licences to expand, thus enlarging the scale of big business in general. In exchange for entering especially risky industries, the government rewarded entrants with other industrial licences in more lucrative sectors, thus furthering the development of the diversified business group in particular.

11 Chang (1993) notes, 'whatever little knowledge the early Korean economic bureaucracy had was not neoclassic economics but the economic theories of Friedrich List, Joseph Schumpeter, and Karl Marx, which dominated Japanese academia and policy-making circles in the first half of the twentieth century'.

12 For the liberalist critique of failed 'Confucian capitalism' in Asia, see, for example, Francis Fukuyama's (1998) 'Asian Values and the Asian Crisis' and *The Economist* (25 July 1998), 'Asian values revisited: what would Confucius say now?'

13 With regard to the 1997 crisis and following reform policies, Lee K.-U. (1999) argues, 'Crisis is a chance'. Similar tones and nuances were to be seen in innumerable articles and papers in Korea between 1998 and 2000.

14 The following critical description of neoclassical and neo-Institutionalist firm theories is a summary of Chandler (1992a, 1992b) and Foss (1993).

15 Amsden (1997a) suggests that the approach suggested by neo-Institutionalist economists such as Williamson (1985), North (1990), Stiglitz (1989) and Chang (1994, 2000) cannot explain the role of the state and business groups in late industrializing countries. She argues that this is because the technological learning associated with production and R&D is much more important than transaction costs and other information-related problems in late industrializing countries.

16 See also Penrose (1959), Nelson (1991, 1994), Foss (1993), Teece *et al.* (1994), Teece, Pisano and Shuen (1997), Chandler, Hagström and Sölvell (1998) and Hodgson (1998).

17 See Fransman (1998), who criticizes information-based approaches to the firm, and suggests a knowledge-based approach.

18 Teece (1980) says that 'successful firms possess one or more forms of intangible assets, such as technological or managerial know-how'.

19 Amsden (1989) and Chang (1994, 2000) regard the developmental state as a quasi-entrepreneur. However, this Schumpeterian tone may be inconsistent with the neo-Institutionalist interpretation of the developmental state suggested by Chang (1994) and Haggard and Lee (1995). See Chandler (1992a, 1992b), Teece (1993) and Amsden (1997a) regarding critiques of the neo-Institutionalist approach.

2   The Asian Crisis in 1997 and its Causes

1   About the ideological character of the debate on the East Asian crisis, Sachs and Woo (2000b: p. 13) note:

> American triumphalists loudly proclaimed that Asian capitalism, just like Soviet-type socialism a decade ago, had come to the end of its logic. The Asian economies that had long been hailed by many analysts as models for the rest of the developing world were depicted by some of the same analysts during the crisis as unsustainable nests of crony capitalism.

2   Pincus and Ramli (1998), for example, explain that the effects of the East Asian financial crisis have been the most severe in Indonesia because of the combination of the ill-designed financial liberalization and the traditionally weak 'patrimonial' Indonesian state.

3   The World Bank once interpreted the public guarantees for banks by East Asian governments as the main source of the financial stability in the economies. See World Bank (1993: p. 16).

4   Jeffrey Sachs (1997) criticizes the IMF policy to Korea for inflaming panic:

> A better approach would have been for the IMF to stress the strengths rather than the weaknesses of the Korean economy, thereby calming the markets rather than further convincing them of the need to flee the country. Months ago, when the financial crisis began, the Fund could have quietly encouraged Japan, the US, and Europe to provide some credit support to the Bank of Korea. It might well have worked with the major banks to encourage them to roll over their short-term debts without inflaming the panic. With appropriate confidence-building measures, Korea could probably have got by with a modest slowdown in growth, no credit crunch, and a realistic time horizon of a few years to complete its needed financial reforms.

5   Following the moral hazard criticism of implicit deposit insurance, US bank regulators changed the policy. In 1991, the US Congress passed the Federal Deposit Insurance Corporation Improvement Act (FDICIA), according to which the Federal Deposit Insurance Corporation protects individual and business depositors only up to the insured maximum of $100,000 for each insured account. Previously, the Federal Deposit Insurance Corporation in effect had insured all depositors of most large banks.

6   LTCM had market exposures of over US$200 billion while its capital base was only about US$4.8 billion.

7   According to Kindleberger (1989), the Great Depression in 1929–39 was so deep and damaging primarily because there existed no international lender of last resort, a function that Britain could not, and the USA would not, assume in the interwar period.

   He points out also that the controversy about the role of national central banks as the lenders of last resort and its moral hazard potential has existed since the times of Napoleonic France and Victorian Britain, or earlier. In the 1970s and 1980s, the Third World debt crises and international rescue operations raised similar controversies. The rescue of the US S&L banking sector was no exception. About financial crisis, lender of last resort, and moral hazard, see also Kindleberger and Laffargue (1982).

8 About the self-fulfilling boom as well as self-fulfilling crisis, see also George Soros (1998), *The Crisis of Global Capitalism*.

9 Short-term debt refers to a debt whose maturity is shorter than one year.

10 Whittaker and Kurosawa (1998) locate the primary source of the Japanese banking crisis of the 1990s in the (partial) financial liberalization process and policy mistakes of the 1980s.

11 Kregel (1998) suggests that bank derivative contracts were related to the sudden increase in short-term bank lending to East Asia. He argues that European banks, especially German and French ones, were also heavily involved in derivatives trading in East Asia. Citing a *New York Times* report of 29 January 1998, with the title 'Huge German banks covering risks in Asia', he writes that 'Deutsch Bank set aside [double its loss provisions for 1996] to cover losses of as much as $100 million on derivatives trading in South Korea, Thailand, Indonesia and Malaysia. Société Générale is reported to have set aside $164 million, against a total exposure of $6.8 billion.' In addition, he notes, 'Commerz Bank has $3 billion in Asian loans, 37 percent of its equity value, Dresdner Bank 26 percent, and Deutsche Bank 27 percent.'

12 Despite this, American banks were involved in a large amount of derivative trades with Asian financial companies, probably more than other banks. Wade (2000) reports that, for example, J.P. Morgan had a $116 billion total credit risk from derivatives at the end of 1997, and 90 per cent of its non-performing loans were defaults from East Asian derivatives counterparts.

13 Even worse, half of Korea's short-term foreign borrowings had a maturity of 90 days or less, and hence Korea's foreign reserves were not enough even to cover these extremely short-term debts. See Palma 1998.

14 Paul Krugman, who had attributed the East Asian crisis to cronyism and state intervention in late 1997, completely changed his opinion from early 1998. Like Sachs, he also criticized the IMF for 'screaming fire in the theatre'. See Krugman (1999), *The Return of Depression Economics*. In this book, he also argues that the panic in the global financial markets was the primary cause of the Asian financial crisis, in spite of the relatively healthy macroeconomic conditions of the East Asian economies. In early 1998, he even supported the idea of the reintroduction of capital control, which was initiated by Mahathir, the Malaysian Prime Minister, but was harshly criticized by the IMF and the US Treasury.

15 In late 1997 and early 1998, Mahathir, the Malaysian Prime Minister, publicly blamed George Soros, the most prominent currency speculator in the world, for causing a foreign exchange crisis in East Asia. However, the US Treasury and the IMF backed up Soros, insisting on the merits of liberalized global financial markets. Subsequently, however, Soros himself warned about the dangers of the global capitalism in his book (1998), *The Crisis of Global Capitalism*.

16 Ito (1999) calls the East Asian crisis the second financial crisis of 'the 21st century type', following the first one in Mexico and Argentina during 1994–5.

3   Korea's Economic Institutions and the Crisis

1   Associated with the panic in the global financial markets as a primary cause of the Asian financial crisis, Wade (2000) relates the 'gestalt shift' in East Asia research to the 'panic': 'we see either one or the other, not some of one and some of the other, and the shift takes place instantaneously, not by degree. This is a long way from the idea of rational, weighing-up-risks-and-rewards calculation. The notion of gestalt shift lends support to the "panic" theory.'

2   For the sake of consistency, Korean family names will precede given names, (e.g., Park Chung-Hee instead of Chung-Hee Park).

3   Debt/equity ratio is the ratio of total liabilities to total equity capital. Total liabilities are defined as the sum of all current liabilities and long-term liabilities. Total equity capital is the sum of capital stock, capital surplus, retained earnings and capital adjustment.

4   Taiwan's heavy and chemical industries, such as heavy machinery, shipbuilding, engineering, steel, aluminium, petroleum, synthetics and fertilizers, have been dominated by state-owned large enterprises. They have concentrated on import-substitution, rather than export-orientation, and supplied raw materials and equipments for export industries led by small and medium-sized companies. See Amsden (1985) and Wade (1990).

5   *Yushin* means restoration. Thus President Park Chung-Hee consciously followed the model of Meiji Restoration in Japan.

6   The assassination of Park Chung-Hee was conducted by the head of the Korean Central Intelligence Agency (KCIA), the second most powerful man in the regime. But the political motive for his action was not clear. He claimed to want democratic reform, but nobody believed him. Hence, it has been argued that the US Central Intelligence Agency supported him. In the latter half of the 1970s, when the USA planned to reduce its military presence in South Korea, President Park wanted to develop nuclear weapons against North Korea and a secret project to develop a nuclear bomb capability was in progress, even though the Carter administration strongly opposed it. See Johnson (1999), for example, about this story.

In this respect, on the other hand, President Park had a 'nationalist' military policy which, in combination with his nationalist economic polices, aimed at creating a 'rich nation, strong army'. Chun Doo-Hwan stopped the nuclear bomb project immediately after his seizure of power and then followed US military doctrine in the 1980s.

7   Kang Kyong-Sik later became one of the designers of the comprehensive liberalization and deregulation under Kim Young-Sam (1993–7). He was Minister of Finance and Economy during 1996–7 and hence was the responsible minister at the time of the 1997 crisis. The National Department of Prosecutions investigated him but he was soon released because the authority concluded that the crisis did not result from a crime but from economic policy.

8   The most famous corruption scandal was the affair of the Hanbo group, in which the President's son was directly involved. Hanbo was a small company which soared to fourteenth- largest *chaebol* within only few years, and entered into iron and steel with the political aid of the President. The President's son, even though he had no official position in the government, directly intervened in some commercial banks' lending decisions to Hanbo. The abolition of

industrial policy made such unofficial intervention possible. In a similar unofficial way, the son also intervened in the licensing procedure for merchant banks, the number of which increased rapidly during 1993–5.

9   The bond market was an exception; it was totally protected from foreign investment until mid-1998.

10 The definition of 'foreign debt' in Chang *et al.* (1998) follows that of the World Bank, and is different from 'external liabilities' in Table 3.7. In addition, GNP is different from GDP, naturally.

11 One trillion won was equivalent to around US$1.25 billion in 1996.

12 According to Hanna (2000: p. 56), NBFIs in Malaysia and Thailand had higher levels of non-performing loans than commercial banks. In Korea, too, the non-performing loans ratio in NBFIs was 15 per cent as of June 1998, compared with 10 per cent in commercial banks. This shows that lax deregulation of NBFIs was significantly responsible for the crisis.

13 In October 1999, after Daewoo's default, a regulation on direct offshore borrowing was introduced. As a result, the amount of direct offshore borrowings by the offshore subsidiaries of *chaebol* from international banks decreased to US$21 billion by late 2001. See *Maeil Economic Daily*, 31 March 2002.

14 The IMF policy of maintaining high interest rates was criticized by a number of economists as one of main failures of the IMF during the Asian crisis. See, for instance, Radelet and Sachs (1998) and Ito (2000).

4   The *Chaebol*'s Corporate Governance and the Crisis

1   Hyundai, Korea's biggest *chaebol* group, divided itself into three smaller groups when the three sons of the founder inherited it early in 2000. These groups are Hyundai Group, Hyundai Motors Group and Hyundai Heavy Industry Group. Among them, Hyundai Group contracted radically in 2001 because of severe cash-flow problems. Its main subsidiaries, Hyundai Construction and Hyundai Electronics (renamed Hynics), became independent companies. In contrast, the other two groups are flourishing. Hyundai Motors Group was ranked sixth largest in 2001 and is growing.

2   The countries included in the survey of La Porta, Lopez-De-Silanes and Shleifer (1999) are Argentina, Austria, Australia, Belgium, Canada, Denmark, Finland, France, Germany, Greece, Hong Kong, Ireland, Israel, Italy, Japan, Mexico, the Netherlands, New Zealand, Norway, Portugal, Singapore, South Korea, Spain, Sweden, Switzerland, UK and the USA. Among them, only some countries went into financial crisis.

3   Mayer's finding is criticized in later studies. Edwards and Fischer (1994) argue that, in terms of the supply flow of investment funds to firms, German companies also finance themselves internally, to a very great extent. Furthermore, the Japanese financial system has been undergoing substantial changes since the 1990s, and strong industrial companies used retained earnings or raised funds on equity markets, while they paid off large amounts of their bank debt. See, for example, Lazonick (1998), Koen (2000) and Raupach-Sumiya (2000).

4   In this respect, Mayer (1988) argues that liquid and competitive financial markets, such as those in the USA and UK, inhibit the use of external

finance because there are not the long-term relationships between firms and external fund providers which are found especially in Japan. The argument was in the context of debate in the 1980s on the short-termism of capital market-based system and the long-termism of bank-based systems.

5 The rapid growth in IPO markets in the USA in the 1990s, particularly in the NASDAQ, however, suggests that Mayer's argument based on the survey for the period 1970–85 should be partly revised for the 1990s.

6 See also Carlin and Mayer (2000) about the relationship between financial systems, corporate systems, and types of economic activity.

7 But the corporate governance mechanism in Japan and Germany is currently being transformed, and the driving force of this change is the financial market globalization, which, in turn, includes partial Americanization of institutional norms for finance and governance. See Lazonick (1998) and Raupach-Sumiya (2000) about changes in the Japanese main banking system, and Jürgens, Rupp and Vitols (2000) and Jürgens and Rupp (2002) about the change of the German *Hausbank* system.

8 The corporate system reform driven by the Korean government and IMF since 1998, however, permits hostile takeover and the rights of outsider shareholders are extensively strengthened. See Black *et al.* (2000) about the corporate governance reform.

9 The limit of 10 per cent of bank's equity was raised to 15 per cent in 1998. Nonetheless, banks are still not allowed to own more than 15 per cent equity in target corporations.

10 Through the extensive financial and corporate reforms during 1998–2000, the IMF and the Korean government established a capital market-based model of governance and financial systems in Korea. This seems to have solved the problem of a vacuum of corporate governance. See Chapter 10.

11 Shleifer and Vishny (1999) note, 'but in actual practice, production capital is highly specific and sunk . . . as a result, the people who sink the capital need to be assured that they get back the return on this capital. The corporate governance mechanism provides this assurance.'

5 Korea's Automotive Industry: The 1960s–90s

1 Remember the neoclassical trade economists' critique of the import substitution regime, as mentioned in Chapter 1.

2 With the beginning of democratization in 1987, Korea's labour movement experienced an unprecedented growth in its power.

3 Stimulated by booming sales of its Pony Excel model, Hyundai built a transplant in Bromont in Canada to produce subcompact and compact cars. It opened in 1989, and assembled Sonata, a compact car model, from CKD kits. However, by 1990 Hyundai's image started to be severely damaged by quality problems. In 1993, the plant stopped operation. In 1997, the factory equipment was shipped to India where it was installed in the company's new overseas plant.

4 Kia's plan to build its first overseas plant with a capacity of 50 000 in Indonesia was cancelled after the outbreak of the financial crisis in 1998.

6   Hyundai Motor Company

1   See Steers (1999) for a detailed history of Hyundai Group and its founder, Chung.

2   Because of the small size of the car repair shop during the 1940s, with a dozen employees, Chung sometimes had had to repair cars personally. Later, this technical experience helped Hyundai Motor Company greatly with its strategy for technological learning.

3   HHI, the shipbuilder, was originally one of the largest business units of HECC. It separated from the latter in the 1980s. Because of their historical role in the group's birth and growth, and because they were its cash cows, HHI and HECC became quasi-holding companies.

4   The ownership transition of HMC in 1999 was not smooth. Because Chung Se-Young had been the nominal CEO for decades and, at the same time, had the largest family shareholding of the company, he expected that his family (i.e., his son) would inherit the company. But the eldest son of Chung Ju-Young also expected to inherit the company. In order to prepare for the management of the auto business, he established Hyundai Precision Company (HPC) which began manufacturing recreational vehicles in the early 1990s.

The founder Chung appeared to stay neutral in the beginning of the conflict between his younger brother and his son. But finally he opted for his own son, and the younger brother, once again, obeyed the eldest brother. In accordance with the founder's wishes, the shares owned by HECC and HHI were transferred to HPC, which is now the quasi-holding company of Hyundai Motors Group. HPC was renamed Hyundai Mobis. Hyundai Motors Group, one of the three small groups inherited from the Hyundai Group, includes more than 20 subsidiaries, but its main focus is automobile manufacturing, including Kia Motors. In return for the abandonment of HMC, Chung Se-Young, the younger brother, inherited Hyundai Industrial Development & Construction (HIDC), a construction firm.

5   The officer was Kim Jae-Gwan, who is now a university professor of mechanical engineering. In an interview with me in August 2001, he talked about his experiences in the 1960s–1970s. He studied machine design in Germany in the 1950s. After completing a PhD, he worked for Demag, a German machine manufacturer. When the company joined a consortium with Krupp and Thyssen to establish a steel furnace in Korea in the mid-1960s, he came into contact with the Korean government. In 1967, the Korean government established KIST (Korea Institute of Science and Technology) and invited scores of Korean people who had studied in the USA, Japan, and Europe to join. At the time, well-educated experts were a scarce resource. He was also invited and employed by the institute.

In 1972, while the government was preparing for the Big Push, he began to work as a technocrat in the planning bureau of the Ministry of Commerce and Industry. He was in full charge of all heavy industries. He organized the establishment of Posco, now the world's largest steel and iron producer. He was also the practical organizer of the Long-term Plan for the Promotion of the Automobile Industry in 1973. Likewise, a dozen specialists in (amongst others) the machine, electrics, electronics, material, chemistry and physics sectors who had studied and worked in the industrialized countries participated in the planning and execution of the Big Push as working-level organizers of the industrial promotion in various ministries.

6 It is important to note that at the time there were few technological experts in the targeted industries. The case of Hyundai Motor Company shows that even the engineer who was selected as the best engineer and who accompanied Chung Se-Young to Europe had little industrial expertise. As mentioned above, the technocrats working in the government were the most competent, and played the leading part in the initial stage of industrial promotion.

7 MMC was established as a spin-off of MHI in 1971. In order to overcome its difficulties as a latecomer, the company cooperated with Chrysler from the beginning, the latter owning 15 per cent equity. MMC learned from Chrysler about automatic transmission, mass production, and other technologies. In return, MMC supplied Chrysler with its subcompact car for export to the US and European markets on an OEM basis. But because of MMC's dependence on Chrysler in the US market sales, it could not increase exports during the 1970s–1980s, while other Japanese carmakers doubled exports. MMC and Chrysler's 50:50 joint American venture, set up in 1985, did not succeed, either. This probably led MMC to fuller cooperation with HMC in the 1980s even though HMC was becoming a rival. Chrysler terminated the equity participation in MMC in 1993.

8 It was known that the Japanese carmakers succeeded in doubling their US exports because their cars were much more fuel-efficient than American cars. The Pony, which had a Mitsubishi-designed engine, was naturally similar to the Japanese cars.

9 The cooperation between HMC and MMC in technology was comprehensive. For example, four production engineers from HMC were allowed to visit MHI for months to learn about the technology of advanced transfer machines. That was important as it allowed HMC to manufacture components for both engine and transmission with precision processing. After on and off the job training, the engineers acquired the blueprints of the transfer machines from MHI. Consequently, the machining department of HMC built transfer machines for engine and transmission by themselves, in 1983. See HMC (1992).

10 As the directorial board of Korean firms did not have power over the *chaebol* owner-managers, however, as mentioned in Chapter 4, the role of the Mitsubishi-dispatched directors was more symbolic and formal than substantial.

11 See HMC (1992, 1997). See also Steers (1999: pp.87–9) for details of the various difficulties faced by HMC in America. Steers emphasizes the problem of cross-cultural communication and conflicts between the top management at the Seoul headquarters and the US executives.

12 See also Chapters 1 and 4 about the world market pressure as an economic governance mechanism.

13 The Korean firm organization is similar to its Japanese counterpart. Individual employees belong to sections, sections belong to departments, and departments belong to divisions. A section usually consists of five to ten employees.

14 This account is based on our interviews with HMC engineers.

15 From the net decrease in the capital at HMC, we can assume that the company recorded net losses for the two years 1996–7. Nonetheless, Figure 6.6 shows that the company made a positive net profit for these years. This contradiction

suggests a possible manipulation of financial statements. In our interviews with HMC staff, we were told that the company had already faced a significant financial contraction in 1996.

7   Daewoo's Global Management

1   Kim's shareholdings include the shares owned by various foundations. Because of diverse tax advantages, *chaebol* families usually established foundations for public and cultural purposes as a means of asset management. In the case of Daewoo, the Daewoo Foundation and the Daewoo Medical Foundation were such organizations.

2   Besides Kim's shares, Daewoo's other subsidiaries also owned 7 per cent of shares of DC, and hence the total intragroup shareholding of DC was 11.7 per cent. It was 7.3 per cent in the case of Daewoo Electronics. Because the remaining stocks of both companies were held by widely scattered shareholders who were not concerned about corporate control, the chairman's authority was not challenged.

3   Most of the rest of DMC's shares, 26 per cent, were owned by ARTEC Ltd, a fund owned by the government of the United Arab Emirates. Besides, in contrast to HMC and Kia, DMC was never listed on the Korean stock market. This was because of GM dominance until 1992, and thereafter because the company did not succeed in meeting the requirement for listing, which was three successive years of positive net profit.

4   Hyundai, however, failed in its negotiation with Ford at this time. See Chapter 6.

5   The corporate laws in Korea at the time banned foreign companies from acquiring more than 50 per cent equity in local firms. In most cases of joint ventures, the Korean partners held at least 51 per cent equity and were able to keep the formal majority for corporate control.

6   Chevrolet CKD kits were imported from GM Holden of Australia. The low fuel economy of the car's engine was so serious that GM-Korea decided to install engines manufactured by Kia – and designed by Mazda – in the Maepsina, the successor of the Chevrolet, in 1981.

7   Daewoo was not enthusiastic about joining GM-Korea, a loss-making company under foreign control. As no *chaebol* was interested, the government tempted Daewoo by licensing the shipbuilding business, a lucrative sector that Daewoo wanted to enter. On the *chaebol's* diversification and its relation to industrial policy, Amsden (1989: p. 14) notes: 'In exchange for entering especially risky industries, the government rewarded entrants with other industrial licences in more lucrative sectors, thus furthering the development of the diversified business group in particular.'

8   In 1972 when it negotiated with Shinjin, GM promised full content localization to the Korean government. However, GM did not keep its promise as GM America itself fell into trouble when the first oil crisis hit.

9   The Opel Kadett would be chosen as 'European Car of the Year' in 1985.

10   Because of waves of labour strikes in 1987, DMC was not able to improve on 38 cars an hour. The number stayed unchanged until 1993 when the labour movement became weaker and Daewoo began, after separation from GM, its 'New Management Campaign'. The number had increased to 60 cars an

hour in the same assembly plants by 1995. That meant deteriorating working conditions for labourers. See Lee E.-S. (1996).

11 According to Ryu J.-H. (1989), the production costs of the LeMan were 30 per cent higher than those of Hyundai Excel.

12 This account is based on our interviews with DMC engineers and technicians who had worked on the LeMan project.

13 Complaints about engine noise were so frequent that, after its separation from GM in 1992, DMC made every effort to solve the problem. When Daewoo developed its first proprietary engine (1993–6), engine noise reduction was one of the major design requirements.

14 This account is taken from the same interviews.

15 Badaracco (1988: p. 9) describes the influence of Adam-Opel on DMC as follows: 'The influence of Opel engineers was evident in a number of the production processes: an assembly line that tilted sideways for easier installation of brake, fuel, and exhaust parts and a one-piece assembly of the driver instrument panel, steering column, and wheel were innovations not found in American plants.'

16 DMC imported manufacturing facilities from European companies that Opel recommended, at first. This was not due to the licensing agreement but simply because DMC did not yet have knowledge about modern machines for car plants. In 1983, DMC established a technical institute for manufacturing technology, which was responsible for buying and setting up new machinery and facilities. As engineers at the institute learned relevant technologies, they became capable of deciding on the proper specifications and prices of necessary facilities by themselves. As a result, Japanese manufacturers gradually became major machinery suppliers for DMC.

17 In her famous book, *Rude Awakening – the Rise, Fall, and Struggle for Recovery of General Motors* (1989), Maryann Keller says not a word about DMC and Daewoo. This suggests that GM headquarters were little interested in the Korean joint venture in the late 1980s when the book was in preparation. GM's management was more interested in the Nummi project, the joint venture with Toyota, by which they hoped to learn from Japanese successes, and the Saturn project.

18 The international banks made great losses due to the credits to Daewoo's overseas projects. After the financial default of Daewoo in August 1999, only 35 per cent of the total overseas credits were repaid and the rest was written-off. See the *Maeil Economic Daily*, 26 March 2000.

19 In Chapter 8, we will discuss in more detail DMC's organization and strategy for product development.

20 According to the break-up agreement between Daewoo and GM in 1992, Daewoo was allowed to begin independent distribution of its proprietary cars to developing countries from 1993, to West European countries from December 1994, and to North America from 1995. This was because the cars Daewoo exported or assembled abroad during 1993–6 were still based on the LeMan technology, whose property rights belonged to GM-Opel.

21 Daewoo achieved capacity utilization rates of over 100 per cent mainly by prolonged operating hours. Korea's car plants generally operated for 5,000–5,500 hours a year, while the internationally relevant uniform operating hours are 4,240 hours a year (16 hours × 265 days).

22 As we will see later, the Financial Supervisory Commission of Korea (FSC) revealed that Daewoo had carried out a large-scale manipulation of financial statements from 1998, due to difficulties arising from the Asian financial crisis.

23 In Daewoo, overseas production plants were under the control of DC. Thus, their operations were not included in DMC's financial statements.

24 According to an FSC press release, the total sum of the manipulated financial statements made by the BFC amounted to 7 trillion won (US$6 billion in 2000). *Hankyeore Sin-Mun*, 1 September 2000.

25 Choe J.-Y. (1998) points out that Daewoo, particularly DC, made losses in overseas automotive investments between 1993 and 1997. Nonetheless, he remained optimistic that DC would compensate by organizing regional barter trading and triangular trading in the emerging market countries.

26 Ssangyong Motor Company's sales dropped to half their 1997 level in 1998, making it one of Daewoo's largest loss-making companies in that year.

27 The exchange rate of the US dollar against the Korean won had remained about 1:800 until 1997, but it soared to over 1:1,600 in the first months of the financial crisis. In mid-1998, it fell to 1:1,400 and stayed at around that level.

28 As we saw in Chapter 3, the sharp growth in market interest rates was the result of the IMF measures. As the measures raised borrowing costs and worsened cash flow, the bankruptcy rate of Korean firms skyrocketed. Therefore, the IMF bears some responsibility for Daewoo's bankruptcy.

29 The KDI (Korea Development Institute) is a government-controlled economic research institute for policy development. The report was initially released only to some high-ranking policy-makers. See *Korea Economic Daily*, 22 August 2001.

30 In fact, most of the investment trust companies went bankrupt or were on the verge of bankruptcy as soon as Daewoo collapsed in August 1999. The government had to inject huge public funds into these companies in order to prevent a possible second financial crisis.

31 The bankruptcy of WorldCom in the USA in mid-2002, with total debts of more than US$100 billion, broke this record.

8 Comparison of Hyundai and Daewoo in Research and Development

1 Relying on European experiences in the late nineteenth century and early twentieth century, Gerschenkron (1962) assumed that, given proper institutional systems of capital supply, latecomers could rapidly industrialize their economies by exploiting an international pool of existing technology, which was available at low cost. Consequently, he is criticized for ignoring costs (and, hence, the importance of active investments) and difficulties in technological learning in late industrializing and developing countries.

2 Besides Amsden (1989) and Wade (1990), see also Odagiri and Goto (1996): *Technology and Industrial Development in Japan: Building Capability by Learning, Innovation, and Public Policy*; Chin (1996): *The Economics of the Latecomers: Catching-up, Technology Transfer and Institutions in Germany, Japan and South Korea*;

Kim L.-S. (1999): *Learning and Innovation in Economic Development*; Zhao (1992): 'Relationship Between Indigenous Technological Capability and Imported Technology: Evidences in China, India, Japan, South Korea and Taiwan'.

3 When Daewoo acquired the Worthing Institute many of the staff left the firm, but more than half of the existing experts remained and worked for Daewoo because of a recession which affected car design houses, particularly in Europe, at the time. Daewoo was also able to keep its British engineers because of the difference in wages between Korea and the UK (higher in the former at the time).

4 By 2000, Daewoo had no proprietary engine for cars of 1.8–3.5 litres. Engines for the Nubira (1.8 litres), Leganza (1.8–2.0 litres) and Magnus (2.0–2.4 litres) were all imported from GM Holden of Australia. But for the Lanos (1.3–1.5 litres), Nubira (1.5 litres) and Matiz, Daewoo had proprietary engines developed by European engine design houses and improved by DMC.

5 Hyun's survey of DMC (1997) differs from this. Even though he apparently knew that styling design of all cars and body and chassis design of the Lanos and Nubira were outsourced from ItalDesign, IDEA, etc., he wrote as if Daewoo had done the work itself.

6 Clark and Fujimoto (1991: p. 77) distinguish 'planning lead time' (the time between the beginning of concept generation and the end of product planning including styling design) from 'engineering lead time' (the time between the beginning of product engineering and the start of commercial production and sales).

7 This account is based on our interviews with DMC engineers who had worked for the Nubira and Matiz projects.

8 HMC employed highly qualified engineers for testing and analysis. Engineers in the testing department were capable of advising engineers in the design department on improvements to the design. In contrast, the testing personnel at the Bupyong Institute were simply operators of testing equipment, and their job usually ended with providing reports on test results to designers. They were neither capable of evaluating test results nor of advising on design improvements. DMC's engineers in simulation (virtual test) had qualifications comparable to their counterparts in HMC. However, they were separated from the real testing unit. Hence the Bupyong Institute had serious organizational conflicts between the design department and the testing department on the one hand, and between the real testing unit and the simulation unit on the other hand. This was due to the weakness of the real testing unit, which, in turn, was caused by Bupyong's dependence on outsourced testing and analysis.

9 The engineers of the Ulsan R&D centres in particular opposed the idea of building full engine-development capabilities. This was one reason why HMC established the Mabukri Institute as a new and separate body. Kim G. (1994) interpreted the opposition from the Ulsan Institute as a case of 'organizational rigidity' arising from its established organizational routine based on learning from Mitsubishi. The birth of the Mabukri Institute was thus an organizational innovation necessary to break the 'path dependency' of the Ulsan Institute.

10 Mitsubishi proposed a lower royalty for car sales. See HMC (1992).
11 See Artzner, Szafir and Whitney (1997) about the activities of the world's automotive engine specialists.
12 Basic design concerns engine structure while detailed design has to do with engine components such as the piston, cylinder, cylinder head, etc.
13 A former Ricardo instructor was employed by HMC – at higher pay – to continue work on the Alpha project alongside HMC engineers. As shown in Chapter 6, Hyundai employed many foreign experts in the 1970s for the Pony project. The employment of foreigners and foreign-educated Koreans shows how eager Hyundai was to learn foreign technology. This was not the case at Daewoo and Kia, which simply relied on their foreign partners who provided only limited training.
14 This account is based on our interviews with HMC engineers who had worked for the engine development projects.
15 After the OEM-production of the Ford Festiva in the late 1980s, Kia launched its first and second proprietary cars, the Sephia (1.5 litres) and the Credos (1.8–2.0 litres), in 1992 and 1996. European design houses developed the engines. Kia was responsible only for minor changes of detailed design to ensure manufacturability.
16 This account is based on our interviews with DMC engineers who had worked for the engine development projects.
17 A Hyundai engineer who participated in the Alpha project said:

> in the agreement with Ricardo, there was naturally a clause about training. The total payment to Ricardo was 1.3 billion won at the time. It was not much money compared to the total 100 billion won invested in the engine development and production. By contrast, DMC is known to have paid 12 billion won to Lotus only for providing a prototype engine and its blueprints.

18 A Daewoo engine engineer said:

> Daewoo made no official agreement about engineer training with Lotus because it would cost further money. Daewoo sent only one or two engineers to Lotus. They were not allowed to participate in the development process. Their role was limited to coordination between Bupyong and Lotus, as mediating translator for different languages and different technologies. An official training programme for Daewoo's engineers by Lotus would have cost only 1 million dollars at most. But the top management wanted to use the money for other purposes of globalization.

19 A Daewoo engineer explained the low capability in engine development as follows: 'To speak concretely and simply, there is no chief engineer in the engine department, who is able to integrate the whole process of developing engine system and parts. Hyundai has chief engineers for engine development now.'
20 Kia also launched its first proprietary cars in the 1990s. The Sephia, a sub-compact car, was developed during 1986–91 and the Credos, a compact car, between 1991 and 1995. The company also used a light product manager system, similar to that of HMC.

21 The Matiz project began a little later, in September 1995.

22 But the control scope of project managers was limited to body, chassis, electric system and trim. They had only indirect influence on engine and vehicle testing. Furthermore, while the Worthing Institute and other European specialized companies carried out styling design and the main testing and analysis, the power of the project managers was limited to within the Bupyong Institute.

23 In July 1994, at the Bupyong Institute, the Lanos project team had 101 members, the Nubira team 120, and the Leganza team had 86. 70 of the Nubira members were stationed in the Worthing Institute, and worked together with the British engineers.

24 See also Fujimoto (1998): 'Reinterpreting the Resource-Capability View of the Firm: A Case of the Development-Production Systems of the Japanese Auto-Makers', in Chandler, Hagström and Sölvell (1998).

25 See Cusumano and Nobeoka (1998) about multi-project management policy in new car development.

26 In Kia also there existed a product commission whose role was similar to that of HMC, but it did not meet as often because the company developed only three proprietary cars in the 1990s before its collapse.

27 The top management of Kia also sometimes directly intervened in product development. A product engineer said:

> in the case of the Sephia (1.3–1.5 litres), Kia's first proprietary car, personal taste of old senior managers significantly penetrated in the style design. Consequently, the car does not much attract young drivers, the primary target customers in the segment. Furthermore, due to several changes of style design initiated by the top management, which working-level engineers regarded as useless or worse, the beginning of pilot production was delayed several times.

28 Among Korea's *chaebol* groups, Samsung is known to have developed and elaborated organizational procedures. Samsung's entry into car production was, of course, an exception in this orientation. HMC also has emphasized the importance of establishing bureaucratic procedures, instead of relying on the entrepreneurship of the founder Chung. His younger brother, Chung Se-Young, initiated this transformation from the 1980s.

9 The *Chaebol*'s Diversification: Ssangyong and Samsung

1 As mentioned in Chapter 6, Hyundai Precision Company (HPC) belonged to Chung Mong-Gu, the eldest son of the Hyundai founder Chung Ju-Young. But HMC was managed by Chung Se-Young, the founder's younger brother. HPC and HMC did not cooperate with each other because of the inheritance conflict between the son and brother. Even though both companies officially belonged to the Hyundai Group, they were rivals in reality. Due to the RV unit of HPC, HMC could not diversify into the RV segment, although it thought that this was necessary. The founder Chung, as the ultimate decision-maker in the Hyundai Group, allowed his son's RV business, for

the purpose of succession. In 1999, the son succeeded in inheriting HMC from the founder Chung and HPC became the quasi-holding company of HMC.

2 The immediate cause of Kia's collapse in August 1997 was also the insolvency of Kia Engineering and Construction Company and Kia Steel Company, which had been part of Kia's diversification into construction and steel in the 1990s.

3 The growing criticism of diversification (both related and unrelated) is significantly related to the rise of institutional investors in the globalized financial markets. These investors are particularly dominant in the USA and UK. Given sharp incentives for short-term performance, these investors – fund managers, for example – strongly demand maximum profitability from targeted firms. As firms diversifying into a wide variety of product markets have some underperforming business units, the investors required the firms to sell off or close down such units. See, for example, Vitols (2002) about the relationship between the shareholder value theory, institutional investors, and firms specializing in a few core markets.

4 See also Claessens, Djankov and Lang (2000) for a neoclassical critique of diversification by Asian firms.

5 See Chandler (1962, 1990), Chandler, Amatori and Hikino (1997), Teece *et al.* (1994) and Teece, Pisano and Shuen (1997) for the 'dynamic capabilities approach' to diversification.

6 For a comprehensive and comparative overview of discussion and literature on diversification, see Bruche (2000).

7 Williamson (1985) provides a theoretical ground for the efficiency of unrelated diversification and the conglomerate form of business. He regards the conglomerate as a superior governance structure, an internal capital market. According to him, an internal capital market can reduce informational asymmetry problems (hence transaction costs) more efficiently than an external capital market. But his theory also concentrates on 'moral hazard' problems arising from managerial opportunism and, hence, neglects the capabilities aspect of diversification. See Chandler (1992a, 1992b) and Teece (1993) for critiques of transaction cost theory.

8 Neoclassical critics of the *chaebol* tend to neglect the fact that related diversification by the *chaebol* is as significant as unrelated diversification. Samsung Group, for example, as shown in Table 9.4, had 10 companies in electronics, which were technologically interrelated with each other.

9 See Chang and Chang (1994), Kang (1996), and Chung, Lee and Jung (1997) about the role and organization of the general planning office of the *chaebol*.

10 But the concepts of move and countermove that belong to the game theory of business strategy are not sufficient to explain diversification. See Teece, Pisano and Shuen (1997).

11 Lee began his career in Samsung in 1968 when he became an executive director of the Joong-Ang Ilbo and Tong-Yang Broadcasting. In 1978, he was promoted to vice chairman of the group and, after the death of his father, he inherited the position of group chairman.

12 About the relationship between the weakening of state developmentalism and the growth of cronyism under president Kim Young-Sam, Chang (2000)

says that '[the weakening] made it easier to abuse whatever residual influence that the state still had through bribery or nepotism. The result was a spilling-over of political corruption from the traditionally corrupt areas (such as urban planning and defence contracts) into the main manufacturing industries.'

13 The Nissan Maxima was the base model for the SM5.

References

English and German language works cited

Alchian, Armen A. (1950): 'Uncertainty, Evolution and Economic Theory', *Journal of Political Economy* (58), pp. 211–21.

Alchian, Armen A. and Harold Demsetz (1972): 'Production, Information Costs, and Economic Organization', *The American Economic Review* (LXII), No. 5, pp. 777–95.

Allen, Franklin and Douglas Gale (2000): 'Corporate Governance and Competition', in Vives (2000b).

Amihud, Yakov and Baruch Lev (1981): 'Risk Reduction as a Managerial Motive for Conglomerate Mergers', *Bell Journal of Economics* (12), pp. 605–17.

Amihud, Yakov and Baruch Lev (1999): 'Does Corporate Ownership Structure Affect Its Strategy toward Diversification?', *Strategic Management Journal* (20), pp. 1,063–9.

Amsden, Alice H. (1985): 'The State and Taiwan's Economic Development', in Evans, Rueshemeyer and Skocpol (1985).

Amsden, Alice H. (1989): *Asia's Next Giant: South Korea and Late Industrialization.* Oxford: Oxford University Press.

Amsden, Alice H. (1997a): 'Bringing Production Back In – Understanding Government's Economic Role in Late Industrialization', *World Development* (25), No. 4, pp. 469–80.

Amsden, Alice H. (1997b): 'South Korea: Enterprising Groups and Entrepreneurial Government', in Chandler, Amatori and Hikino (1997).

Amsden, Alice H. (2001): *The Rise of 'The Rest' – Challenges to the West from Late-Industrializing Economies.* Oxford: Oxford University Press.

Amsden, Alice and T. Hikino (1994): 'Project Execution Capability, Organization Know-how and Conglomerate, Corporate Growth in Late Industrialization', *Industrial and Corporate Change* (3), No. 1, pp. 111–47.

Aoki, Masahiko and Hugh Patrick (eds) (1994): *Japanese Main Bank System: Its Relevance for Developing and Transforming Economies.* Oxford: Oxford University Press.

Artzner, Denis, Ezequiel Szafir and Daniel Whitney (1997): *A Possible Scenario for the Future of the Automotive Engine Industry.* Massachusetts Institute of Technology, Financial Year 1997 IMVP working papers, International Motor Vehicle Program, Engine Plant Study, August 1997.

Badaracco, Joseph L. (1988): *General Motors' Asian Alliances.* HBS Case Services N9-388-094. Cambridge, MA: Harvard Business School.

Balassa, Bela (1981): *The Newly Industrializing Countries in the World Economy.* New York: Pergamon Press.

Balassa, Bela (1991): *Economic Policies in the Pacific Area Developing Countries.* London: Macmillan.

Bennett, Douglas C. and Kenneth E. Sharpe (1985): *Transnational Corporations versus the State: The Political Economy of the Mexican Automobile Industry.* Princeton, NJ: Princeton University Press.

Berglof, Eric, and Enrico Perotti (1994): 'The Governance Structure of the Japanese Financial Keiretsu', *Journal of Financial Economics* (36), pp. 259–84.

Berle, Adolf and Gardiner Means (1932): *The Modern Corporation and Private Property.* Chicago, IL: Commerce Clearing House.

Biersteker, Thomas J. (1981): *Distortion or Development?: Contending Perspectives on the Multinational Corporation.* Cambridge, MA: MIT Press.

Black, Bernard S., Barry Metzger, Timothy O'Brien and Young Moo Shin (2000): *Corporate Governance in Korea at the Millennium – Enhancing International Competitiveness. Final Report and Legal Reform Recommendations to the Ministry of Justice of the Republic of Korea.* Downloaded from the website of Social Science Research Network electronics library at: http://papers.ssrn.com/paper.taf?abstract_id = 222491.

Brendel, Gregor (2001): *Zur Macht der Banken in Deutschland: Eine empirish-historishe Untersuchung.* Muenster: LIT Verlag.

Bruche, Gert (2000): 'Corporate Strategy, Relatedness and Diversification', Working Paper, No. 13, Business Institute Berlin at the Berlin School of Economics (FHW-Berlin). Downloaded from the website of the institute at: http://www.fhw-berlin.de.

Bursa, Mark, Hugh Hunston, Anthony Lewis and Chris Wright (1998): *Transplant and Beyond – the Internationalization of the World's Automotive Manufacturers.* FT Automotive, Financial Times Business.

Carlin, Wendy and Colin Mayer (2000): 'How Do Financial Systems Affect Economic Performance?', in Vives (2000b).

Chandler, Alfred D. Jr (1962): *Strategy and Structure: Chapters in the History of the American Industrial Enterprise.* Cambridge, MA: MIT Press.

Chandler, Alfred D. Jr (1990): *Scale and Scope: The Dynamics of Industrial Capitalism.* Cambridge, MA: The Belknap Press of Harvard University Press.

Chandler, Alfred D. (1992a): 'Organizational Capabilities and the Economic History of the Industrial Enterprise', *The Journal of Economic Perspective* (6), No. 3, pp. 79–100.

Chandler, Alfred D. Jr. (1992b): 'What is a Firm? – A Historical Perspective', *European Economic Review* (36), pp. 493–4.

Chandler, Alfred D., Franco Amatori and Takashi Hikino (eds) (1997): *Big Business and the Wealth of Nations.* Cambridge: Cambridge University Press.

Chandler, Alfred D. Jr, Peter Hagström and Örjan Sölvell (eds) (1998): *The Dynamic Firm – The Role of Technology, Strategy, Organizations and Regions.* Oxford: Oxford University Press.

Chang, Chan-Sup and Nahn-Joo Chang (1994): *The Korean Management System – Cultural, Political, Economic Foundations.* London: Quorum Books.

Chang, Ha-Joon (1993): 'The Political Economy of Industrial Policy in Korea', *Cambridge Journal of Economics* (17), No. 2, pp. 131–57.

Chang, Ha-Joon (1994): *The Political Economy of Industrial Policy.* New York: St Martin's Press.

Chang, Ha-Joon (1998): 'Korea – The Misunderstood Crisis', *World Development* (26), No. 8, pp. 1,555–61.

Chang, Ha-Joon (1999): 'The Economic Theory of the Developmental State', in Woo-Cumings (1999).

Chang, Ha-Joon (2000): 'The Hazard of Moral Hazard: Untangling the Asian Crisis', *World Development* (28), No. 4, pp. 775–88.

Chang, Ha-Joon and Hong-Jae Park (2000): 'An Alternative Perspective on Government Policy towards the *Chaebol* in Korea: Industrial Policy, Financial Regulations, and Political Democracy', in Jwa and Lee (2000).

Chang, Ha-Joon, Hong-Jae Park and Chul-Gyu Yoo (1998): 'Interpreting the Korean Crisis: Financial Liberalization, Industrial Policy and Corporate Governance', *Cambridge Journal of Economics* (22), pp. 735–46.

Chin, Jang-Sup (1996): *The Economics of the Latecomers: Catching-up, Technology Transfer and Institutions in Germany, Japan and South Korea*. London: Routledge.

Choi, Young-Rak (1996): *Dynamic Techno-Management Capability: The Case of Samsung Semiconductor Sector in Korea*. Aldershot: Avebury.

Chung, Kae-H. and Hak-Chong Lee (1989): *Korean Managerial Dynamics*. New York: Praeger.

Chung, Kae-H., Hak-Chong Lee and Ku-Hyun Jung (1997): *Korean Management – Global Strategy and Cultural Transformation*. Berlin/New York: Walter de Gruyter.

Chung, Myeong-Kee (1998): 'Hyundai Tries Two Industrial Models to Penetrate Global Markets', in Freyssenet *et al.* (1998).

Claessens, Stijin, Simeon Djankov and Larry H.P. Lang (2000): 'East Asian Corporations: Heroes or Villains?', World Bank Discussion Paper No. 409. Washington, DC: World Bank.

Claessens, Stijn, Simeon Djankov and Lixin Colin Xu (2000): 'Corporate Performance in the East Asian Financial Crisis', *The World Research Observer*, (15), No. 1 (February 2000), pp. 23–46.

Claessens, Stijn and Marion Jansen (eds) (2000): *Internationalization of Financial Services: Issues and Lessons for Developing Countries*. The Hague: Kluwer Law International.

Clark, Kim B. and Takahiro Fujimoto (1991): *Product Development Performance – Strategy, Organization, and Management in the World Auto Industry*. Cambridge, MA: Harvard Business School Press.

Coase, Ronald H. (1937): 'The Nature of the Firm', *Economica* (4), pp. 386–405.

Coase, Ronald H. (1960): 'The Problem of Social Cost', *Journal of Law and Economics*, October, pp. 1–44.

Cohen, Stephen and Gavin Boyd (eds) (2000): *Corporate Governance and Globalization – Long Range Planning Issues*. New York: Edward Elgar.

Corsetti, Giancarlo, Paolo Pesenti and Nouriel Roubini (1998a): 'Paper tigers? A Model of the Asian crisis', NBER Working Paper No. 6783, November 1998.

Corsetti, Giancarlo, Paolo Pesenti and Nouriel Roubini (1998b): 'What caused the Asian Currency and Financial Crisis?', mimeo, Yale University, New Haven, CT.

Cusumano, Michael A. and Kentaro Nobeoka (1998): *Thinking beyond Lean: How Multi-project Management is Transforming Product Development at Toyota and Other Companies*. New York: The Free Press.

Delhaise, Philippe (1998): *Asia in Crisis – The Implosion of the Banking and Financial Systems*. Singapore: John Wiley & Sons (Asia) Pte.

Demigruc-Kunt, A. and V. Maksimovic (1996): 'Stock Market Development and Firm Financing Choices', *The World Bank Economic Review* (10), No. 2, pp. 341–69.

Demsetz, Harold (1967): 'Toward A Theory of Property Rights', *The American Economic Review*, May 1967 (2), pp. 347–59.

Demsetz, Harold (1983): 'The Structure of Ownership and the Theory of the Firm', *The Journal of Law and Economics* (26), pp. 375–90.

Deyo, Frederic C. (ed.) (1987): *The Political Economy of the New Asian Industrialism.* Ithaca, NY, and London: Cornell University Press.

Dietl, Helmut M. (1998): *Capital Markets and Corporate Governance in Japan, Germany, and the United States: Organizational Response to Market Inefficiencies.* London: Routledge.

Dornbusch, Rudiger (1997): *Financial Crisis in East Asia and the Prospects for Recovery.* A special lecture at the Korea Institute of Finance in December 1997. Seoul: Korea Institute of Finance.

Dos Santos, Teotonio (1970): 'The Structure of Dependence', *The American Economic Review* (60), No. 5, pp. 235–46.

Dosi, Giovanni, David J. Teece and Josef Chytry (eds) (1998): *Technology, Organization, and Competitiveness – Perspectives on Industrial and Corporate Change.* Oxford: Oxford University Press.

Edwards, Jeremy S. and Klaus Fischer (1994): *Banks, Finance and Investment in Germany.* Cambridge: Cambridge University Press.

Edwards, Sebastian (ed.) (2000): *Capital Flows and the Emerging Economies: Theory, Evidence, and Controversies.* Chicago, IL, and London: The University of Chicago Press.

European Corporate Governance Network (1997): *The Separation of Ownership and Control: A Survey of 7 European Countries Preliminary Report to the European Commission,* Volumes 1–4, by European Corporate Governance Network, Brussels. Downloaded from the network's website at http://www.ecgn.ulb.ac.be/ecgn/.

Evans, Peter B. (1979): *Dependent Development: The Alliance of Multinationals, State, and Local Capital in Brazil.* Princeton, NJ: Princeton University Press.

Evans, Peter B. (1987): 'Class, State, and Dependence in East Asia: Lessons for Latin Americanists', in Deyo (1987).

Evans, Peter B., Dietrich Rueshemeyer and Theda Skocpol (eds) (1985): *Bringing the State Back In.* New York: Cambridge University Press.

Fallows, James (1995): *Looking at the Sun: The Rise of the new East Asian Economic and Political System.* New York: Vintage Books.

Fischer, Stanley (1998): 'The Asian Crisis: A View from the IMF', address by Stanley Fischer, first deputy managing director of the IMF, at the Midwinter Conference of the Bankers' Association for Foreign Trade, Washington DC, 22 January 1998. Downloaded from Nouriel Roubini's Asian Crisis home page at http://www.stern.nyu.edu/globalmacro/.

Fishlow, Albert, Catherine Gwin, Stephan Haggard and Dani Rodrik (eds) (1993): *Miracle or Design – Lessons from the East Asian Experience.* Washingten, DC: Overseas Development Council.

Foss, Nicolai J. (1993): 'Theories of the Firm: Contractual and Competence Perspectives', *Journal of Evolutionary Economics* (3), pp. 127–44.

Frank, A. Gunder (1967): *Capitalism and Underdevelopment in Latin America.* New York: Monthly Review Press.

Frankel, Jeffrey A. (1998): 'The Asian Model, the Miracle, the Crisis and the Fund', a speech delivered at the US International Trade Commission, 16 April 1998. Downloaded from Nouriel Roubini's Asian Crisis home page at http://www.stern.nyu.edu/globalmacro/.

Fransman, Martin (1998): 'Information, Knowledge, Vision and Theories of the Firm', in Dosi, Teece and Chytry (1998).

Freyssennet, Michael, Andrew Mair, Koichi Shimizu and Giuseppe Volpato (1998): *One Best Way? – Trajectories and Industrial Models of the World's Automobile Producers*. Oxford: Oxford University Press.

Fujimoto, Takahiro (1998): 'Reinterpreting the Resource-Capability View of the Firm: A Case of the Development-Production Systems of the Japanese Auto-Makers', in Chandler, Hagström and Sölvell (1998).

Fujimoto, Takahiro (1999): *Evolution of A Manufacturing System at Toyota*. Oxford: Oxford University Press.

Fukuyama, Francis (1998): 'Asian Values and the Asian Crisis', *Commentary*, February, pp. 23–7.

Furman, Jason and Joseph E. Stiglitz (1998): 'Economic Crises: Evidence and Insights from East Asia', *Brookings Papers on Economic Activity* (2), pp. 1–135.

Galbraith, John Kenneth (1967): *The New Industrial State*. Boston, MA: Houghton Mifflin.

Gerschenkron, Alexander (1962): *Economic Backwardness in Historical Perspective: A Book of Essays*. Cambridge, MA: Harvard University Press.

Greenspan, Alan (1998): 'Testimony of Chairman Alan Greenspan, Before the Committee on Banking and Financial Services', US House of Representatives, 30 January 1998. Downloaded from Nouriel Roubini's Asian Crisis home page at http://www.stern.nyu.edu/globalmacro/.

Haggard, Stephan (1990): *Pathways from the Periphery – the Politics of Growth in the Newly Industrializing Countries*. Ithaca, NY, and London: Cornell University Press.

Haggard, Stephan (1993): 'Politics and Institutions in the World Bank's East Asia', in Fishlow, Gwin, Haggard and Rodrik (1993).

Haggard, Stephan (2000): *The Political Economy of the Asian Financial Crisis*. Washington, DC: Institute for International Economics.

Haggard, Stephan and Chung H. Lee (eds) (1995): *Financial System and Economic Policy in Developing Countries*. Ithaca, NY, and London: Cornell University Press.

Hahm, Joon-Ho (1998): 'Financial System Restructuring in Korea: The Crisis and its Resolution', a paper presented at the AT 10 Conference on 'Evolution of the Financial Systems in East Asia – Beyond the Financial Crisis', Tokyo, Japan, 26–27 February 1998. Published by Korea Development Institute.

Hahm, Joon-Ho and Frederic S. Mishkin (2000): 'Causes of the Korean Financial Crisis: Lessons for Policy', in Shin (2000).

Hanna, Donald (2000): 'Restructuring Asia's Financial System', in Woo, Sachs and Schwab (2000).

Hart, Oliver (1989): 'An Economist's Perspective on the Theory of the Firm', *Columbia Law Review* (89), pp. 1757–74.

Hattori, T. (1989): 'Japanese *Zaibatsu* and Korean *Chaebol*', in Chung and Lee (1989).

Hellwig, Martin (2000): 'On the Economics and Politics of Corporate Finance and Corporate Control', in Vives (2000b).

Hodgson, Geoffrey M. (1998): 'Competence and Contract in the Theory of the Firm', *Journal of Economic Behavior and Organization* (35), pp. 179–202.

Holderness, Clifford and Dennis Sheehan (1988): 'The Role of Majority Share-holders in Publicly Held Corporations – An Exploratory Analysis', *Journal of Financial Economics* (20), pp. 317–46.

Holderness, Clifford, Randall Kroszner and Dennis Sheehan (1999): 'Were the Good Old Days that Good? Changes in Managerial Stock Ownership since the Great Depression', *Journal of Finance* (54), 435–69.

Hughes, Helen (ed.) (1988): *Achieving Industrialization in East Asia*. Cambridge: Cambridge University Press.

Hwang, Hye-Ran (1998): 'Organizational Capability and Organizational Rigidities of Korean *Chaebol* – Case Studies of Semiconductor (DRAM) and Personal Computer (PC) Products', PhD thesis submitted to the University of Sussex.

Hyun, Young-Suk (1997): 'New Product Development Series: Daewoo Motor – From Joint Venture to Multiple-Project Developer'. Working Paper of IMVP (International Motor Vehicle Program). MIT, Center for Technology, Policy and Industrial Development.

Hyun, Young-Suk (1999): 'The New Product Development Capabilities of the Korean Auto Industry: Hyundai Motor Company', *International Journal of Vehicle Design* (21), No. 1, pp. 7–20.

IMF (1997a): 'Korea Memorandum on the Economic Program', 3 December. A Letter of Intent from the government of Korea, which describes the policies that Korea intends to implement in the context of its request for financial support from the IMF. Downloaded from the IMF website at http://www.imf.org/ external/ country/KOR/.

IMF (1997b): *World Economic Outlook. Interim Assessment. A Survey by the Staff of the International Monetary Fund*. (December). Washington, DC: IMF.

IMF (1998a): 'Korea's Economic Adjustments under the IMF-supported Program', Presentation by Kunio Saito, Director, IMF Regional Office for Asia and the Pacific, at the Sogang University/*Korea Economic Daily* Conference, 21 January. Downloaded from the IMF website at http://www.imf.org/external/np/ speeches/.

IMF (1998b): 'Korea Updated Memorandum on the Economic Program', 2 May. A Letter of Intent from the government of Korea, which describes the policies that Korea intends to implement in the context of its request for financial support from the IMF. Downloaded from the IMF website at http://www.imf.org/ external/ country/KOR/.

IMF (1998c): *World Economic Outlook, A Survey by the Staff of the International Monetary Fund*. (May). Washington, DC: IMF.

Iqbal, Farruhk and Jong-Il You (2001): *Democracy, Market Economics, and Development: An Asian Perspective*. Washington, DC: World Bank.

Ito, Takatoshi (1998): 'What can Developing Countries Learn from East Asia's Economic Growth?', *Annual World Bank Conference on Development Economics*, pp. 183–200.

Ito, Takatoshi (1999): 'Bail-out, Moral Hazard, and Credibility: IMF and World Bank policies in Crises of the 21st Century Type' (May), a paper prepared for the Wharton Conference on Asian Twin Financial Crises in Tokyo on 10 March 1998.

Ito, Takatoshi (2000): 'Capital Inflow in Asia', in Edwards (2000).

Ito, Takatoshi and Anne O. Krueger (eds) (1996): *Financial Deregulation and Integration in East Asia*. NBER East Asia Seminar on Economics, Volume 5. Chicago, IL: University of Chicago Press.

Jang, Ha-Sung (2001): 'Corporate Governance and Economic Development: The Korean Experience', in Iqbal and You (2001).

Jenkins, Rhys (1984): *Transnational Corporations and Industrial Transformation in Latin America*. New York: St Martin Press.

Jensen, Michael C. (1988): 'Takeover: Their Causes and Consequences', *Journal of Economic Perspectives* (2), pp. 29–48.

Jensen, Michael C. and William H. Meckling (1976): 'Theory of the Firm: Managerial Behavior, Agency Costs and Ownership Structure', *Journal of Financial Economics* (3), pp. 305–60.

Jensen, Michael C. and Richard S. Ruback (1983): 'The Market for Corporate Control – the Scientific Evidence', *Journal of Financial Economics* (11), pp. 5–50.

Joh, Sung-Wook (1999): 'The Korean Corporate Sector: Crisis and Reform', KDI Working Paper No. 9912. KDI, November 1999.

Johnson, Chalmers (1982): *MITI and the Japanese Miracle – The Growth of Industrial Policy, 1925–1975*. Stanford CA: Stanford University Press.

Johnson, Chalmers (1984): *The Industrial Policy Debate*. San Francisco, CA: Institute for Contemporary Studies Press.

Johnson, Chalmers (1995): *Japan: Who Governs? – The Rise of the Developmental State*. New York: W.W. Norton.

Johnson, Chalmers (1998): 'Economic Crisis in East Asia: The Crash of Capitalisms', *Cambridge Journal of Economics* (22), pp. 653–61.

Johnson, Chalmers (1999): *Blow Back – The Costs and Consequences of American Empire*. New York: Metropolitan Books.

Jones, Leroy and Il SaKong (1980): *Government, Business, and Entrepreneurship in Economic Development: The Korean Case, Studies in the Modernization of the Republic of Korea: 1945–1975*. Cambridge, MA: Harvard University Press.

Jung, Ku-Hyun (1991): *Diversification and International Competitiveness of Korean Business*. Seoul: Korea Economic Research Institute.

Jürgens, Ulrich, Yannick Lung, Giuseppe Volpato and Vincent Frigant (2002): 'The Arrival of Shareholder Value in the European Auto Industry – A Case Study Comparison of four Car Makers', *Competition & Change* (6), No. 1, (March), pp. 61–80.

Jürgens, Ulrich, Thomas Malsch and Knuth Dohse (1989): *Moderne Zeiten in der Automobilfabrik: Strategien der Productionsmodernisierung im Länder- and Konzernvergleich; Ergebnis eines Forschungsprojects des Wissenschaftszentrums Berlin für Sozialforschung (WZB)*. Berlin: Springer.

Jürgens, Ulrich and Joachim Rupp (2002): 'The German System of Corporate Governance – Characteristics and Changes'. WZB Discussion paper FS II 00–202.

Jürgens, Ulrich, Joachim Rupp and Katrin Vitols (2000): 'Shareholder Value in an Adverse Environment: The German Case', *Economy and Society* (29), No. 1, pp. 54–79.

Jwa, Sung-Hee and In-Kwon Lee (eds) (2000): *Korean Chaebol in Transition: Road Ahead and Agenda*. Seoul: KERI (Korea Economic Research Institute).

Kang, Myung-Hun (1996): *The Korean Business Conglomerate – Chaebol Then and Now*. Institute of East Asia Studies, University of California, Berkeley, CA: Center for Korean Studies.

Keller, Maryann (1989): *Rude Awakening – the Rise, Fall, and Struggle for Recovery of General Motors*. New York: William Morrow.

Kim, Eun-Mee (1987): 'From Dominance to Symbiosis: State and *Chaebol* in the Korean Economy, 1960–1985'. PhD thesis submitted to the Department of Sociology at Brown University, USA.

Kim, Hyun-Jeong (2001): 'The Korean Automobile Industry: Vertical Disintegration and Competitive Success'. PhD thesis submitted to Department of Economics, University of Cambridge, UK.

Kim, Joon-Kyung and Deockhyun Ryu (1998): 'Debt and Financial Instability in Korea', KDI Working Paper No. 9808. Seoul: KDI.

Kim, Jun-Il (1994): 'The Korean Economy 1994–96: Policy Development and Prospects', KDI working paper, December.

Kim, Jun-Il (1995): 'The Korean Economy 1995–96: Recent Trends and Future Prospects', KDI working paper, December.

Kim, Jun-Il and Jong-Ryn Mo (1998): 'Democratization and Macroeconomic Policy', in Mo and Moon (1998).

Kim, Lin-Su (1997): *Imitation to Innovation: The Dynamics of Korea's Technological Learning.* Boston, MA: Harvard Business School Press.

Kim, Lin-Su (1999): *Learning and Innovation in Economic Development.* Cheltenham: Elgar.

Kim, Suk-Ran (1997): *Vom Schwellenland zur Spitzennation: Entwicklungs- bedingungen und –prozesse der Halbleiterindustrie Suekoreas.* Berlin: edition Sigma.

Kim, Tae-Koo (1997): *The Global Management of Daewoo Motor Co. – Global Configuration and Coordination.* The Center for Case Development. Case Study No. 9-297-026. Seoul: College of Business Administration, Seoul National University.

Kindleberger, Charles P. (1989): *Manias, Panics, and Crashes: A History of Financial Crises.* New York: Basic Books (2nd ed.).

Kindleberger, Charles P. and Jean-Pierre Laffargue (eds) (1982): *Financial Crises – Theory, History, and Policy.* Cambridge: Cambridge University Press.

Koen, Carla I. (2000): 'The Japanese "Main Bank" Model: Evidence of the Pressures of Change.' A paper prepared for the 2000 WZB Workshop in Berlin.

Kohli, Atul (1999): 'Where Do High-Growth Political Economies Come From? The Japanese Lineage of Korea's "Developmental State"', in Woo-Cumings (1999).

Koo, Bon-Chun (1998): 'Corporate Restructuring and Financial Reform in Korea', KDI Working Paper, November.

Kregel. J. A. (1998): 'Derivatives and Global Capital Flows: Application to Asia', *Cambridge Journal of Economics*, 22, pp. 677–92.

Krueger, Anne O. (1979): *The Developmental Role of the Foreign Sector and Aid.* Cambridge, MA: Harvard University Press.

Krueger, Anne O. (1980): 'Export-led Industrial Growth Reconsidered', paper presented to the Eleventh Pacific Trade and Development Conference, 1–4 September, Seoul: KDI.

Krueger, Anne O. (1990): *Perspectives on Trade and Development.* New York: Harvester Wheatsheaf.

Krueger, Anne O. (1995): *Trade Policies and Developing Nations.* Washington, DC: The Brookings Institution.

Krugman, Paul (1998a): 'What happened to Asia?', mimeo, Cambridge, MA: Massachusetts Institute of Technology.

Krugman, Paul (1998b): 'Will Asia bounce back?', a speech for Credit Suisse First Boston, Hong Kong, March. Downloaded from the Krugman home page at http://web.mit.edu/krugman/www/suisse.html.

Krugman, Paul (1999): *The Return of Depression Economics.* New York: W. W. Norton.

La Porta, Rafael, Florencio Lopez-De-Silanes and Andrei Shleifer (1999): 'Corporate Ownership Around the World', *The Journal of Finance* (LIV), No. 2 (April), pp. 471–517.

Lazonick, William (1998): 'The Japanese Financial Crisis, Corporate Governance, and Sustainable Prosperity', Jerome Levy Economics Institute Working Papers No. 227: 1–55.

Lazonick, William and Mary O'Sullivan (1997a): 'Finance and Industrial Development. Part I: The United States and the United Kingdom', *Financial History Review* (4), pp. 7–29.

Lazonick, William and Mary O'Sullivan (1997b): 'Finance and Industrial Development: Evolution to Market Control. Part II: Japan and Germany', *Financial History Review* (4), pp. 117–38.

Lee, In-Kwon (2000): 'Excess Capacity and Big Deals', in Jwa and Lee (2000).

Lee, Young-Ki and Young-Jae Lim (1998): 'In Search of Korea's New Corporate Governance System', revised conference paper on 'An Agenda for Economic Reform in Korea: International Perspective', KDI.

Leipziger, Danny M. (ed.) (1997): *Lessons from East Asia*. Ann Arbor, MI: The University of Michigan Press.

Leipziger, Danny M. and Peter A. Petri (1993): *Korean Industrial Policy – Legacies of the Past and Directions for the Future*, World Bank discussion paper 197, East Asia and Pacific region series. Washington, DC: World Bank.

Leonard-Barton, Dorothy (1992): 'Core Capabilities and Core Rigidities: A Paradox in Managing New Product Development', *Strategic Management Journal* (13), Special issue, pp. 111–25.

Leonard-Barton, Dorothy (1995): *Wellsprings of Knowledge – Building and Sustaining the Sources of Innovation*. Cambridge, MA: Harvard Business School Press.

Lim, Hyun-Chin (1985): *Dependent Development in Korea, 1963–1979*. Seoul: Seoul National University Press. (A reprint of his 1982 PhD thesis), 'Dependent Development in the World-System: The Case of South Korea, 1963–1979', at Harvard University.

Lorianux, Michael (1999): 'The French Developmental State as Myth and Moral Ambition', in Woo-Cumings (1999).

Lundvall, Bengt-Åke (1992): 'User-Producer Relationships, National System of Innovation and Internationalization', in Lundvall (ed.), *National System of Innovation – Toward a Theory of Innovation and Interactive Learning*. London, Pinter.

Magnusson, Lars (ed.) (1994): *Evolutionary and Neo-Schumpeterian Approaches to Economics*. Boston: Kluwer Academic.

Mayer, Colin (1988): 'New Issues in Corporate Finance', *European Economic Review* (32), pp. 1167–89.

McKinnon, Ronald I. (1991): *The Order of Economic Liberalization – Financial Control in the Transition to A Market Economy*. Baltimore, MD, and London: Johns Hopkins University Press.

McKinnon, R. and H. Pill (1996): 'Credible Liberalization and International Capital Flows: The "Overborrowing Syndrome" ', in Ito and Krueger (1996).

McKinnon, R. and H. Pill (1998): 'International Overborrowing – A Decomposition of Credit and Currency Risk', *World Development* (26), No. 7, pp. 1267–82.

McLeod, Ross H. (1998): 'Indonesia', in McLeod and Garnaut (1998).

McLeod, Ross H. and Ross Garnaut (eds) (1998): *East Asia in Crisis: From Being a Miracle to Needing One?* London: Routledge.

Minsky, Hyman P. (1982): 'The Financial-Instability Hypothesis: Capitalist Processes and the Behavior of the Economy', in Kindleberger and Laffargue (1982).

Mo, Jongryn and Chung-in Moon (eds) (1998): *Democracy and the Korean Economy*. Stanford, CA: Hoover Institution Press.

Moon, Chung-In (1998): 'Democratization and Globalization as Ideological and Political Foundation of Economic Policy', in Mo and Moon (1998).

Moon, Chung-In and Sang-young Rhyu (2000): 'The State, Structural Rigidity, and the End of Asian Capitalism: A Comparative Study of Japan and South Korea', in Robison Richard, Mark Beeson, Kanishka Jayasuriya and Hyuk-Rae Kim (eds), *Politics and Markets in the Wake of the Asian Crisis*. London: Routledge.

Morikawa, Hidemasa (1992): *Zaibatsu – The Rise and Fall of Family Enterprise Groups in Japan*. Tokyo: University of Tokyo Press.

Nam Il-Chong, Kim Joon-Kyung, Kang Yeong-jae, Joh Sung-Wook and Kim Jun-Il (1999): 'Corporate Governance in Korea', a paper presented at the Conference on Corporate Governance in Asia: A Comparative Perspective, sponsored by the OECD and KDI, March 1999.

Nelson, Richard R. (1972): 'Issues and Suggestions for the Study of Industrial Organization in a Regime of Rapid Technical Change', in V. Fuchs (ed.): *Policy Issues and Research Opportunities in Industrial Organization*. New York: NBER.

Nelson, Richard R. (1991): 'Why Do Firms Differ, and How Does It Matter?', *Strategic Management Journal, Special Issue* (12), pp. 61–74.

Nelson, Richard R. (1994): 'The Role of Firm Differences in an Evolutionary Theory of Technical Advance', in Magnusson (1994).

Nelson, Richard R. and S. G. Winter (1982): *An Evolutionary Theory of Economic Change*. Cambridge, MA: The Belknap Press of Harvard University Press.

Nester, William R. (1998): *A Short History of American Industrial Policies*. New York: St Martin's Press.

Newfarmer, Richard (1985): *Profits, Progress, and Poverty: Case Studies of International Industries in Latin America*. Indiana: University of Notre Dame Press.

North, Douglas C. (1990): *Institutions, Institutional Change and Economic Performance*. Cambridge: Cambridge University Press.

O'Brien, Peter (1998): *Korea's Automotive Future*. An FT management report published and distributed by FT Automotive. London: Financial Times Business.

Odagiri, Hiroyuki and Akira Goto (1996): *Technology and Industrial Development in Japan: Building Capability by Learning, Innovation, and Public Policy*. Oxford: Clarendon Press.

Palma, Gabriel (1998): 'Three and A Half Cycles of "Mania, Panic, and [Asymmetric] Crash": East Asia and Latin America Compared', *Cambridge Journal of Economics* (22), pp. 789–808.

Park, Chan-Hi (1998): *Daewoo's Globalization: Uz-Daewoo Auto Project*. HBS Case Services N9-598-065. Cambridge, MA: Harvard Business School.

Park, Hong-Jae (1999): 'The *Chaebol* and Economic Growth in Korea', a PhD thesis presented to the Department of Economics, School of Oriental and African Studies, University of London.

Penrose, Edith (1959): *The Theory of the Growth of the Firm*. Oxford: Basil Blackwell.

Perry, Guillermo E. and Daniel Lederman (1998): *Financial Vulnerability, Spillover Effects, and Contagion: Lessons from the Asian Crises for Latin America*. Washington, DC: World Bank, Latin American and Caribbean Studies.

Pfeiffer, Hermannus (1993): *Die Macht der Banken*. Frankfurt: Campus-Verlag.

Pincus, Jonathan and Rizal Ramli (1998): 'Indonesia: From Showcase to Basket Case', *Cambridge Journal of Economics* (22), pp. 723–34.

Pomerleano, Michael (1998): 'The East Asian Crisis and Corporate Finances – the Untold Micro Story.' *Emerging Markets Quarterly* Winter (2), No. 4, pp. 14–27.

Prahalad, C.K. and George Hamel (1990): 'The Core Competence of the Corporation', *Harvard Business Review* (68), pp. 79–91.

Radelet, Steven and Jeffrey Sachs (1998): 'The East Asian Financial Crisis: Diagnosis, Remedies, Prospects', *Brookings Paper on Economic Activity* (28), No. 1, pp. 20–58.

Raupach-Sumiya, Joerg (2000): *Reforming Japan's Corporate Governance System: Will the Markets Gain Control?*, Working Paper 00/2, Tokyo: Deutsches Institut Für Japanstudien.

Reber, Arthur S. (1996): *Implicit Learning and Tacit Knowledge: An Essay on the Cognitive Unconscious*. Oxford: Oxford University Press.

Rohwer, Jim (1995): *Asia Rising*. New York: Simon & Schuster.

Sachs, Jeffrey (1997): 'IMF is a power unto itself'. A column in *The Financial Times* on 11 December.

Sachs, Jeffrey (1998): 'The IMF and the Asian Flu', *The American Prospect* (37), March–April.

Sachs, Jeffrey and Wing Thye Woo (2000a): 'A Reform Agenda for a Resilient Asia', in Woo, Sachs and Schwab (2000).

Sachs, Jeffrey and Wing Thye Woo (2000b): 'Understanding the Asian Financial Crisis', in Woo, Sachs and Schwab (2000).

Samuels, Richard J. (1987): *The Business of the Japanese State: Energy Markets in Comparative and Historical Perspective*. Ithaca, NY, and London: Cornell University Press.

Schmidt, Hartmut and Jochen Drukarczyk (1997): *Corporate Governance in Germany*, HWWA-Institute für Wirtschaftsforschung, Band 31. Baden-Baden: Nomos Verlagsgesellschaft.

Shin, In-Seok (ed.) (2000): *The Korean Crisis: Before and After*. Seoul: KDI.

Shin, In-Seok and Yun-Jong Wang (1999): 'How to Sequence Capital Market Liberalization: Lessons from the Korean Experience', Working Paper 99–30, Korea Institute for International Economic Policy.

Shleifer, Andrei and Robert Vishny (1986): 'Large Shareholders and Corporate Control', *Journal of Political Economy* (94), 461–88.

Shleifer, Andrei and Robert Vishny (1997): 'A Survey of Corporate Governance', *The Journal of Finance* (LII), No. 2, pp. 737–83.

Soros, George (1998): *The Crisis of Global Capitalism: Open Society Endangered*. New York: Public Affairs.

Steers, Richard M. (1999): *Made in Korea – Chung Ju Yung and the Rise of Hyundai*. New York: Routledge.

Sternberg, Robert J. and Joseph A. Horvath (eds) (1998): *Tacit Knowledge in Professional Practice: Researcher and Practitioner Perspectives*. New York: Lawrence Erlbaum Associates.

Stiglitz, Joseph E. (1989): 'Markets, Market Failures and Development', *American Economic Review* (79), No. 2, pp. 196–203.

Stiglitz, Joseph E. (2001): 'From Miracle to Crisis to Recovery: Lessons from Four Decades of East Asian Experience', in Joseph E. Stiglitz and Shahid Yusuf (eds), *Rethinking the East Asian Miracle*. Oxford: Oxford University Press and World Bank.

Stiglitz, Joseph E. and A. Weiss (1981): 'Credit Rationing in Markets with Imperfect Information', *American Economic Review* (71), pp. 393–410.

Teece, David. J. (1980): 'Economies of Scope and the Scope of the Enterprise', *Journal of Economic Behavior and Organization* (1), pp. 223–47.

Teece, David J. (1993): 'The Dynamics of Industrial Capitalism: Perspective on Alfred Chandler's *Scale and Scope*', *Journal of Economic Literature*, (XXXI) (March) pp. 199–225.

Teece, David J. and Gary Pisano (1998): 'The Dynamic Capabilities of Firms: An Introduction', in Dosi, Teece and Chytry (1998).

Teece, David J., Gary Pisano and Amy Shuen (1997): 'Dynamic Capabilities and Strategic Management', *Strategic Management Journal* (18), No. 7, pp. 509–33.

Teece, David J., Richard Rumelt, Giovanni Dosi and Sidney Winter (1994): 'Understanding Corporate Coherence – Theory and Evidence', *Journal of Economic Behavior and Organization* (23), pp. 1–30.

Vartiainen, Juhana (1999): 'Successful State Intervention in Industrial Transformation', in Woo-Cumings (1999).

Vickrey, William (1994) (edited by Richard Arnott *et al.*): *Public Economics: Selected Papers by William Vickrey*. Cambridge: Cambridge University Press.

Vitols, Sigurt (2000): 'The Reconstruction of German Corporate Governance: Reassessing the Role of Capital Market Pressure', a background paper for the debate 'Höpner vs. Vitols v. Zugehör: Do financial markets matter?'. Wissenschaftszentrum Berlin für Sozialforschung. Downloaded from the WZB home page at http://medea.wz-berlin.de/vitols.htm/.

Vitols, Sigurt (2002): 'Shareholder Value, Management Culture and Production Regimes in the Transformation of the German Chemical Pharmaceutical Industry'. Wissenschaftszentrum Berlin für Sozialforschung. Downloaded from the WZB home page at http://medea.wz-berlin.de/vitols.htm/.

Vives, Xavier (2000a): 'Corporate Governance: Does It Matter?', in Vives (2000b).

Vives, Xavier (ed.) (2000b): *Corporate Governance – Theoretical and Empirical Perspectives*, Institut d'Anàlisi Econòmica, CSIC Barcelona. Cambridge: Cambridge University Press.

Wade, Robert (1990): *Governing the Market: Economic Theory and the Role of Government in East Asian Industrialization*. Princeton, NJ: Princeton University Press.

Wade, Robert (1993): 'Selective Industrial Policies in East Asia: Is the East Asian Miracle Right?', in Fishlow, Gwin, Haggard and Rodrik (1993).

Wade, Robert (2000): 'Gestalt Shift: From "Miracle" to "Cronyism" in the Asian Crisis', in Leonardo Burlamaqui, Ana Celia Castro and Ha-Joon Chang (eds), *Institutions and the Role of the State*. Cheltenham: Edward Elgar.

Wade, Robert and Frank Veneroso (1998): 'The Asian Crisis: The High Debt Model Versus the Wall Street – Treasury – IMF Complex', *New Left Review* (228), pp. 20–44.

Walter, Ingo (2000): 'Capital Markets and Control of Enterprises in the Global Economy', in Cohen and Boyd (2000).

White, Gorden and Robert Wade (eds) (1985): *Developmental State in East Asia*. Institute of Development Studies Research Report, 16, Brighton.

Whitley, Richard (1992): *Business Systems in East Asia: Firms, Markets and Societies*. London: Sage.

Whittaker, D. Hugh and Yoshitaka Kurosawa (1998): 'Japan's Crisis: Evolution and Implications', *Cambridge Journal of Economics* (22), pp. 761–71.

Williamson, Oliver E. (1975): *Markets and Hierarchies*. New York: Free Press.

Williamson, Oliver E. (1985): *The Economic Institutions of Capitalism: Firms, Markets and Relational Contracting*. New York: Free Press.

Womack, James P., Daniel T. Jones and Daniel Roos (1990): *The Machine that Changed the World*. New York: Rawson Associates.

Woo, Jung-en (1991): *Race to the Swift: State and Finance in Korean Industrialization*. New York: Columbia University Press.

Woo, Wing Thye, Jeffrey Sachs and Klaus Schwab (eds) (2000): *The Asian Financial Crisis: Lessons for a Resilient Asia*. Cambridge, MA: The MIT Press.

Woo-Cumings, Meredith (ed.) (1999): *The Developmental State*. Ithaca, NY, and London: Cornell University Press.

World Bank (1993): *The East Asian Miracle: Economic Growth and Public Policy*. Oxford: Oxford University Press.

World Bank (1998): *East Asia: The Road to Recovery*. Washington, DC.

World Bank (1999): *Global Development Finance: Analysis and Summary Tables*. Washington, DC.

Yoo, Seong-Min (1999): *Corporate Restructuring in Korea: Policy Issues Before and During the Crisis*. KDI working paper, February.

Zhao, Hongxin (1992): 'Relationship Between Indigenous Technological Capability and Imported Technology: Evidences in China, India, Japan, South Korea and Taiwan', a PhD thesis at Washington University, Washington DC.

Korean language works cited

Board of Public Inspection (1999): 'Analysis of Causes of the Currency Crisis in 1997', *Monthly Chosun* in October 1999, a special report.

Cho, Seong-Jae (2000): 'Corporate Governance and Industrial Relations: The Case of Kia Motors', a PhD thesis submitted to Seoul National University.

Cho, Yoon-Je and Joon-Kyung Kim (1997): *Credit Policies and the Industrialization of Korea*, KDI Research Monograph 9701, Seoul: Korea Development Institute.

Cho, Young-Chul (1999): 'Debt-Dependent Economy and the *Chaebol* Reform', *Sahoekyongjepyonglon* (12), pp. 124–56.

Cho, Young-Chul (2001): 'Review of the Restructuring of the Korean Economy and Alternative Policies', a paper presented at the conference of the Korean Economics Association, 31 March.

Choe, Jeong-Pyo (1999): *End of the Chaebol Era*. Seoul: Gowon.

Choe, Jong-Yun (1998): 'Financial Alchemy of Daewoo's Global Management', in Seo, Kwack and Song (1998).

Economic Planning Board (1988): *White Book on External Debts*.

Fair Trade Commission: *The Designation of Big Business Groups*, yearly, Seoul: Fair Trade Commission of Korea.

Financial Supervisory Commission (1999): *Process of Corporate and Financial Restructuring and Policies for the Future*, Press Release, 24 August.

Hu, Sang-Su (1994): *Samsung and Automobile Industry*. Seoul: Saenal.

Hyun, Young-Suk (1988): 'An Empirical Survey of the Technological Development in the Korean Automobile Industry during 1962–1986', a PhD thesis submitted to KAIST (Korea Advanced Institute of Science and Technology).

Hyundai Motor Company (1992): *Twenty Years of Hyundai Motor Company*. Seoul: Hyundai Motor Company.

Hyundai Motor Company (1997): *History of Hyundai Motor Company*. Seoul: Hyundai Motor Company.

Jung, Ku-Hyun (1987): *Growth Strategy and Management Structure of Korean Companies*. Seoul: Korean Chamber of Commerce and Industry.

Kang, Chul-Kyu (1995): 'An Estimation of the *Chaebol*'s Rent based on Interests Rate Difference', in Chung Yun-Hyung, Chul-Hwan Chun and Geum-Su Kim, *National Economic Theory and the Korean Economy*. Seoul: Changjakkwabipyongsa.

Kang, Chul-Kyu, Jeong-Pyo Choe and Ji-Sang Chang (1991): *Chaebol – The Leader of Growth or the Incarnation of Greed?* Seoul: Bibong Press.

Kang, Myong-Han (1998): *Korean Auto Industry Facing Difficulties*. Seoul: Jeonghaksa.

Kim, Dae-Hwan and Kyun Kim (eds) (1999): *On Reform of the Korean Chaebol*. Seoul: Nanam.

Kim, Gyun (1994): 'A Study on the Technological Capability of Korea in the 1980s – with the emphasis on the development of "In-House" R&D systems', a PhD thesis submitted to Seoul National University.

Kim, Ki-Won (1999): 'Abolition of the *Chaebol* System and Establishment of Responsible Professional Management System', in Kim and Kim (1999).

Kim, Tae-Woo (1996): *Daewoo's Strategy to Advance in Emerging Markets – The Case of Daewoo Motor Co. in East Europe*, The Center for Case Development, 9-296-009, College of Business Administration, Seoul National University.

Korea Automobile Manufacturers Association, *Automotive Statistics*, yearly, Seoul: KAMA.

Kwack, Eui-Jae (1999): 'A Study on the Changing Autonomy of Korean Firms – With Regard to the Ability of the *Chaebol* to Mobilize Financial Sources', a PhD thesis submitted to Yon-Sei University.

Lee, Eun-Suk (1996): 'Change of Corporate Strategy and Industrial Relationship – The Case of Daewoo Motor Company', a master's thesis submitted to Sukmyong Women's University.

Lee, Jin-Ju and Young-Suk Hyun (1985): 'The Process of Technological Development in the Korean Automobile Industry', *Jagobo*, December 1984–April 1985.

Lee, Keun (ed.) (1997): *The Technological Capabilities and Competitiveness of Korean Industry*. Seoul: KyongMunSa.

Lee, Kyu-Uk (1999): 'Comments on the *Chaebol* Reform and Policy Goals', a paper presented at the conference of the Korea International Economy Research Institute, on 3 December.

Lee, Yong-Woo (1998): 'Exploiting the World Markets', in Seo, Kwack and Song (1998).

Oh, Ku-Chang and Chul Cho (1997): *The History of the Korean Automobile Industry and its Growth Potential*. Seoul: KIEP (Korea Institute for International Economic Policy).

People's Solidarity for Participatory Democracy (1999): *White Book on the Five Largest Chaebol* in Korea – 1995–97. Seoul: Nanam Press.

Ryu, Jae-Hun (1989): 'The Development of the Korean Automobile Industry and the Historical Characteristics of the Firms', in Ryu *et al.* (1989).

Ryu, Jae-Hun, Hyung-Je Cho, Sang-Suk Shin, Yong-U Lee and Byung-Yu Chun (1989): *The Korean Capitalism and Automobile Industry*. Seoul: Pulbit.

Seo, Jae-Myong, Su-Il Kwack and Il Song (1998): *Kim Woo-Joong's Global Management*. Seoul: Haenam.

Shin, Sang-Suk (1988): 'A Study of the Shifting Characteristic of Capital Accumulation in the Korean Automobile Industry', a master's thesis submitted to Seoul National University.

Song, Il (1998): 'Daewoo, Kim Woo-Joong, and Global Management', in Seo, Kwack and Song (1998).

Yoo, Chul-Gyu (1998): 'Financial Crisis and Problems of the IMF-initiated Financial Reforms', *Donghianggua Jeonmang* (37), pp. 73–92.

Yoo, Chul-Gyu (2000): 'Political Economy of Restructuring: 1998–99', in Jin-Ho Yun and Chul-Gyu Yu (eds), *Political Economy of Restructuring and the Korean Economy in the 21st Century*. Seoul: Pulbit.

Yun, Jin-Ho, Chang-Pyo Hong, Byung-Hee Lee, Seong-Jae Cho and Yong-Sun Chung (1998): *Structural Change of the Korean Automobile Industry and Problems*. Seoul: Saenal.

Japanese language works cited

Kim, Gyun (2000): 'Product Development of Korean Carmakers', in Maruyama Yoshinari and Hyung-Je Cho (eds): *An Overview of the Japanese and Korean Automobile Industry*. Tokyo: Corporation Torai.

Kim, Wan-Pyo (1999): 'Restructuring of the Korean Automobile Industry in the 90s and Problems'. Samsung Economic Institute. Downloaded from electronic database of the institute's web site at *http://seriecon.seri.org/*.

Index

Note: f = figure; n = note; t = table; **bold** = extended discussion or heading emphasized in main text.